OFFICE MANAGEMENT

P. W. Betts is Director of the Management Centre at Harrow College of Technology. His experience in office management extends to fifteen years in industry; he has undertaken research in administrative management, and is actively engaged on various national and local committees associated with this function. In particular he is a member of the National Examinations Board in Supervisory Studies, and a member of the Council and of the Education Committee of the Institute of Administrative Management.

He has also arranged and led various management groups on Study Tours abroad.

TEACH YOURSELF BOOKS

OFFICE MANAGEMENT

Peter W. Betts

M.Tech., F.Inst. A.M.(Dip), M.B.I.M., F.I.W.M.,
M.I.M., M.I.S.M.

TEACH YOURSELF BOOKS
Hodder and Stoughton

First printed 1975
Second impression 1976

ISBN 0 340 19496 0

Printed and bound in Great Britain
for Teach Yourself Books, Hodder and Stoughton, London,
by Richard Clay (The Chaucer Press), Ltd.,
Bungay, Suffolk

Contents

Preface

Administrative management is gradually becoming more recognised as an essential component of the senior executive team. This change has occurred through the upsurge in information technology and its vital effect on the survival of a concern in a rapidly evolving and increasingly competitive business world.

The daily grind of administrative machinery at lower levels in the organisation structure, however, continues to be controlled by departmental office managers with considerable but often unrecognised responsibility. The on-going business is entirely dependent upon successful administrative operations at these levels, as is strategic research into long-term policy and new projects which should be undertaken by a specialist at senior executive level.

This book is designed to indicate the information and techniques that are needed by a successful departmental office manager and to introduce the overall situation in administrative management, which is often not appreciated by many students studying this subject. Developing managerial skills, however, depends upon considerable practice and experience, and upon further reading in depth the many features mentioned throughout the chapters. Moreover, the office manager should continually up-date his knowledge, and an excellent way is to join the Institute of Administrative Management and take advantage of the facilities offered. In addition he should not overlook the opportunity of qualifying in this function by studying for the Diploma examinations offered by the Institute.

The text will be particularly useful for three main groups of people: the student who intends to take up office management as a career, the office supervisor who wishes to develop himself for further promotion, and the departmental office manager who desires to know more about his job and its broader, modern responsibilities.

The title *Office Management* is interpreted in a specific way: the management of an office. The term 'office' is used here to mean an office where a procedure or a number of procedures is operating. The term is *not* used to describe all the clerical activities in a concern which often implies the inclusion and control of all areas where these activities are conducted; thus the *office* as a general term is excluded. This distinction is drawn to separate the work of a departmental office manager from that of an administrative manager at senior executive level who naturally will possess much broader responsibilities. The exception to this distinction is apparent in the small concern. An office manager in this type of firm will also find the contents very useful, especially where company growth prospects are high.

1 Introduction to office management

The background

The rapidly increasing interest in office management is well-known today. This function has undergone a series of changes over the past fifty years, each phase becoming progressively shorter and more important as the so-called administrative revolution intermittently accelerates.

A competitive concern cannot afford to ignore information and this fact has induced a large increase in office staff, along with an evolution in information technology and the development of an unfortunate situation where management capability to cope with administrative change is tending to lag behind. This type of situation is not unusual in the business world. To the potential office manager it presents an interesting challenge, together with the possibility of high rewards in the long term.

The mood of change in the structure of senior executive teams is also evident. For those companies who suffer from inertia in developing office management, the need for change will eventually be forced upon them through the sheer impact of information technology in forthcoming years, and through the necessity to employ a specialist in this field at a high level in the organisation.

A wealth of knowledge in various disciplines and techniques is an essential requirement for the information technologist. When these are applied through the use of various managerial skills he progresses to managerial status (office manager) and finally he reaches senior executive level (administrative manager) when sufficient expertise has been gained. The term 'administrative management' is now accepted as an extension of office management at senior executive level, which includes other relevant activities discussed later.

At present, managers of high calibre in this function are rare. Education and training facilities have lagged behind and institutes associated with the function have not taken full advantage of the changing scene. Meanwhile, information technology forges ahead, managers attempt to apply the techniques and often fail through no fault of their own. Indeed, the techniques are also labelled as failures, and until managers update themselves and recognise reality it is doubtful whether the situation will adjust itself.

Opportunities in office management are now plentiful. The benefits to a company through the effective use of this function are considerable and there is now ample evidence to prove it. Although modern machines, sophisticated equipment and efficient systems are important, the effectiveness of the function depends mainly upon trained staff of high calibre. The main areas of knowledge and techniques can be learned and used in conjunction with management skills. The skills have to be practised continually, however, to achieve full competence. In addition, the first appointment above clerical level to, say, a senior clerk or supervisor involves taking responsibility for the work of others. This broadening of responsibility is particularly demanding and success depends mainly upon the art of dealing with people. Moreover, the value of office supervisors is often overlooked, as is the importance of training schemes to improve their effectiveness. The office manager should be sure that his supervisors are highly trained and many courses are available for this purpose. The National Examinations Board in Supervisory Studies scheme, for example, is offered by many colleges throughout the country.

The main topics which follow are discussed to clarify the general background within which an office manager operates in order to:

1 Consider the various definitions of office management so that any misconceptions relating to organisation roles may be removed.

2 Examine the typical duties and responsibilities of managers who work within the administration function at various levels in the organisation so that the breadth of the job may be appreciated.

3 Discuss some of the critical aspects relating to the operational effectiveness of office management in a concern.

4 Define the purpose of clerical activity in conjunction with the main elements of office management and the office function.

5 Outline some of the current problems that present a strong but absorbing challenge to practising office managers.

Office management

A definition of office management is: to apply effectively all the managerial skills towards achieving the objectives associated with the office function of providing appropriate information and a communication network to all sectors of the organisation.

The term 'office management' is interpreted in various ways:

1 At senior executive level, which implies overall responsibility for all office activities. This function is now termed 'administrative management' in many concerns.

2 At middle management level, where responsibility is usually for a system consisting of a number of procedures. The term 'departmental office manager' is generally used, 'sales office manager' being a typical example.

3 At lower management level, where responsibility for one or a few procedures generally applies. The title in a large firm could be 'office supervisor' or 'chief clerk', whereas

in a small concern the person may often be called an 'office manager'.

Thus there is a wide range of responsibilities which vary according to the size, nature and organisation structure of the concern. The titles of individuals also vary considerably because often this function overlaps with other functions. For example, a chief accountant may also be responsible for administrative management in a medium-sized concern and so may a company secretary in a large firm.

The office manager

To avoid misunderstandings the term 'office manager' is used to describe the middle management level operating within the administration function. The office manager's role may be recognised by considering the typical duties and responsibilities of the four distinguishable levels in administrative organisation:

1 The administrative manager

The office manager is responsible to the administrative manager, who is located in the organisation at a point where all the systems and clerical activities peak, which is at senior executive level. The administrative manager, who may be called an administrative director or chief administrator, is responsible to the managing director, i.e. to the head of the concern. A typical list of responsibilities assigned to an administrative manager is:

(a) To effectively control the administration function throughout the organisation at minimal cost.
(b) To co-ordinate and integrate all clerical activities with a view to optimising the main objectives of the concern.
(c) To ensure full use is made of information technology consistent with cost-benefits.
(d) To provide an efficient communication network.

   (e) To approve a master budget for all administrative activities and submit it to the managing director.

   (f) To comply with legal requirements.

Within each one of the above-mentioned composite responsibilities there are many other associated responsibilities. This applies also to the office manager's and the office supervisor's responsibilities detailed below. The administrative manager will generally have a number of office managers reporting to him as well as other specialists such as an O and M manager, an OR officer, a computer manager and the chief of an information team. Fig. 1 illustrates a typical line-up.

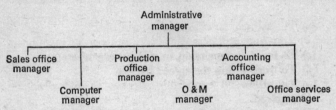

Fig. 1 A typical administrative management team

2 The office manager
At departmental level it is likely that a number of supervisors will be reporting to the office manager. Each supervisor will be responsible for a section which may be limited to dealing with one procedure or may deal with more, depending upon the size of the organisation. The total number of procedures form a system controlled by the departmental office manager. Examples are an accounting system, a cost accounting system, a production control system and a sales system. A typical organisation structure is shown in Fig. 2.

A representative list of the office manager's responsibilities would be:

   (a) To control the system and procedures within his department.

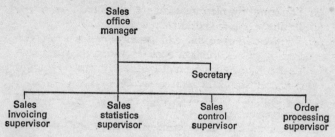

Fig. 2   A typical departmental office management structure

    (*b*) To co-ordinate the clerical activities with other departments.

    (*c*) To maintain an effective group of staff.

    (*d*) To ensure optimum use of all machines and equipment.

    (*e*) To build and maintain an efficient organisation.

    (*f*) To work within the agreed budget.

    (*g*) To utilise all supporting services as and when required.

    (*h*) To attempt the achievement of all objectives.

    (*i*) To keep up-to-date on all aspects of office management and make recommendations accordingly.

    (*j*) To maintain a close link with the administrative manager.

3 The office supervisor

Sometimes the office supervisor is referred to as a section leader and he may be responsible for six to ten group leaders or senior clerks, each one dealing with a segment of the procedure which is known as an activity. Typical activities are invoice checking, filing copy orders, posting entries in the bought ledger, time card calculations, entering sales statistics, scheduling production, issuing inspection tickets, issuing share dividends and maintaining records documentation.

A typical list of his responsibilities would be:

    (*a*) To run the section on a day to day basis.

(*b*) To control the clerical staff in his section.

(*c*) To advise, guide and instruct staff.

(*d*) To maintain discipline and sanction staff where necessary, bearing in mind the need for good human relations.

(*e*) To set a good example and lead staff towards achieving the objectives of the section and the concern.

(*f*) To maintain close links with his superior and fellow supervisors.

(*g*) To control output in terms of quantity and quality of work, timeliness and cost.

(*h*) To develop the effectiveness of the procedures by ensuring that up-to-date methods, machines and equipment are recommended.

(*i*) To utilise supervisory skills in the most efficient way.

(*j*) To encourage staff and help them in every possible way to improve their performance and to increase job satisfaction.

4 Group leader or senior clerk

Although the senior clerk is responsible for a group of about three to six clerks, it is not unusual for him to spend as much as 80% of his time on clerical duties. Thus his supervisory activities are restricted and his authority is correspondingly limited generally to issuing work, checking for errors, helping out where necessary, advising the staff, and maintaining output and quality.

He is not generally involved in any financial aspects such as budgetary control and operating costs of the section, but his influence when coupled with the supervisor's leadership qualities can have considerable effect on staff morale and the effectiveness of the group.

Critical aspects

Some of the main aspects affecting office management are the modern approach to the management process, which places much emphasis on certain networks; the question of company size, which often limits the administrative organisation structure; the vital need for information in the business world of today; and the rapid development of information technology. Each of these aspects is now discussed.

The modern management process
The importance of effective information and communication networks in a thriving business may be assessed by considering how a modern manager operates. The process of management is, briefly stated, to set objectives and attempt to achieve them. In more detail, this basic process implies the use of a number of main managerial skills which form a complete cycle in the following order: anticipating, planning, establishing suitable conditions, acting to achieve the plans, motivating employees, checking performance, solving problems, setting and revising objectives, and making decisions.

The development of these skills depends upon three main factors:

(*a*) The opportunity to practise, making training and experience essential.
(*b*) Acquiring sufficient knowledge in the disciplines associated with each skill, making education vital.
(*c*) Learning associated techniques and keeping up to date on new techniques.

Although skill development rests on the above three factors the effectiveness of skills in operational conditions depends largely upon an adequate supply of appropriate information and an efficient communication network within which the manager can work. In addition to assessing the information, he must also sense the true situation. Clearly each skill he employs demands information: modern managers cannot rely upon judgement alone.

A brief look at each skill and the disciplines and techniques associated with it now follows.

1 Anticipating. This skill is often neglected. Disciplines such as economics, human relations, econometrics and knowledge of the particular business are certainly helpful. Developing a sensitivity towards situations and being able to forecast ahead is particularly difficult, and time allocated to this skill is essential. On the bright side, however, it is surprising how accurate some people can be at 'crystal ball gazing'. Even more astonishing is the fact that when some of these people are asked how they manage to achieve such foresight, they eventually reveal quite simple methods such as the study of trends. The lesson to be learned is that they actually devote time to thinking about possible problems that will arise and using information with this idea in mind. The way procedures are operated and the use of reporting is helpful, and these aspects are discussed in Chapter 5.

2 Planning. Anticipation of changes leads to planning, which involves among many features the setting of standards (discussed in Chapters 9 and 10), disciplines associated with quantitative techniques such as statistics and mathematics, the use of logic and planning principles.

On the operational side the whole question of data processing, systems and procedures is fundamental to the plan, and these are dealt with in Chapters 4 and 5. Legal aspects must also be considered; the main Acts affecting office management are listed in Appendix I. In addition, a useful aid in establishing standards is offered by the British Standards Institution who publishes a number of pamphlets relating to office work. The main topics together with the BS number are listed in Appendix II.

3 Establishing suitable conditions. When the plan is completed or revised the composite skill of establishing suitable conditions under which the plan can materialise is applied. These conditions include creating the right organisation (Chapter 2) within which carefully selected and suitably trained staff (Chapter 7) can operate in an appropriate office environment (Chapter 8). The disciplines associated with these aspects are organisation, psychology and sociology.

4 Act to achieve plans. The next skill in the cycle is to take action by communicating the plans and activities desired to achieve the objectives to all concerned. The main disciplines involved are command and communication (Chapter 6) and it should be carefully noted that this skill is limited to making staff aware of intentions, plans, objectives, the procedures to adopt and so on.

Awareness or possessing knowledge on all the aspects associated with a job does not necessarily mean that any particular work will be undertaken, although naturally there should be a strong impulse to do something when an individual fully understands his job and the role he should play.

5 Motivating employees. The importance of the skill of motivating employees should never be underestimated. Motivation brings the organisation to life through the upsurge of drive in each individual who is motivated. At this stage work commences in the sense that clerical activities are now undertaken after all the planning and arranging is completed, which is another form of work in itself, carried out by managers and supervisors. The important features are leadership, financial and non-financial incentives, psychology, sociology and motivation concepts, all of which are covered in Chapter 3.

6 Checking performance. When clerical operations are under way it can be guaranteed that the activities and procedures will not go according to plan. Almost invariably errors will occur, problems will appear and continual correction becomes necessary. The skill of inspection or checking is part of the control feature (Chapter 9) and particular care is necessary to avoid destroying enthusiasm. The main disciplines involve psychology, but techniques associated with statistical method and quality control approaches must also be studied.

7 *Solving problems.* When errors are known and deviations from the plan become obvious, the need to solve problems and to find the causes becomes a separate skill which is particularly demanding. Involved approaches varying in complexity may be undertaken and these form sufficient material to fill many text-books. A mention of these procedures is given in Chapter 6.

8 *Setting and revising objectives.* When the causes of deviations from the plan are located, it may be desirable to revise the associated policy and to reset objectives if the deviations are very serious. Minor causes can easily be remedied by the supervisor, who can make adjustments from day to day. Major causes, however, may upset the whole plan and demand extensive revision at executive level. Various disciplines such as corporate planning, budgeting and economics might govern the executive's thoughts when utilising this skill.

9 *Decision-making.* When problems are solved, the causes known and objectives revised if necessary, the skill of decision-making (Chapter 6) is undertaken. The complexity of the skill is similar to that of problem-solving and many books have been written on this subject. The disciplines are very involved and depend upon the type of decision. New techniques are constantly appearing, such as the use of decision trees.

Finally, when the decision is made, the time to consider the outcome follows which completes the cycle and returns to anticipating or forecasting what will happen as a result.

In conclusion, it should be remembered that no manager is highly proficient in all managerial skills, many of which have not been mentioned in this précis approach to the subject. Invariably he will be weak in some areas and particularly strong in others. Some skills come far more naturally: it depends on the individual.

Company size
Some organisations consist mainly of clerical activities while others of a similar size have only a small number of office staff. The deciding factor is the nature of the business, such as, on the one hand, insurance, banking and tour operating and, on the other hand, manufacturing concerns, building constructors, mining firms, laundries and hospitals.

Although four levels are distinguishable in administrative management in a large organisation, there is a tendency for the number to be reduced as the small organisation is approached. Similarly, the smaller the organisation is the fewer administration specialists will be found. Both occur through economic necessity and operational effectiveness. An indication of the type of structure in three theoretical concerns is now given.

The small concern. In the small business the jobs are generally known and are capable of being performed by everyone. In emergencies even the owner helps out, doing simple tasks to maintain the flow of work. The duties which are combined in a job in the small firm are normally split into separate jobs in medium- and large-sized firms. This combination often makes the work more varied and interesting. An example of a small business is given in Fig. 3 and a small office in Fig. 4.

The medium-sized concern. As a company grows, the tendency is for the office to develop in a haphazard way. When the demand for more information cannot be met in time by existing

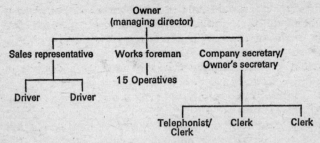

Fig. 3 A small business—organisation structure

staff, more clerks have to be engaged on a crisis basis instead of in a planned scheme of development. In the absence of an office management specialist, the likelihood of an uneconomic, poorly organised office emerging is very strong. Empire-building is a temptation for most managers during growth periods, although one organisation concept actually encourages this practice for the purpose of developing managers. Eventually the day of reckoning causes an unhealthy upheaval in the organisation which could have been avoided.

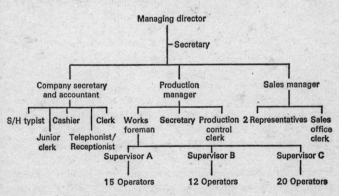

Fig. 4 A small office—organisation structure

In some companies regular dislocation occurs in the organisation, indicating a weak management structure which is out of balance and poorly staffed at senior executive level. The fact that the company is actually growing might negate such a statement. Unfortunately companies often grow through the appearance and change of situations over which there is no real control. The company is often swept up on the crest of a lucky wave with no bed-rock to support it and, unless staff of the right calibre are employed and trained, the company may just as easily fall back and fail completely. Effective office management during growth is a critical feature of survival, although generally neglected as attention is concentrated on increasing production, for example, or on expanding marketing.

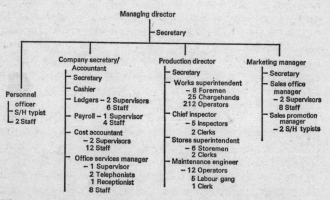

Fig. 5 A medium-sized concern—organisation structure

Fig. 5 indicates a typical example of a medium-sized concern. The administrative manager at senior executive level is intentionally omitted as most concerns have not yet reached this stage of development. The need is obvious, but the managers are not trained and available at this stage.

The large-scale concern. Many teething problems of an organisation have often been overcome by the time a company reaches large-scale proportions. By this time appropriate costing systems have been installed and top management has a good idea of expense areas in each function. Cost-conscious managers help to reduce uneconomic areas and in many large firms administrative managers at senior executive level play an important role in the top management team. This change has only occurred in recent years, however, and many firms are still only on the threshold of this new era of functional change. An indication is given in Fig. 6 of a theoretical organisation in a large company.

The need for information
Although the need for information may seem obvious and essential considering the modern approach to management, there still persists a feeling among some managers that hunches and experience are sufficient for high performance. This group generally is found among the so-called 'experienced managers,' who are not professionally trained and sometimes tend to resent the scientific and other sophisticated approaches to management.

The growth of management thought in this century has passed through a number of phases commencing with the concept of scientific management initiated by F. W. Taylor and developed by Frank and Lilian Gilbreth, Henry Gantt and others. This concept was based on applying various scientific techniques in an attempt to assist managers in solving problems and making decisions, and is known as the Scientific Management School.

In the middle 1920s another phase stands out among the many which there have been over the past seventy years. This concept is often called the Human Relations School and was developed by George Elton Mayo and others who were associated with the famous Hawthorne Experiments at the Western

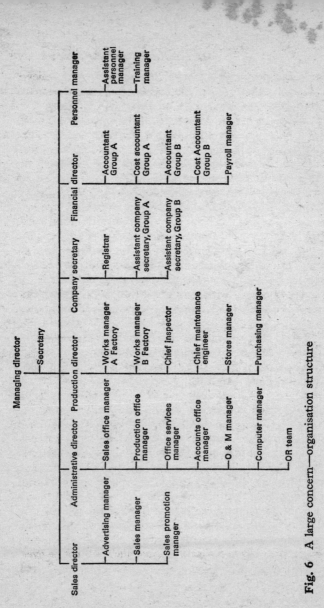

Fig. 6 A large concern—organisation structure

Electric Company near Chicago. Briefly, this school believes in the importance of recognising human beings and their needs as paramount in achieving high productivity.

Since then there have been various combinations of the two schools' basic concepts and offshoot concepts such as communication, higher business control, joint consultation, welfare work, incentives and motivation. Gradually, the need for more sophisticated information was recognised as essential if managers were to operate scientific techniques successfully and to utilise employees effectively. The development of information technology to cope with the problems of obtaining, classifying, storing and giving information, has now reached a point where the management dilemma associated with problem-solving and decision-making in particular can be reduced considerably. The use of the computer, system design and many information-processing machines and techniques can, when utilised with expertise, remove much of the uncertainty in management.

The rapidly increasing complexity of industry and commerce in recent years has also accelerated interest and development in information technology. The trend towards large-scale concerns and diversity of trades within conglomerates has increased the need for highly sophisticated information networks to cope with such aspects as rapid change in markets, competitors' varying tactics and strategic research. Co-ordination and communication are vital for the survival of businesses and information is the lifeblood of these arteries. There is far more to it, however, than simply pumping information in vast quantities to managers and staff. The danger of overloading managers with information is already apparent. There is a limit to the amount of data that can be absorbed in a working day. Thus other problems such as analysis and presentation, for example, become equally important. The information explosion has produced a state of flux which will not be overcome for many years.

Incidentally, the term *information* is generally assumed to represent all the details on a multitude of topics including the term *data*. *Data*, however, generally refers to the detail whereas *information* is often used to describe the data which have been processed, sifted and re-presented in a more suitable form for management. In fact, managers are receiving data and information most of the time through the natural process of communicating with people.

The ability to classify information instinctively into worthwhile and useless categories is an asset to any manager. So much information he receives is never used. The argument that it should be recorded 'in case' is not very sound when all aspects are considered, such as the time component, the economics of storage and the probability of its use. It is worthwhile to develop the habit of questioning each piece of information quickly to see whether it is relevant and worth recording.

Information technology

Information technology is the art (and science) of locating, collecting, analysing, recording and transmitting all necessary information and data to every part of the organisation on time and in the most suitable form to satisfy the requirements of everyone. These requirements should provide managers, supervisors, clerical staff, specialists and manual operators with sufficient information to operate effectively, provided, of course, that the other essential features affecting performance are fully developed.

The breadth of information technology is extremely wide and includes a number of basic disciplines such as economics, mathematics and statistics, and many techniques such as operational research, systems analysis, accountancy, management accountancy, cost accountancy, neurology, the study of servo-mechanisms and ergonomics. Office mechanisation and automation feature prominently in this technology. The original all-purpose clerk is gradually disappearing and being replaced by the specialist clerk who uses a variety of machines and concentrates on such activities as posting accounts, typewriting, filing, calculating, card punching, duplicating, verifying and sorting. The computer is gradually overcoming the mechanical problems of information processing such as recording quickly, moving information, and rapidly calculating and summarising.

The overall aim of information technology is to provide information so that everyone's knowledge is up to date but, at the same time, to ensure that managers do not suffer with an overload of information. The problem of overloading can only be solved through the study of the specific knowledge that managers actually use to become more effective. This dynamic aspect is associated with the choice of information and the impression created on managers, which in total provide the dynamism of information technology.

The communication aspect. There is a critical reliance upon communication in the achievement of company objectives. Communication failures immediately destroy the information technologist's efforts, therefore it would seem appropriate to absorb communication within information technology in view of its importance.

A balanced approach. Although information technology is an essential requirement in an effective organisation, the danger of overdevelopment at the expense of the human side of organisation must be considered. Both technological and human aspects are important and deserve equal attention. Thus topics such as styles of leadership, incentives, motivation, authority, responsibility and welfare merit consideration, as well as the more bureaucratic aspects such as the organisation structure, systems, procedures and computers. Effectiveness depends upon the right combination of the two.

The information technologist. The upsurge in information technology in recent years has attracted a number of professional people who are developing expertise within their own comparatively narrow spheres and who are responsible to a senior executive. Typical examples are electronic data processing managers, communication managers, cyberneticians, O & M managers, management services managers, senior systems analysts, corporate planning managers, long-range forecasters, economic intelligence officers and technical intelligence officers. These technologists in turn are operating alongside a number of technicians with responsibilities for various segments of the basic technology. Typical technicians *within this category* are accountants, cost accountants, registrars, O & M officers, programmers, systems analysts and departmental office managers.

Above the information technologists appears the higher technologist. He may be called *the* office manager or administrative manager and his role as *the* information technologist in the concern should be distinguished from that of *an* information technologist at a lower level.

The purpose of clerical activity

The purpose of any activity may be defined as the design of effecting something, or the thing it is designed to effect. Therefore the use of the office as a general term is to provide and maintain an effective information service through an established communication network. This definition includes all the main elements of office management described below, provided that the term *service* is employed in its broad meaning to include information technology and all its associated activities. Alternatively, the office may be considered as a producer of information. In many ways the production or processing of information is similar to producing an article and is equally important in a business.

In many concerns the office function is expected to be responsible for the effective flow of information to everyone through appropriate communication channels. This heavy and important responsibility indicates a function which is equal to other functions, interdependent, interrelated and goes beyond the narrow concept of a service. Thus clerical activities help the organisation to achieve its objectives and to cater for any legal obligations associated with the environment, financial aspects, documentation and contracts. The clerical activity often attempts to achieve its purpose by conducting operations not only in accommodation specifically designed for clerical work but also in many unsuitable places, such as the driving cab of a van, open storage sites, the workshop and customers' premises.

The main elements of office management

To clarify the main elements of office management a definition of what the term involves should be examined and divided into constituent parts. These are outlined below:

1 Managerial skills. These must be applied effectively, making office management both an art and a science.

2 Administrative knowledge. An abundance of knowledge in the various disciplines and knowledge areas is essential.

3 Clear objectives. The aims must be concise and in perspective with the other main functions.

4 The office function. This function represents the work the office is designed to perform, namely to receive, record, arrange and give information wherever and whenever it is needed throughout the organisation.

5 The communication network. The flow of information in many diverse directions depends upon the provision of a formal and informal comprehensive network of communication channels.

6 The staff and environment. The successful operation of the function rests with administrative staff and their degree of effectiveness within the environment that they are expected to work in.

7 Software and hardware. The provision of suitable forms, systems, procedures, other paperwork, machines, equipment and techniques is an essential support feature which demands constant attention and safeguarding.

The office function

The office function mentioned above is an element which illustrates clearly the complexity of clerical activities that may be divided into the following components:

1 Inward information flow. The inward flow of information takes many forms such as letters, telegrams, telephone calls, newspapers, callers, orders, invoices, credit notes, radio messages, various reports, teleprinter messages and so on. Collection of information, in addition to the normal inward flow, is also needed to satisfy the requirements of managers.

2 Recording appropriate information. Some of the information flowing into the concern must be recorded for the use of management when required at a later date. Recording all the information would be an enormous task and uneconomic, therefore decisions are necessary to avoid chaos. Some records must be kept to satisfy legal requirements. Typical records normally maintained in concerns include financial accounts, cost accounts, orders, work in progress, price lists, stock, invoices, personnel records and correspondence.

3 Processing information. Information must be distributed to managers *in the most suitable form* to satisfy their requirements. The correct way to consider this aspect is to relate the activity in terms of marketing a product. A product must conform to the consumer's needs otherwise he is not interested in buying it. The office has an important responsibility in a similar fashion and highly trained staff are essential to satisfy this demand. Typical examples are issuing statistical statements, budgets, costings, preparing invoices, financial statements and reports in general.

4 Information retrieval. The office should provide everyone with information as and when required, provided that there is a legitimate reason. The two main classifications are routine information used for operating procedures and special information for such uses as problem-solving and policy-making. Examples of routine information are orders for various materials, quotations, prices and stock statements. Special information would include emergency instructions, financial analyses not usually available and statistical analysis of a non-routine nature.

5 Administrative control. A particular duty not generally recognised is to maintain a constant watch on the affairs of the business in general and to warn management of any deviation, deficiency or unusual occurrence which is reported. This duty extends to safeguarding the property, protecting any cash, intelligently interpreting any information and reporting any occurrence which could be construed to be of importance to management.

Current problems in office management

Practising office managers will be well aware of the main difficulties associated with their function. Some of these problems are insoluble at present because technological development has not yet reached a high level of sophistication. Moreover, the lag in the development of effective office managers and higher executives and general scepticism among managers tend to aggravate these problems. The potential office manager must be prepared to accept the difficulties which underlie the job and he should work towards overcoming them eventually. The insurmountable problems of today are manipulative material for young managers who may become successful in the future by finding suitable answers. The challenge is clear and the opportunities are manifold. Ten typical problem areas are now illustrated.

1 Recognition

Although there are indications that more and more concerns are recognising the importance of the administration function, many organisations are still not geared towards acceptance of this concept. Many administrative costs are easily lost among other functions' expenditure. The true cost, therefore, remains hidden and the function is not considered sufficiently important. Until the true costs are revealed there is little hope of convincing anyone, except the few converted managers, that large savings and increased managerial effectiveness are possible.

2 Development of information technology

The teething troubles with any new technology tend to detract from its immense possibilities. Probably it is true to say that information technology is still in its infancy, but this does not mean that it can be ignored. The opportunities offered in its present form are already considerable and should be grasped now.

3 Assignment of blame

There is a distinct tendency to blame the technology if a scheme associated with it fails. A closer study often reveals that the failure is due to the inadequacy of individuals. Expertise in a new function takes a long time to develop and it is not unusual for the blame to be pinned on the inanimate object (the technology) that cannot protest and defend itself.

4 Indistinct objectives attainment

Objectives are easy to state but it is very difficult to prove that they are being approached or achieved if the results are not measurable in quantitative terms.

Unfortunately some of the objectives in office management and administrative management are qualitative. Their achievement often depends upon personal opinion and it is impractical and probably impossible to separate other influencing factors which affect the outcome of operational effectiveness in this function. It is essential to have goodwill and an understanding of the evolving situation in which the function plays its part.

5 Cost-benefit analysis

Closely connected with the problem mentioned above is the complexity of rising costs in office work. Constant rises in salaries, the cost of materials, machines, equipment and many other items place a heavy burden on a person who attempts to evaluate the benefit of expenditure on office management to the concern as a whole. The use of the cost-benefit analysis technique identifies the crucial issues and presents a comprehensive picture of the real situation. No doubt the logic of assessing the value of expenditure in terms of reward and effectiveness is quite sound. However, thinking in terms of both quantity and quality analysis, their justification is purely subjective and there may be some difficulty in convincing senior management.

6 Overall control

The problem of actually finding a suitable senior executive who possesses the high capability necessary to control this

function effectively is difficult to solve at present. There are
not sufficient specialists in this field; the demand is low mainly
through ignorance or an unpleasant experience when the
experiment was previously tried. This 'chicken and egg' situation is commonplace and disasters often occur before the syn-
drome is finally broken.

The answer has to be found, however, as administration is
the fastest growing sector in the working population, although
the professional and technical sectors are also increasing very
rapidly. Paradoxical as the situation may seem with automation
and mechanisation being introduced and the administrative
working population increasing at the same time, the insatiable
demand for information is overtaking both at present. Whether
the demand is justifiable is another matter.

7 Information requirements

One of the unfortunate features of administrative inefficiency
is that managements' information requirements are not
accurately known. The cause of this problem is debatable.
There are two extreme schools of thought: one feels that each
manager should say what information he requires and the
other feels that the administrative manager should decide. The
situation in practice is not so clear-cut. For example, some
managers for various reasons do not know what their information requirements are. In addition, some administrative
managers are unable to say what information should be given
either. One solution is to discuss information requirements
together, thus using both parties more effectively.

8 The leadership problem

An entirely different form of leadership is needed to cope with
the current situation in industry and commerce compared with
thirty years ago. The emergence of the welfare state, the rising
level of education, the increasing standard of living and the
growth of trade union power have all contributed to a marked

change in attitude and behaviour on the part of the working community. High staff turnover, continual demands for higher salaries, less will to do a fair day's work for a fair day's pay and a more belligerent mood are commonplace in companies today. Knowing how to motivate staff is the key to good leadership, but this task is exceptionally difficult. Although a thorough knowledge of the behavioural sciences is an important feature, the secret of success goes far beyond this stage.

The situation is aggravated by the continuing loss of status of office staff through the levelling-up process in manual occupations and the tendency for office jobs to be less interesting. Also, many women have entered offices, resulting in a high percentage of staff who are, perhaps, less ambitious and less conscientious.

9 Technological change
A problem which is shared by all specialists is one involving the work of keeping pace with technological change. Unless the office manager is prepared to allocate his time carefully, including an allowance for reading and generally up-dating his knowledge by other means, there is a real risk of falling behind.

Decisions affecting various aspects of office management, such as the purchase of hardware and software, demand up-to-date knowledge. Rapid obsolescence is a fact of life, mistakes can be very costly and a reputation can easily be lost through a few errors of this nature.

10 Co-ordinating company activities
The professional administrator is fast becoming involved in the co-ordination and steering activities of the business alongside other professionals. This professional team has the critical role of strategic planning and devising suitable tactical operations to achieve the plans. For the office manager who aspires to participate in these activities there are high prospects, but

to be eligible, years of hard and intensively interesting work are necessary.

This role which is now being adopted by the new specialist in administration was undertaken in the past first by the production expert, who promised increased output of higher quality goods, and secondly by the marketing expert, who undertook to sell, in increasing quantities, in new markets. In later times the specialist engineer and marketing manager worked closer together, creating new products and developing or revitalising marketable outlets. The two continue to strive for fresh goals, now alongside the new professional administrator who joins the team together with the essential support of the financial specialist.

As the team grows in size the overall co-ordination problem increases considerably. The managing director has to undertake this task, but he must be backed by efficient co-ordination at levels immediately below and at departmental level. Thus the office manager cannot escape his responsibilities for co-ordination within his own area of operations and he must be able to work closely with other co-ordinators in an ever-increasing complexity of business activity.

2 Administrative organisation

Introduction

One of the main skills in office management is to establish suitable conditions within which employees can operate successfully. These conditions may be considered to be static (or cold) when isolated from the human aspect. There is no life or dynamism attached to them until they are vitalised by people. These conditions have no economic benefit, no productivity and no purpose other than to favourably affect employees' performance. A possible exception is that they tend to increase the asset value of a concern, considering that suitable conditions include maintenance and decoration of premises, all office machinery, equipment, systems and furniture, as well as organisation. Suitable conditions are considered to be established only when the objectives are clear beforehand and company policies are carefully formulated to achieve them. Theoretically, therefore, a sound organisation plan will enable employees' activities to interlock successfully towards achieving a common aim.

Definition of organisation

If organisation is considered for the moment to be static it may be defined as a plan of the concern's structure, indicating all the jobs, their relationships with each other, their function and the duties involved, as well as the authority and responsibilities associated with them. This definition implies continuity of jobs, which is an essential requirement regardless of the individuals who may be performing them at any point in time.

The organisation designer must face the fact that people are not indispensable; as soon as they are born it is a certainty that they will die. In addition, staff movement from company to company is becoming more usual and acceptable. This does not mean that employees can be ignored, for they are vital, but continuity of jobs within the concern is also important. Company survival is one objective to remember, and if certain individuals appear to be indispensable the danger signal should be recognised.

If organisation is envisaged from the dynamic or operational viewpoint a more appropriate definition is: a system indicating all the structural interpersonal relationships between staff who have a common aim. Both definitions are limited and suffer from problematic relationships, as will become apparent during the discussions that follow.

Main aspects

The departmental office manager may become involved in organisational problems in various ways. In a growing concern he may easily be implicated in redesigning his own organisation and be asked to give advice on the general administrative organisation structure. During the normal routine some jobs may have to be restructured through staffing difficulties and he should always be striving to improve the organisation whenever the opportunities occur.

The essential information he will require is outlined in the rest of the chapter, which includes preliminary considerations, structures associated with organisation design and the main characteristics of conventional organisations. Before continuing with organisation relationships, a section on the administration function describes the subfunctions and the operation of the administrative machine. The principles of organisation are next examined, which leads into organisation analysis and a typical approach that can be adopted by the office manager.

Designing an organisation

Preliminary considerations

Before reaching the design stage an important aspect should be considered. If the organisation is not already operating an opportunity exists to start at the job design stage, but this is most unlikely in the majority of situations. Most design work involves an established organisation which includes personalities who have developed certain situations that will strongly influence proposed changes. The alternative in these conditions is to design an ideal organisation, which involves considering the jobs themselves rather than the employees in the jobs at present, and to work gradually towards the so-called ideal.

This feature is most important considering the remarks in the introduction above. Thus it is possible for a well-designed organisation to run badly and a poorly designed organisation to run very smoothly. It depends on the employees, their treatment, selection, training and many other apparently obscure factors. This fact does not mean, however, that organisation design is unimportant; a combination of good design and the right employees is ideal and this should be the objective.

There should be a clear understanding that changes in the organisation, although sound in theory, will not guarantee increased effectiveness. The outcome may be the introduction of disrupting influences and emotional upheavals caused by existing personalities, who may object for various reasons to the alterations, and by the breakdown of effective informal groups. Indeed, it is essential to consider and consult employees who are already involved in operating the section of the organisation under review. Unless drastic action is essential, such as severe redundancy, rapid expansion or a change in site location, it is safer to visualise the ideal organisation and to work gradually towards it as opportunities occur through natural wastage of employees, promotions and development transfers.

Before continuing with the tools and principles associated with organisation design, an examination of organisation structures and their relationships with administration should be of assistance.

Organisation structures

The main aspects of organisation structures that have direct effect on the administration function are responsibility for the administration function and direct responsiblity at various levels in the organisation for administrative staff. The treatment of these two aspects considerably affects the role of the office manager and his method of operating.

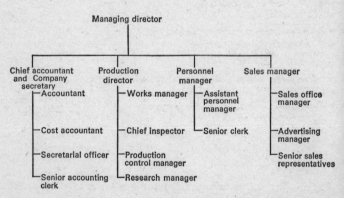

Fig. 7　Organisation structure—administrative responsibility held by chief accountant

A typical structure illustrating the situation where the chief accountant, in addition to his specialist accounting and company secretarial function, has responsibility for administration is given in Fig. 7. In this case all administrative staff are responsible to the line managers: production director, personnel manager and sales manager. The sales office manager's role is a difficult one considering that he is responsible to the sales manager for the control of the office and to the chief accountant for administrative matters. Thus the functional responsibility for administration is centralised, but the operating responsibility is decentralised to each line manager.

A similar structure might operate with no senior executive being responsible for the administration function throughout the concern. In this case it must be assumed that administration responsibility, although not recognised or stated, appears at that point in the organisation where all the systems meet, namely at managing director level.

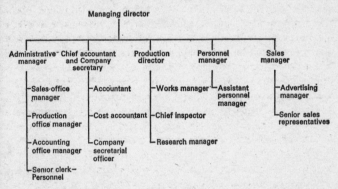

Fig. 8 Revised organisation structure—administration function established

In Fig. 8 the structure is revised to show the establishment of direct responsibility at all levels of administration staff. The line managers are no longer directly involved in administrative matters and can now spend all their time in their specialist activity. Thus administration is fully centralised.

Bearing these aspects in mind, the characteristics and principles of organisation are now examined.

Characteristics of conventional organisation

The majority of concerns still tend to conform to a pattern as regards a number of characteristics, such as the conventional grouping process for tasks and jobs, the establishment of main functions, the employment of one or more of the recognised formal relationships, recognition of informal relationships and the organisation pyramid. In addition, the tendency to use conventional principles of organisation continues, although one school of thought insists that a change is occurring. New concepts are being adopted in some large concerns and these seem to indicate a breakdown of certain organisation principles. Both approaches will be examined later.

Another important feature of conventional (or classical) organisation is the principle of delegation, which theoretically should provide each employee with an even workload, allow for individual development and prevent overloading at more senior levels. This principle will also be discussed later.

Finally, the question of span of control figures prominently. Theoretically, a supervisor or a manager has difficulty in effectively controlling more than six staff when their duties interlock. The argument is based on the idea that each time an additional member is added to the group under control the number of relationships rises as a geometric, not arithmetic, progression. In practice, the controllable number depends more upon the superior's capabilities, but the stress factor must be considered as group size increases.

The natural approach

With no knowledge of organisation many people find the natural way to design an organisation is:

1 To consider the basic elements. In the case of office work these are reading, writing, calculating, filing, sorting, collating, typing and duplicating.

2 To group the elements together to perform a task such as calculating a basic wage, say 40 hours at 50p an hour.

3 To group tasks together to form a job such as calculating net weekly wages.

4 To group jobs together to form a section such as the payroll.

5 To arrange for section supervision.

6 To group sections together to form a department such as the accounting department.

7 To arrange for departmental management.

8 To group departments together to form a main function, such as finance.

9 To arrange for functional management.

10 To group main functions under a managing director.

The size of the organisation and the amount of office work will mainly determine whether the full structure described above would be necessary. Each characteristic is outlined below, bearing in mind the natural approach described above.

The grouping process

A vast number of tasks is distinguishable in an organisation. In office work typing a letter, filing a document, answering the telephone, calculating income tax, posting an entry in a ledger and writing a receipt are typical examples. These tasks may be grouped together to form a job and the method of grouping decides the breadth of the job. If *series* grouping is used the job is inclined to be narrow and specialised because the principle is to group as few tasks together as possible so that the employee can become more skilful in performing them, is more easily trained and, in theory, should be more efficient. Thus one clerk may simply write out orders every day. Obviously this type of job soon becomes boring and loss of interest inevitably affects performance. A similar situation on the shop floor such as turning nuts with a spanner every day has caused a tremendous amount of industrial unrest in recent years.

If *parallel* grouping is used the employee will be engaged in a greater number of tasks which make up the job. For example, he may receive telephoned requisitions and written enquiries, make out orders, process the orders, check delivery, write out goods received notes, pass the invoice and check payment. The difference between the two methods is that with *series* grouping each employee performs a task and passes on the work to the next one who performs another task, and so on. With *parallel* grouping each employee performs a number of tasks which form a segment of a procedure. Other clerks will also be engaged on similar work in another segment.

Following this task grouping process, which is generally called job design, the next stage is to group the jobs to form subfunctions such as an invoicing section, a sales statistics section and payroll section. Eventually the subfunctions are gathered together to form a main function such as accountancy, sales or production. This aspect is now discussed.

The main functions

The establishment of main functions is vital to the success of an organisation and yet it is one of the most neglected aspects and often planned in a completely haphazard way. The conventional arrangement is based upon three so-called main functions immediately recognisable in industry, namely sales, production and finance. In commerce the main functions are based upon the specialism of the concern, such as insurance, which replaces the production function.

Recognition of a function in a concern seems to depend upon the use of an activity that requires a sufficiently wide breadth of knowledge to warrant the engagement of a specialist. The existence of such an activity hinges mainly on the size of the concern, the type of business, the structure of the organisation and recognition of the need for it. This indicates that recognition of this need rests with managerial knowledge and internal policies.

Regardless of recognition, specialist activities often exist and are operated either by an existing member of the staff as a side-line or by an outside expert on an occasional basis. If a specialist activity is undertaken as an extra duty by another specialist, malfunctioning may occur because he will not be able to devote all his time to his original specialism and it is unlikely that he will possess sufficient knowledge of the second specialism or have the time to practise it. This presupposes that company size and other factors mentioned above are viable.

A specialist who controls a main function has a particular responsibility to keep up to date so that he may practise and advise accurately. A structure based upon specialisms ensures that the boundaries between functions are naturally formed with no overlaps or gaps. If one essential specialism is omitted, however, there is a risk of chaos and empire-building.

The administration function

The evolvement, increasing interest in, and the importance of the administration function has already been discussed. Through its nature this activity permeates all other functions. Paperwork appears everywhere in a concern, even at the extremities such as in transport vehicles, open storage depots, the boiler-house and the cleaners' cupboard. If the definition of an office is anywhere where paperwork is processed, the spread of the administration activity is obvious, as is the risk of uneconomic operation if it is not effectively controlled.

The subfunctions already discussed, which make up a main function, may be grouped under the headings of O & M, computer operations, office services, operational research, systems analysis, departmental office managers and management information services. The wealth of knowledge demanded by these subfunctions in total is sufficient to warrant the sole attention of one man who can specialise. Full competence and the formation of the function immediately relieves the load on the rest of the specialists, who may now apply themselves fully in their own sector.

Arguments often encountered are that the administration function is a service, it is a secondary activity, it is a servant to other functions and it has no value in isolation. Unfortunately the same applies to all functions. Producing goods is pointless unless they can be sold; marketing is useless unless there is a service or goods on offer. Placing any group at a psychological disadvantage is dangerous and invites trouble. Each employee has a part to play and he likes to know that his job is as important as the next.

A peculiar characteristic of the administration function is that a large variety of costs connected with it can be easily cloaked under many guises throughout the concern. Unless a good costing system is functioning the true cost of operating the activity can be very difficult to assess. The wastage, degree of benefit, overall effect on management and actual cost are easily overlooked. There is no doubt that if the true picture were known in many firms the need for a rearrangement of main functions would be obvious.

Each of the subfunctions of administrative management are described below, bearing in mind that a subfunction may be described as a group of activities that are closely related and collectively have a clear objective and end-product which allies itself completely with other subfunctions and a main function.

Organisation and methods

The application of work study which for many years has been solely associated with the factory is now extended to include

office work. The title often used for work study in the office is
O & M: organisation and methods. Similar techniques to those
employed in the factory are used along with specialists who
concentrate on improvement programmes. The main fields of
study are work measurement so that standards may be established for many clerical activities; method study to ensure that
the most efficient way of performing clerical duties is adopted;
organisation study to consider better ways of controlling and
structuring the sections; and other more sophisticated techniques.

Computer operations
The use of a specialist to cope with the continuing advancement
in data processing technology is essential because of the direct
involvement in processing information which is, of course,
fundamental to administration activities.

The high cost of computers, including hardware, software
and operating costs, demands particular expertise in being able
to advise and control with accuracy. Effective management of
a computer, the attendant staff, data transmission, storage and
information retrieval is an exacting responsibility.

Office services
This term is widely interpreted and is sometimes called management services. Office services may include the maintenance
and redecoration of offices, office cleaning, various activities
such as filing, typing, reproducing, communication services,
reception and mailing, and other activities of this nature.

A feature of these services is that they are often centralised,
meaning controlled from one point or physically brought together. The advantages of centralising this type of activity are
that more effective control can be applied to the service by
establishing supervision, dealing with fluctuations in workload,
higher utilisation of machines and equipment, and more
specialised use of employees. The tendencies to avoid when

centralising are over-rigidity of control features, loss of status by employees who are transferred from other jobs and the possibility of a reduction in the service offered to the organisation.

Operational research

An essential part of information technology is the use of operational research, which assists managers in making more reliable decisions where there are many, and often opposing, aspects to be considered and balanced. Operational research work is expensive; it demands a specialist or a team of specialists, it is an evolving science and its application has been limited mainly to large concerns so far. There are many sophisticated techniques, the most familiar being network analysis, linear programming and queuing theory. The technique that has received most publicity is network analysis, which was used on the Polaris project in 1961, the project being completed in record time. This scientific approach is not fully utilised in solving industrial problems, but very large concerns are continuing to experiment with the techniques.

Systems analysis

Redesigning existing procedures is an essential step before they can be adapted to the computer. Systems analysis, therefore, is strongly connected with the computer and the analysts have to work closely with the computer programmers. A system may be referred to as a number of procedures which are carefully planned to reach established objectives, such as preparation of final accounts, budgetary control figures and personnel policy application. All the systems should form a master system, which is often called systems-integration or total-system. Their importance lies in the constant reminder of aims, the application of control, the knitting together of all sectors, the co-ordinating effect and the valuable assistance given in preparation of plans.

Management information services

This generic term often includes the operation of costing systems, communication channels and techniques of reporting, parts of O & M, ways of managing, systems analysis, information theory, random observation and cybernetics. The main aspects of the work are trying to assess the information requirements of managers, endeavouring to provide information at the right time, recording and processing information, and providing appropriate channels for transmitting and receiving information. These complex requirements are sometimes grouped under the title of Management Information Systems (MIS).

The administrative machine

The brief survey given above of the subfunctions that make up the administration function could indicate the emergence of three key components: the communication network, appropriate information and organisational points. The function of the administrative machine in this sense would be to provide communication channels and systems which have a capability of supplying information to all points in the organisation.

The communication network should allow for smooth two-way flow along all channels and interconnecting points by providing both personal and mechanical or electrical means.

The provision of appropriate information covers both internal and external sources. Deciding on whether a particular item of information is needed is fundamental to this component. How it is presented is also critical. The determination of organisational points may appear to be simple. In practice, account must be taken of strategic and tactical operations and various projects, all of which involve groups of people whose progress often depends upon information. Thus the administrative machine has a critical effect on all activities in a concern. This feature is often not realised or appreciated in many companies.

Organisation relationships

To achieve co-ordination each job must be related to other jobs at a similar level and to jobs at levels below and above. In this way networks are established throughout the organisation and they may be categorised as formal or informal.

Formal organisation relationships

The formal authority relationships are divided into three categories: line, functional and staff. Their existence implies that a hierarchy exists and they are illustrated in Fig. 9. In addition, a committee relationship can be seen in some concerns. This arrangement is often disputed and abused, but there is a tendency to think in terms of team organisation as against the line or command-type organisation.

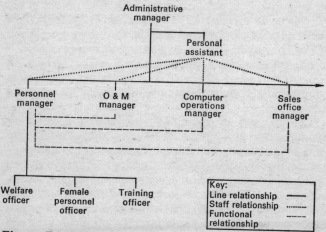

Fig. 9 Formal authority relationships

The need for various specialists to get together and discuss strategy and new projects is becoming increasingly obvious and essential for long-term survival. Some of these individuals will already be engaged in the on-going business which is concerned with manufacturing and marketing already proven products. Thus they will be engaged in dual roles which establish varying relationships with each other. This dynamic fluid situation which utilises people's expertise more effectively illustrates a totally different form of organisation. Lines of command, many principles and conventional thought on organisation structures tend to fall into the background, while everyone is expected to display far more self-discipline, self-control and inner responsibility in his highly flexible role.

1 Line relationship. Line relationship is often called the hierarchy, the scalar process or the scalar chain. This main communication link which flows from top to bottom of the organisation in the form of a complete network is based upon military organisation. These lines of command imply direct authority between the various levels; the principle is clear and each line commander has complete responsibility for his subordinates.

2 Functional relationship. A specialist who is not exercising any direct authority over subordinates but is consulted on his specialism is said to be engaged in a functional relationship with those line commanders he advises. Using the expertise of specialists is an important aspect of a line commander's job, but he should clearly understand that the functional specialist exercises no direct authority and it is up to the line commander to accept or reject the advice. The line and functional relationship may be coupled if a specialist also has staff directly responsible to him.

3 Staff relationship. This relationship describes the type of authority which is essentially representative. Typical examples are where an executive engages a staff officer or personal assistant whose job is to ease the burden by ensuring that the executive's subordinates interpret his policies and decisions correctly. The staff officer has no direct authority; his responsibility is advisory and he must work through his superior.

4 Committee relationship. In some concerns a committee is established in place of an executive post. This arrangement may be seen in hospitals and local authorities, and it is not unusual for a management committee to appoint a number of standing advisory committees, subcommittees and working parties. The line of command may remain or be abandoned and replaced by various functional relationships. The outcome of this arrangement is that it is time-consuming for all the committee members, some of whom may not be able to contribute for various reasons. Also, responsibility is difficult to attach to a group of members compared with one individual, procedure may be slow and decisions are often a compromise or limited through the domination of one person. There are advantages, however, through the increased brain power, the co-ordinating effect and fuller use of specialists who may be co-opted.

Informal organisation relationships
To ease the rigidity and restrictiveness of formal relationships three types of informal relationship can be recognised. These are illustrated in Fig. 10.

1 Lateral relationship. Both co-ordination and co-operation are achieved between jobs at a similar level within a group through the operation of a lateral or horizontal relationship. The relationship may exist at any level in the organisation and be between a group of clerks, supervisors or managers.

2 Ad-hoc relationship. To avoid the tedium of using the line of command between sections or departments an *ad-hoc*

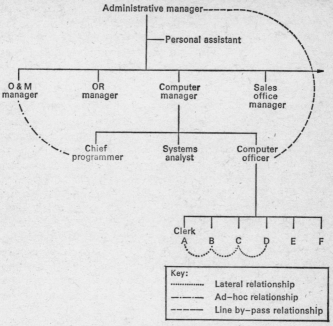

Fig. 10 Informal organisation relationships

relationship should exist between groups not only on similar levels but also at differing levels. This form of harmony and shortening of communication lines relieves the line commanders of unnecessary contact.

3 Line by-pass relationship. Another informal approach is to by-pass the scalar chain completely and establish contact direct; thus two or more levels may be short-circuited. This relationship is often essential if the true situation at a much lower level is to be fully appreciated by an executive who, for example, contacts a clerk personally.

The organisation pyramid

The grouping of jobs together to form subfunctions and eventually main functions creates the problem of how to arrange them into various levels for supervisory and managerial purposes. The general outcome of grouping within the functional approach is the formation of the following structures which, of course, will vary in size and number of levels depending on the individual concern.

1 The primary group
These groups form the base of the pyramid. Each one consists of about six to twelve staff under the control of a supervisor.

2 The section
At the next level sections known as secondary groups consist of about six supervisors associated with their primary groups under the control of a section supervisor.

3 The department
The pyramid continues to narrow by repeating the same process. At this level about six sections are grouped together under a manager. This stage is often termed middle-management level.

4 The functional head
The final grouping of departments or subfunctions under a senior executive nearly completes the pyramid, which is capped by the managing director.

With this approach it is possible to accommodate large numbers of employees as the concern grows by simply creating new primary groups and appropriate groups to complement them at section and departmental level.

Principles of organisation

The conventional principles of organisation are assumed to apply in any concern and may be described as general rules or guides. They also apply to the operational aspects and to manning the organisation, as well as creating the structure. Principles can be recognised in most organisation structures and the main ones are now outlined:

(*a*) Set realistic objectives.

(*b*) Establish a sound working plan to achieve the objectives. The following seven principles (*c*) to (*i*) are closely associated with this main principle.

(*c*) Ensure stability by seeing that instructions are carefully considered before issuing them.

(*d*) Preserve balance in terms of allocating sufficient time to all the tasks within a job and in terms of staffing each function.

(*e*) Maintain orderliness within the organisation.

(*f*) The scalar process should be adopted.

(*g*) *Reports* should be conscientiously completed as required.

(*h*) *Records* should only be kept when the purpose is known.

(*i*) Ensure *continuity* of staff by operating suitable schemes to cope with terminations, death and retirement.

(*j*) Establish suitable leaders. The following seven principles in (*k*) to (*q*) are closely associated with this main principle.

(*k*) Progressiveness should be encouraged so that staff feel the need to be effective and forward-looking.

(*l*) Authority must be allocated, which should be consistent with the responsibilities within the job.

(*m*) Responsibility is essential and implies being answerable to a superior for either getting work done by subordinates or actually doing the work allocated to the job.

(n) Duties must be allocated to each job and be clearly defined.

(o) Discipline underlines the concept of organisation within which individuals are expected to conform to established codes of conduct and operational rules. In the ideal situation people exercise self-discipline; unfortunately, in practice, supervisors and managers have to exercise their authority to achieve varying degrees of discipline and control.

(p) Fairness and justice should be seen, exercised and recognised by *all* employees.

(q) Policy, rules and regulations should be made clear to everyone.

(r) Flexible working arrangements ensure that no task falls between two jobs. This is made possible by ensuring that all the areas of responsibility impinge on each other.

(s) Individual capability, status and personality should be borne in mind when allocating jobs.

(t) Effective delegation is explained in detail below because of its importance.

(u) Span of control is considered to be the number of staff a manager can effectively control. The factors that govern this number are whether their duties interlock, the complexity of the work, the degree of self-discipline and self-control exercised by the staff, and the capability of the manager.

An important aspect to consider is that each time an extra person is added to the group, the relationships in the group increase geometrically through the interlocking of the various associations between the individuals. An adequate number to control is often quoted as six, but in practice the number is often well above this figure, especially at lower levels.

(v) The concept of centralisation is to establish information flow to a central point where it is processed and then transmitted to appropriate points for further processing. This natural concept is applied in organisms. Conforming to this concept means that managers would be in direct contact with employees at several levels below them, thus conflicting with the scalar process and the concept of delegation. The general outcome is that decentralisation is used so that the subordinates' roles become more important, thus fostering increased job interest.

Delegation

The importance of effective delegation is often either misunderstood or underestimated. To avoid these faults the office manager must appreciate the value of delegation, otherwise his performance will suffer drastically. The principle hinges on the assumptions that no one should be overloaded with work, decisions should be pushed as far down the line as possible consistent with competence and everyone should have the opportunity to develop his abilities by practising more difficult tasks. Delegation, therefore, means that a manager must release lower grade tasks and allocate them to his subordinates so that he has sufficient time to concentrate on higher grade tasks and to continue with his own development.

Delegation does not mean shirking responsibility or 'passing the buck'. Some managers have difficulty with delegation for various reasons, such as their tendency to be lazy and to spend time on easy tasks; natural fear associated with tackling more complex tasks, which is instinctively cloaked by becoming absorbed in detail, thus leaving no time to spare; feelings of insecurity which are compensated by refusal to pass on authority in case a subordinate proves himself to be more capable; and lack of trust in subordinates to tackle higher level work.

Procedure for delegating

Many difficulties in delegating may be overcome by adopting a logical approach. A useful method is given below.

(a) List all the tasks, including those which are not carried out through lack of time.

(b) Rearrange the items in descending order of importance.

(c) Estimate the time for each task. An approximation is sufficient.

(d) Starting from the top of the rearranged list, work down to a point where sufficient tasks can be coped with and draw a line.

(e) Assess subordinates' capabilities, allowing for further development.

(f) Match the tasks with appropriate subordinates and allocate them.

(g) Check on their performance by following up and inspecting periodically.

(h) If there are difficulties, rearrange after a fair trial.

Further observations

The procedure already outlined accounts for the allocation of tasks or duties. Two other aspects are involved, however, which must be considered. These are authority and responsibility.

Although conferring authority is straightforward within the delegation process, the ability of the subordinate to give instructions and receive the right response will vary. The outcome depends upon the subordinate's ability to develop appropriate power. Without this power he will lose control and often be ignored. In the case of responsibility the office manager should understand that he cannot delegate his own responsibility. He will always remain ultimately responsible for all the activities and staff under his control.

The concept of responsibility at various levels involves the absorbing of all lower levels of responsibility into the next level up and so on. Put another way, the responsibility at any level is expanded into lower levels, but the basic responsibility still remains. An example of this concept is now given by considering the preparation of sales statistics:

Managing director:	first-rate responsibility	getting
Administrative manager:	second-rate responsibility	the
Sales office manager:	third-rate responsibility	work
Sales office supervisor:	fourth-rate responsibility	done
Sales statistics clerk:	operational responsibility for doing the work	

An examination of this example indicates the concept of expanding responsibility for getting the work done, down to a point where operational responsibility for actually doing the work takes over.

Organisation analysis

In recent years analysing organisations has resulted in more sophisticated definitions of principles and terms, highly developed methods of studying organisations and a number of new organisational concepts. Unfortunately these cannot be examined in depth, but it should be remembered that, although they are an important part of organisation study, the office manager at departmental level will be more involved in improving his own sector. This work will of necessity be more basic and can possibly follow a proposed procedure which will be discussed later.

Advanced study of organisations indicates a number of approaches to organisation thinking. Organisation may be considered as a structure, as a number of processes or in terms of its product. The people working in an organisation probably see it in various ways. One employee may visualise organisation as a means for him to satisfy his needs; another may see it as a means of providing the community with goods; someone else may feel it is an opportunity for him to mix with other people and yet others may see it as a combination of the afore-mentioned factors. Certainly there are at least two sound pur-poses of organisation: to satisfy needs and to provide goods or services. Of course, people must have the opportunity to earn money to buy the goods and services, and thus there is a complex cycle of events to consider.

The conventional or classical school of thought believes that work should be arranged to achieve the organisational objec-tives and that people will accept the concept and perform as required. The assumption that rational behaviour will auto-matically apply in view of the cycle of events is considered acceptable. The behavioural school or naturalistic school, how-ever, hinges on the natural tendency for people to group to-gether. If they have similar interests or needs there is no need for a consciously planned organisation; they will tend to group according to their collective requirements.

Another concept involves a self-adjusting factor which is often termed the systems concept. Each part of the total system contributes, acts as a balancing factor and is inter-dependent in operation. Thus any friction or upset is taken up by the parts immediately and a new situation evolves. This concept assumes that an organisation is simply a part of in-creasingly larger systems such as areas, countries, groups of countries and so on.

From these concepts mentioned above, certain basic con-siderations emerge. Certainly any organisation has a definite purpose, it is manned by people who are willing to work with an end in view, someone has to establish the organisation for a good reason and co-operation is essential to success. In these circumstances it should be possible to analyse an organisation and redesign it to achieve success. Unhappily, people are not completely rational and they do not think entirely logically. They have emotional overtones that affect their judgement, they become preoccupied quite easily and they suffer from communication problems. Thus co-ordination and co-operation become very difficult to achieve and various specialists are needed to lessen these problems within a concern.

As already mentioned, the office manager's role in organisation analysis is restricted generally to the study of his particular sector. Armed with the concepts of organisation, the principles and the characteristics he requires, a logical approach to improving his organisation and the techniques which are useful in solving organisation problems are now discussed.

A typical approach

One method of studying organisation with a view to installing improvements is to follow a traditional procedure associated with most method study activities. This procedure is discussed in detail later, but for this particular purpose the six main steps are:

(a) Select the area to be studied and clarify the objectives of the analysis.
(b) Record the existing organisation.
(c) Critically examine the organisation by applying all the criteria mentioned previously.
(d) Develop an improved organisation using the knowledge acquired by study.
(e) Install and maintain the new organisation structure.
(f) Follow up, evaluate results and revise as considered necessary.

Main techniques

A few minutes' quiet thought should indicate the aspects where techniques can be applied. For example, starting from the base line that there are many tasks performed by individuals, these tasks are grouped to form jobs, the jobs are grouped to form sections and so on. In addition, the tasks are associated with procedures, these are grouped to form a system and systems are grouped together finally to form the complete administrative organisation. At various control points, senior clerks, supervisors and managers are installed to form an executive hierarchy. This information provides sufficient material to formulate techniques for use in studying the organisation.

1 Job tasks
A simple way of recording the tasks in a job is to complete a form similar to the example shown in Fig. 11. The employee or the supervisor may record the details on a daily basis, and finally a summary should be drawn up showing the total hours in the week allocated to each task performed. Assessing job requirements usually comes under the province of the person-

Job title: Processing clerk – buyers			Name: R.P Osmond
Section: Registrar's office			Day: Monday
Time			**Task**
Start	Finish	Minutes	
0900	0915	15	Sort transfers into class of stock
0915	0955	40	Fix transfer label to transfer form
1000	1135	95	Copy information from form to label
1145	1225	40	Obtain stock certificates, locate transfer, copy details
1225	1310	45	Write certificate No. on brokers memo and detach
1430	1446	16	Calculate stock totals and enter in control book
1446	1451	5	Select new buyers from transfers pass to operator
1451	1522	31	Extract E.P.C's for existing buyers

Fig. 11 Daily task sheet

nel department and an examination of this factor is given in Chapter 7, personnel aspects.

2 Activity analysis

To establish a more comprehensive picture of all the activities conducted in a section the use of an activity analysis is recommended. An example in Fig. 12 illustrates the work of a registrar's section. The information can be obtained from the job tasks forms and tabulated by combining the times devoted to each activity during a period of say one week.

Activity	Supervisor	Hrs	Clerk A	Hrs	Clerk B	Hrs	Clerk C	Hrs	Secretary/Clerk	Hrs
Processing transfers	Auditing	3.20	Buyers	19.20	Sellers	21.00	Probates	22.00	Transfers	6.00
Registrations	Miscellaneous	2.45	Mandates	5.30	Change of Address	10.30	Vouchers	7.45		
Income tax									9th Typing	36.00
Correspondence	Dictation	12.00								
Certifications	Verifying	13.15	Certifying	3.30						
Statistics	Holdings	0.45	Movements	0.45						
Computer Runs	Preparation	2.00								
Dividend reconciliation	Bank Recon	3.30								
Totals										

Section: Registrar's office
Week commencing:

Fig. 12   Weekly activity form

3 Organisation chart

The next step is to draw an organisation chart showing the groupings of staff and the lines of authority at various levels. Fig. 13 shows a simple chart of the company secretary's department. The two-dimensional restriction should be remembered, and to compensate for this disadvantage it is essential to prepare job descriptions.

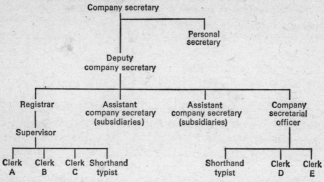

Fig. 13 Organisation of a company secretary's department

4 Job descriptions
These have already been mentioned and examples given. The
main features are the job title, terms of reference, responsibilities, authority relationships, duties and special activities such
as attendance at committees. Preparation of job descriptions
can be an arduous task in itself, but they are an essential element when rearrangements are contemplated.

A critical examination

Armed with the information gathered through the preparation
of job tasks, activity analysis, the organisation chart, and job
descriptions, the office manager may now actually examine the
organisation. He should remember all the information given
in organisation concepts and carefully consider all the possibilities for improvement.

Some questions which might be of assistance are:

(*a*) Are the objectives clear?
(*b*) Does each member know the objectives and the part he
should play in attempting to achieve them?

(c) Are each employee's capabilities and ability known?

(d) Is each section viable considering the objective?

(e) Are there clear channels and networks of communication?

(f) Are the tasks in each job well balanced, considering boredom, and tasks that are either distasteful, enjoyable or demanding?

(g) Are suggestions and ideas welcomed?

(h) Are reports regular, comprehensive and reasonably correct?

(i) Are records up to date and accurate?

(j) Are policy, rules and regulations known to everyone?

(k) Does each employee know clearly his authority, responsibilities and duties?

(l) Is any member overloaded or underloaded with work?

(m) Is the span of control for each supervisor within his capabilities?

(n) Is authority delegated as much as possible?

(o) Is there sufficient staff flexibility to cope with sickness and absence?

Procedures

The answers to some of the questions will not be possible unless the procedures are charted in some way to show the sequence of processes. Process charts are normally used for this purpose. They indicate a series of events which should follow a logical pattern in the performance of a particular activity. These are described later under work study in Chapter 10.

Improving the organisation

The improvement areas should become obvious as a result of examining all the material collected. The important aspects that are occasionally overlooked are mainly associated with the human factor. People are easily upset if they are not consulted in the early stages of contemplated changes. They naturally fear the worst and every possible method of removing this fear is essential. Any alteration in working arrangements may fail without the full support of the staff concerned. Training and capability are also features that cannot be ignored. People do not always recognise their capabilities and sometimes they are not even aware of them. These factors have to be considered.

To avoid unnecessary upheavals of all descriptions a considerable degree of sensitivity towards people is the first consideration when planning changes. The office manager should remember the important part that the informal organisation plays in the maintenance of a smooth running organisation. Studying the informal side and analysing it demands the services of a behavioural scientist, but inevitably the work has to be undertaken by individuals who often work with little knowledge and lots of common sense.

Informal organisation analysis
Probably the first impression that an investigator gets when studying a group is the atmosphere in the working environment. The group which appears to be very busy, bustling about with plenty of fuss, is often not very efficient. The quiet group with an easy-going, smooth appearance who seems to be free-wheeling is in general more efficient. Then there is another form of atmosphere indicating the morale of the group. Although difficult to define and analyse, these factors must somehow be taken into account.

Another indication of informal organisation can be gained from interviewing group members with the aim of identifying the informal leader. Knowing how to use the information when he is located is naturally essential. To identify him a number of preference lines must be charted. The technique is to ask each individual in the group with which other person within the group he would prefer to spend his time. Plotting all the lines connecting the group members should reveal the informal leader: the one on whom the most lines converge.

A similar process using contact lines is sometimes used to indicate informal communication channels and actual procedural operation. Each member involved in a procedure is invited to indicate others he contacts for information retrieval and information passing; in other words, the way he informally operates. The people who are avoided or by-passed are also subjects for further investigation. Other more specialised techniques are time-consuming and very involved. The use of the information obtained has to be treated with care, but at least it provides an indication of possible effects if changes are made without due consideration of the social influences surrounding and intermixing with the formal organisation.

3 Psychological and sociological aspects

Introduction

One of the most bewildering aspects of the office manager's job is how to treat the staff under his control so as to achieve optimum effectiveness. The complexity of this task is generally underestimated, as is its importance and the overall effect it has on the concern. The staff in a company are its lifeblood: success ultimately depends on them. They have the capability to destroy a concern, to wreck plans and to thwart any management action. Well-motivated staff who are aligned with company objectives, however, can pull a concern through most difficulties. This make-or-break capability should convince an office manager of the need to study human behaviour in depth and to develop his skill as a motivator. He should remember that no manager is perfect. Many mistakes and miscalculations are inevitable, but these may be overcome if he has the backing of enthusiastic staff.

Many volumes have been written on the behavioural sciences, the psychological and sociological aspects of human behaviour. The sciences already cover a vast area of topics and are continually growing as large sums of money are spent on research and resulting new concepts emerge. A few years of concentrated study are necessary to reach a really knowledgeable stage on this subject. The development of skill is also long, hazardous and often frustrating, but perseverance is essential.

Any manager's experience in this field is difficult for him to assess. Invariably he will come to the wrong conclusions unless he has sufficient knowledge and has taken many apparently obscure factors into consideration. Specialists have spent a life-time studying the human race, including the reaction of individuals in various situations, but so far complete analysis and acceptable conclusions have eluded them all. The office manager, nevertheless, must tackle the task of trying to understand people.

An appropriate way to study the subject is first to consider the background and the office manager's role in this area, followed by a brief outline of the human body and the way in which it functions. Human characteristics are then examined with a view to studying the human relations approach in depth. This approach includes such aspects as treatment of the individual and the group, leadership, motivation psychology and current theories on motivation. Finally, a section on further considerations summarises and offers an overall picture of the behavioural sciences scene.

The background

An indication of the depth of the subject is possible by listing the disciplines involved and by outlining the research already undertaken. Anthropology, Biology, Political Science, Mathematics, Physics, Ecology, Philosophy, Social and Industrial Psychology, Sociology, Ergonomics and other disciplines all touch on the problem of human relations in business.

Research into ways of improving productivity started on logical lines around the beginning of this century. F. W. Taylor, F. B. Gilbreth and others studied the subject and concentrated on a number of relevant aspects which included the operator, his job, the tools and equipment at his disposal, and working conditions. The outcome of these studies was the introduction of financial incentives, revised methods, the use of time and motion studies, revised rest periods, new types of tools, revised layout and increased specialisation.

A quarter of a century later the Western Electric Company

in the USA decided that the results of applying these techniques were poor, so Elton Mayo was asked to examine the problem. His research into human behaviour at the factory lasted for about five years. His findings became a revelation in this field and are known as the Hawthorne experiments. The evidence proved that, besides wages and working conditions, other factors directly associated with human relations had a significant effect on output. The importance of human relations was recognised, and this investigation eventually triggered off a vast range of research on a broad front which still continues today.

As research progressed, so companies tried out new ways of operating. During the inter-war years the vogue was mainly personnel management. More and more emphasis was placed on welfare, worker participation and a general paternal approach by management. The spotlight was always on the factory worker. Very little mention was made of office staff, most of the research being conducted on the shop floor. At that time there was a gulf between the factory and office worker, but this has gradually narrowed over the years.

Since World War II other topics have risen to fame and slowly died down. Communication, joint consultation, management by objectives, goal-setting, job satisfaction, self-discipline, responsibility-seeking, the mathematical approach, cultural interrelationships, the empirical approach and the decision theory approach are all examples of techniques the popularity of which has fluctuated, but not one of these can really claim to be the answer by itself. One important factor has emerged, however, and is generally accepted now: people in companies are no longer considered as a cold resource or economic tool. They are thought of as human beings, each one possessing unique mental features, demanding individual attention and careful consideration. Acceptance of this view is a major step forward and, if sincerely practised, is very demanding on every manager's and supervisor's time.

The office manager's role

A sincere belief in people and their capabilities will enable the office manager to create a more effective organisation under his control. Sincerity is very difficult to express to others or to convince them of unless there is a genuine belief in people which is continually supported by appropriate actions and recognised ways of operating. People have an uncanny knack of seeing through a façade and the outcome is disastrous. If the office manager is successful, however, he will achieve far more than the total of the disciplines which make up the human relations approach. The way he uses these disciplines through experience and foresight is a personal problem based upon his own personality and approach. In addition to his own role, he should arrange the organisation so that each member of staff can fully play *his* role, not only within his job but also within the group of which he forms a part. Thus participation emerges as an essential element, along with teamwork, which should produce really dynamic groups.

To motivate successfully the office manager should experiment, using a deep knowledge of various motivation concepts. Underlying this approach is the use of communication, application of appropriate leadership and waging the continual battle to achieve a suitable working environment. Many other factors, some of which are outside his control, can upset all his attempts to motivate; but this is business life and he must accept it, otherwise he will be severely frustrated. His skill development in the motivation field will mark his success as an office manager to some extent, but his technical skills must also be developed to cope with policy-making, anticipating, decision-making, general planning, solving problems, and setting and revising objectives. The effective office manager, therefore, must have a capability to utilise both motivational and technical skills in the appropriate combination dependent upon particular circumstances so that all his staff are aligned towards achieving the organisational objectives.

Whether whole-hearted support of staff is really possible is a main consideration for the office manager. If he sees his role as providing employment for white-collar workers, keeping them happy and providing job interest, but no more than that, then he may have to probe more deeply into the question of how to gain full support. Perhaps he should look inwardly to himself and attempt self-analysis to figure out in what circumstances *he* would be prepared to place himself in such a situation offering full support. No doubt many other factors would come into his mind.

The relationships aspect

The motivational effect on staff does not depend alone upon the relationship between the office manager and each member. His relationships with fellow managers, the levels above him and the supervisors who work with him are equally important. The interaction between *all* the groups and individuals sets the scene, provides the atmosphere and creates a dynamism which is either encouraging and enthusiastic or disheartening and apathetic. Varying degrees of these two extremes can occur, of course, but the effect of social organisation throughout the firm and, indeed, the many external social activities, all contribute to the situation.

These situations may be favourable or adverse and they are a contributory factor in the office manager's attempt to achieve motivation. Although research has revealed much on relations between manager or supervisor and operatives, only a few investigations have concentrated on the many other relationships within the concern. Full development of such relationships may relieve the feelings of employees, who often direct their antagonism and blame for injustices towards the concern as an object rather than towards other factors often outside the control of the concern. Thus the role of the office manager is also to apply his social skills towards eliminating as much as possible the misdirected feelings of his staff.

Another very common situation is where the office supervisor is expected to supervise and do the work too. In other words, he is not only responsible for getting the work done in his section but is also expected to do part of it. Such an arrangement conflicts with the motivational role of the supervisor. He cannot establish good relationships, pay individual attention to each staff member, motivate him, control the work and do part of the workload at the same time—especially if a substantial part of the day is spent on work. Malfunctioning will occur in these circumstances and the excuse by management to justify this approach is that more output will result if the supervisor shares the workload. Probably it is difficult to imagine productivity increasing by shifting the workload to a smaller number and allowing someone to spend more time on supervision; alternatively, by engaging another clerk, the pressure on the supervisor is relieved. A motivated group, however, will be far more productive as a team and make a positive contribution far exceeding the normal expectation from, say, eight separate individuals, each one being treated in isolation from the productivity viewpoint.

Considerable time has to be spent on the human relations aspect to create dynamic groups; they do not just happen as many people imagine. A great deal of hard supervisory and managerial work has to be undertaken on a continuing basis which is demanding as regards knowledge, experience and motivational skills. Relationships unfortunately extend to areas that are outside the province of the office manager. Wherever the individual is contacting other people at any time, his outlook and reaction will be affected and, without doubt, will impinge in some way on his relationship within his group at work. Inexplicable behaviour at work is often attributable to this fact and must be considered as an important factor when dealing with employees. The office manager is no exception;

he is also subjected to many outside pressures which will affect his performance. A domestic upset, trouble at the club, family illness and so on all contribute to his behaviour. Human problems cannot be left at home, they travel with people all the time, although some managers still expect their staff to shed them all before entering the office. Such shortsightedness and lack of understanding is deplorable.

Limitation of human relations

The expectations from adopting a policy of establishing good human relations should not be overestimated. Unless people are able to take an active interest in their work with appropriate responsibility and job breadth, it is unlikely that they will be motivated. On the other hand, even with more consideration for the job and opportunity for staff to develop and successfully advance through achievement, poor human relations can override and reduce productivity. An essential approach, therefore, should be on a broad front. Over-emphasis on one sector can produce imbalance and ruin the most sincere attempts to encourage people to work well and be happy at work. On the question of happiness, however, people can be highly productive and unhappy at the same time. Happiness and productivity are not necessarily synonymous. For example, an employee may be unhappy over the question of his salary, but he may also be highly productive at the same time.

A further limitation already mentioned is that human relations research has been restricted mainly to the factory floor and first-line supervision. The findings are often used in general terms to apply to all levels within the organisation, including the office and professional fields. Whether these findings do apply in all organisational situations is debatable and certainly not proven. The office manager must bear this factor in mind when considering the concepts later.

In any business situation there are always accompanying circumstances which are peculiar to that situation alone. Unless

these are thoroughly understood and appreciated during negotiations and dealings with employees, the application of
human relations will be unsuccessful. Without a harmonious
understanding there will often be a negative response. These
limitations outlined above are simply indications of the dangers. Any responsible office manager must accept them collectively as an inevitable hazard and persevere with his efforts
—adjusting as frustrating situations develop.

The human being

The human body

Although the physical side of a human being may be fairly
obvious, often a little more thought is needed to clarify certain
functions of parts of the body when considering human relations.

First of all, the brain seems to possess an infinite capacity to
assimilate information; it constantly seeks information, clarify-
ing and tabulating it for future use. This searching aspect
coupled with capability forms a natural function to acquire
knowledge and to use it. The learning process is strongly
associated with skill development through the use of muscles
and various nervous systems. Again there is a natural tendency
to develop and use skills. Without studying muscles in detail
it is well known that unless they are used regularly they start
to wither. If continually used for a long period, they tire and
need rest to recover. Therefore it seems quite natural for
muscles to work, rest and then work again. This approach
when extended to arms and legs follows a similar cycle. This
cycle of movement or activity and rest appears to apply to most
parts of the body.

The above aspects may appear to be a very elementary,
obvious approach and no more than common sense, but their
applications or significance in business are often ignored by
many managers. If the correct response from an employee is

not forthcoming there is no point in branding him as lazy or unco-operative. Apparent laziness may be due to many factors, such as poor physical health, poor mental health or domestic troubles. While considering the few points mentioned above about the human body, the office manager will have to look elsewhere for the causes of the lack of response.

Stages of growth

To really understand people it is necessary to study what happens in the very early stages of life. The fundamental need of a baby is probably to be loved and looked after so that its basic needs, to eat, drink and move around are satisfied. There seems to be a complete absence of the instincts which are noticeable in lower forms of animal life. These fixed behaviour patterns or instincts severely restrict the learning capacity and socialisation of animals, whereas people, although possessing animal needs, impulses and some innate capacities, also have the capability to use language. This ability only develops, however, when people have the opportunity to mix or socialise. The assumption is that a baby's basic needs are in fact biological drives, not instincts. Therefore the absence of instincts makes it possible for the transmission of culture and the establishment of most individuals into an organised society.

Basic attitudes are formed in the first five years of life. Habits are established and attitudes develop towards parents and other close relatives. These attitudes tend to become models which are used in dealing with other people. If the attitudes work successfully for the child they gradually become traits which are the core of his personality. Examples are aggressiveness, gentleness, greediness, independence, capability, business, noisiness and cruelty.

In about its sixth year the child shows the first signs of a conscience. The phase commences with a love for the parent of the opposite sex; this is followed by the realisation of the futility of this love, then two changes happen. First introjection occurs, which means that the moral attitudes of the parents are absorbed into the child, and secondly the child starts to copy the parent of the same sex. Thus the superego is formed. From this point on, the complicated growth process associated with personality development, repression of emotions, mental mechanisms and so on may be studied under the very involved Freudian theory, which is too extensive to be discussed in detail in this text. The important aspect to note about this theory is that the child is hardly responsible for his traits. The parents in fact mould them for him. Unless an individual realises this and he attempts to overcome the anti-social ones, he may be severely frustrated. Generally the child develops his ego to cope with reality and he adjusts to life accordingly.

To end this very brief survey, what Freud has to say about character should be considered. Three forces are applied to form character; first the id, which is a term used to describe the primitive drives of the infant such as sex and aggression; secondly the ego, which represents the reality of the situation; and thirdly the superego, which indicates the moral requirements of the community to which the individual belongs.

The emergence of character is felt when feelings of guilt are evident if the moral code is broken in some way. Bearing in mind the way the id, ego, and superego are formed, the parents' responsibility for the eventual well-being of the child is considerable. Remembering the well-known saying that people are victims of their own environment and that environmental and educational problems are the responsibility of the community, the office manager should attempt to balance these points in his mind with the actions of employees before condemning them out of hand.

The individual

One person becomes distinguishable from another in many different ways besides the obvious physical differences in appearance. Each individual thinks and reacts differently in similar situations through inherent and developed mental qualities and feelings. Although in most cases physical recognition is very easy, mental recognition is exceptionally difficult. The mental make-up of the individual consists of many facets which are often not perceived at the office. One side only is seen at his place of employment, whereas in total many sides exist. Immediate examples of other facets that come to mind are his domestic life, social life, sporting activities, political activities, hobbies and religious pursuits. Then there are the traits, mental barriers, ideas, concepts, suspicions, conflicting viewpoints and general temperament to add to the picture.

As mentioned previously, the logical outcome is that each individual demands unique treatment, but this is not possible unless his mental differences are known. Tackling this problem involves initially sincere acceptance of this fact. Secondly, the adverse effect on productivity—if it is ignored—must also be accepted. If these two factors are genuinely recognised a philosophy should be developed based on this understanding. Such a philosophy cannot be switched on one day and off the next. It is a way of thinking about people, and treating them, and governs fundamentally the office manager's outlook on life both in business and in general.

Getting to know employees really well is time-consuming yet essential. If the office manager controls a large number of staff he will find there is naturally insufficient time to spend with each one. He will have to organise groups and appoint supervisors, who must be allocated time for this purpose. They in turn should keep him informed.

To gain each employee's confidence there must be sympathetic and fair treatment at all times, due respect, diplomacy and a demonstrated genuine interest both in his work life and in his outside life. There is no doubt that some staff will be highly suspicious of this approach, especially the experienced employee who has suffered under the usual off-hand treatment.

People do recognise sincerity, however, and perseverance is the answer.

The need for careful observation and avoidance of jumping to conclusions should be remembered. Consideration should also be given to the fact that people are very reluctant to show their true feelings: everyone wears a mask to some extent. Seldom are people seen as they really are. They often say things they do not mean, their actions often are impulsive and governed by emotions, and behaviour prejudicial to the concern is often caused by the concern. This should be sufficient to see that hasty judgements are fatal. Rebuffs through the use of this philosophy are inevitable, but these must be weighed against the eventual reward. Only weak managers give up in these circumstances and resort to the so-called 'good old days' method.

Human characteristics

Everyone at times resorts to a casual study of the human race, especially when he is personally involved in a puzzling human situation. A few minutes' thought soon conjures up many peculiarities that fail to hang together to form a set pattern. Some people appear to be predictable, whereas others are totally unpredictable. Some are predictable in one sense, but not in another. Certainly people do not respond in the same way every time. Changes are noticeable in one person, but in another there seems to be little change over many years. Some act like sheep, while others are intensely strong-willed and very independent.

On the one hand, the whole race seems to be very good at killing each other, standing by while others starve, behaving indifferently towards the torture and discomfort of others, and lusting for power. On the other hand, the human race seems to be moving gradually forward towards higher ideals, a more responsible approach and more consideration for mankind. This collective trend, however, still contains groups who continue to act in a barbaric way. Other noticeable features in people are the many likes and dislikes, wide range of hobbies and ideas, inability to think clearly, faith in the unknown, inability to recognise happiness until later when it is gone and strong support for what they help to create.

The characteristics mentioned briefly above can be partially explained by considering the distribution of human differences, basic drives, outlets and mental levels, personality and temperament, which are now outlined.

The distribution curve

Underlying all human characteristics is their conformity to a particular distribution curve known as the Gaussian or Normal Distribution. This applies to all mental characteristics as well as physical ones. An example in Fig. 14 shows the distribution of a sample of adult males indicating the variance in shoe size. Provided that the sample is sufficiently large, a symmetrical bell-shaped curve will appear when the data are plotted on a graph. Although this is perfectly acceptable in relation to the physical characteristics, there is sometimes difficulty in appreciating the significance of this where mental characteristics are concerned.

The main point to note is that in any group one should expect to find a range of intelligence, desires, disposition and so on. Generalising about an individual within the group is dangerous and probably wrong; first impressions will probably be incorrect too. Only by examination, when a person is given the opportunity to demonstrate his capabilities, will the true individual be seen, and not before.

If the office manager agrees with these phenomena the responsibility for giving his staff this opportunity is up to him. He will have to arrange his organisation to cope with the situation. He should also accept that a wide range of different attitudes towards him will be quite normal. Inevitably one out of a group may like him, others may be indifferent towards him, another may hate the sight of him and so on. He will have to be strong-willed and human in his approach if he is to avoid penalising those who are not very well disposed towards him. If he fails to counter his immediate reaction,

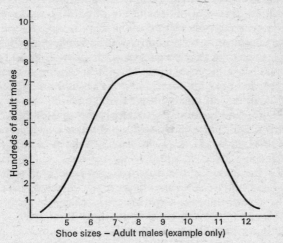

Fig. 14 Distribution of human differences

others will also turn against him. If he succeeds, he will gain the respect of everyone within the group.

Basic drives

A more detailed examination of the drives already mentioned reveals five inclinations which are important in business life. They are significant because suddenly they may appear in the conscious mind and pressurise the individual to take a certain line of action which he might not have taken if he had been given time to think. However, if the drive is suppressed frustration may result, causing loss of energy, unless an adjustment is made.

The five drives referred to are aggressiveness, acquisitiveness, self-assertion, constructiveness and gregariousness.

1 Aggressiveness. The drive to be powerful expresses itself in general hostility, awkwardness, being generally quarrelsome and, in extreme cases, in the use of physical force, shouting and banging the table violently. The drive is very close to the desire to escape when confronted with an intolerable situation. The proximity of these two drives sometimes forces a person into an unhappy state of mind, when he may want to attack a manager and leave the concern if he feels he is unfairly treated. Because of outside commitments he may not be able to take this course, and the resulting conflict causes severe stress. The results often seen are day-dreaming, constant complaints and poor productivity. If he is a popular individual he may even gain support from colleagues, whose productivity also drops. Clearly the answer is to be sure that each member of staff has the opportunity to develop so that he feels he is not just a cog in a very large impersonal machine. The chance to study and expand in his job with equal opportunity to be selected for higher posts naturally needs stressing.

2 Acquisitiveness. The desire for protection and possession are directly associated with this drive. Sometimes it develops as a strong desire to control and possess power over others. Satisfying this drive means that a manager should examine company policy to be sure that employees are adequately protected in the form of secure employment, insurance, superannuation and other welfare benefits.

Factors such as full employment, State benefit schemes, State retraining schemes, powerful trade unions and staff associations, and the general feeling of job security all contribute towards the state of mind of the employee in this connection. There is no guarantee, however, that satisfying this drive will mean high productivity from an employee, this being only one factor out of many that have to be correctly adjusted.

3 Self-assertion. The drive to be important is closely coupled with constructiveness. Receiving due credit for creating something is essential, but when a product or a system is divided into many jobs the feeling of importance lessens because there is no direct association with one individual. To compensate for this remoteness from the end-product an employee may turn to the group within which he is a member and enjoy group spirit if it is strong. Thus group dynamics must be considered; this depends not only on the other people within the group but also on the amount of attention given by management to this factor. Consistently fair and just treatment, careful counselling of each person's problems, development schemes for employees and a human approach all help to foster a keen group spirit.

The office manager should appreciate, however, that the aim is to make *each* employee important. Trying to make a person *feel* important is not enough because the feeling soon disperses and then reality is obvious. Each member of staff must be placed in such a position that he *is* important and that he can actively demonstrate his importance to himself and his colleagues.

4 Constructiveness. The strong drive to create probably causes more trouble in business than any of the other drives. The reason is that in so many jobs the opportunity to create is omitted from the job requirements. Such folly results in severe frustration, yet the whole concept of manufacturing processes and office work in general is based upon narrowing the job down to relatively simple tasks which are not demanding and certainly not creative.

People satisfy the urge to create by suggesting improvements, having job flexibility, preparing and discussing their ideas, and knowing that they actually participate in decisions affecting their jobs. Recognition of their contribution couples up with self-assertion so that they know they are important and that they are actively contributing towards the success of the business. The disastrous effects of frustration if this drive is ignored are discussed later.

5 *Gregariousness.* Another drive which is associated with group behaviour is the urge to belong to and be accepted by the group. Throughout life the tendency to group together is seen everywhere and people will go to great lengths to be included in various social groups. The need to unite is probably close to mating and parental drives, and banning a person from a group is particularly harsh and inhuman. The victim may be driven to near-panic in such circumstances and there are many dangers.

Outlets for drives

The drives just described are aptly named because they make up personality and the essential energy with which a person strives to develop and achieve a continual stream of objectives. This impressive array of driving forces which compel a person to take action in specific ways must be relieved or released through activity. If for any reason they are blocked, then the effect is rather like an excess of steam that cannot escape in a boiler; the pressure builds up until breaking point is reached and the boiler explodes. Alternatively, in some cases, if the boiler is sufficiently strong to withstand the pressure, the steam is contained within a seething cauldron of pressure. In both cases the boiler's function is considerably weakened and the effect is very similar on the human being.

The three main outlets to satisfy drives are expression, repression, and control and redirection. The office manager should be able to recognise symptoms which will indicate which outlet is operating and in some instances he will be able to assist by redirecting a person's energies.

1 Expression. When the drive is freely satisfied by an activity directly associated with it, the term expression is used to describe this normal outlet. An artist painting a picture and a strong-willed individual being appointed chairman of a social club are typical. If examples of aggressiveness are taken, such as murdering an individual or publicly speaking for increasing the pensions of old folk, a distinction is noticeable. One could be called a barbaric or primitive approach to satisfying the drive, while the other could be called a civilised or cultured approach. When free expression is very difficult and the person feels restricted he may unthinkingly repress the drive.

2 Repression. To avoid nervous tension when an impulse is restrained the drive may be repressed unconsciously and transferred out of the conscious mind. Unfortunately, this process of forgetting about it or placing it out of conscious thought is unhealthy or harmful because confusion and a weakening of energy occur; also the painful experience continues at another level. Generally the outcome is only a temporary repression. Suddenly the drive will break through, often at the most inopportune moment which causes embarrassment and an even more painful situation. Partial repression of this nature may result in certain circumstances in various forms of perversion.

Many difficulties experienced in business are the direct result of repression. The office manager has a clear social responsibility to avoid placing his staff in situations where repression may occur. Typical symptoms associated with this state are poor co-operation, apathy, disinterest in the job and the company, maladjustment, antagonism and low concentration. Employees should not be forced into situations where there is no choice but repression. Inevitably verbal or physical violence will result as a retaliation against a manager or, indirectly, the concern. A much better approach is to consider the question of controlling and redirecting the outlet.

3 Control and redirection. For those individuals who possess a well-balanced personality there is ample opportunity to recognise the nature of a drive within them and, with appropriate knowledge and experience, to redirect their natural urges into more satisfying fields. Similarly, the office manager should ensure that his supervisors are able to recognise drives and appropriate symptoms in their staff with a view to encouraging employees to adjust by redirecting not only within the job but also in other social pursuits within the concern.

In the majority of cases redirection or sublimation occurs unconsciously. Thus someone with a strong constructive drive who has no opportunity to exercise it at the office may become involved, for example, in building complex model aircraft. Similarly, someone with a high aggressive impulse may be engaged in clerical duties at work, but in social life outside he will be running a tennis club, organising help for old folk or chairing a local residents' association. Such redirection is quite healthy and desirable. The chances are, however, that in similar situations another individual might develop unhealthy alternatives such as pursuing criminal activities, bullying or perversions.

Mental levels

On reflection most people recognise that their minds seem to be divided into compartments or levels because there is an immediate awareness of surroundings, an area of the mind that holds recent information or experience which can be recalled easily, and a more remote area which acts as a permanent store that is not very easy to contact or recollect at will. These three recognisable areas or levels, and there are probably more, are called the conscious, the subconscious and the unconscious. Whether there are actual divisions is difficult to imagine, and probably there are not, but at least they serve to illustrate the apparent workings of the mind.

The conscious level. An examination of the conscious level indicates that awareness can be divided into the focal area which represents the point of concentration and the peripheral or marginal areas which surround it. Imagine a pilot in an aircraft taking off. He is concentrating on take-off procedure, but at the same time he will be aware of his co-pilot who is adjusting controls, the radio operator who is conferring with flight control, and the increasing roar of the jets. He must not allow any fringe area to distract him or his attention will be lost, perhaps with disastrous results. Similarly, a clerk who is operating a paper guillotine but is suddenly distracted by an unusual noise or movement might lose concentration. Thus local conditions under which staff must work can have an adverse effect on output and this factor demands due consideration.

Some occupations call for people who are able to concentrate easily while others are not so critical. There must be a match between the job and the person because some people do have difficulty in concentrating. The slightest noise is sufficient to switch their focal point and a mistake may occur or they may have to retrace their steps and start again, thus affecting productivity.

The subconscious level. Apparently all information in the form of data, instructions and experiences flows into this area to be held for immediate recollection. This is quite straightforward in theory, but again each individual is different. One may easily recall an event whereas another may experience difficulty; similarly, the process varies within the time-scale. Some may recall easily within a week, others may forget within a day. If a job demands a good memory there is no point in selecting someone with a bad memory. This is perhaps no more than common sense, but it is surprising how often such factors are overlooked.

The unconscious level. Finally, information reaches the permanent store: the unconscious. Without exception, every event
that passes through the conscious and the subconscious levels
is faithfully recorded. Recollection, however, is not automatic;
there seems to be a communication problem with the links
which is sometimes solved by a time lag and also by current
situations sometimes triggering off the process. An interesting
aspect of this is that when meeting a stranger the initial reaction
may be unfavourable. This instant dislike could be due to an
unconscious coupling of the newcomer with a person of similar
features or mannerisms who was associated with a disturbing
or unhappy past event in childhood. In these circumstances
the danger of first impressions is obvious.

Mental experience
The importance of the conscious mental level has been already
stressed, but to complete the outline the actual mental experience associated with awareness will be examined. At any time
there are three closely knit areas operating: feeling, willing and
thinking. These are often called affective, conative and cogni-
tive respectively. Generally one overrides the other two, although they are also activated. For example, a clerk notices a
mistake in another clerk's work; he may *feel* it is his responsibility to report it, but he might *will* himself to take no action
if he reasons or *thinks* that the mistake will go through the
procedure and eventually be spotted.

These three areas or factors of mental experience are very
involved. Thinking, for example, can be on several levels, such
as the perceptual, the ideational and the reasoning level, all of
which are strongly associated with remembering and imagin-
ing. Similarly, feelings become complex when moving on to
the question of emotions and temperament. The temperament
of a person is determined by inherited affective nature and by
the environment. The emotional changes associated with
temperament have to be considered from many angles, such

as the rate of change, the strength of emotion, its stability and its place among the other emotions involved. Coupled with other factors such as the control feature known as sentiments, the influential feature known as disposition and the complexes associated with them, the subject of mental experience can only be glanced at. There is a tremendous amount of material under this heading, but condensed to a minimum it means that people cannot be held responsible for their nature or temperament. With help, however, they can learn to adjust and become more acceptable citizens and employees.

Within the scope of employment the office manager unfortunately does not have the time to take on the role of psychiatrist or psychologist, but he should not lose sight of the opportunity to advise staff to seek specialist help when the need is obvious.

The human relations approach

The importance of the human being and his characteristics have already been considered. The need for a balanced approach by the office manager in terms of the technical and human aspects of his managerial job is fundamental. How to improve human relations is probably the biggest problem after acceptance of the general concept. The main areas to consider are, firstly, how to deal with each individual; secondly, how to deal with the group within which each person operates; thirdly, how to apply appropriate leadership within this concept; and, fourthly, how to motivate employees. Each area is now discussed.

Dealing with the individual

The short survey on human beings given previously has indicated the importance of physical and mental make-up. Some indications have been given of the need to avoid as many stresses and strains as possible, otherwise performance suffers. These factors are bound up with emotion which involves three responses: a physical or organic change, an impulse to act and a feeling which may quicken the impulse. Thus if these three responses are considered together they can give a good indication of temperament. In other words, a clear indication is offered through the way a person controls his emotions, his display of moods and outbursts, and his overall emotional approach in various business situations.

The fairly unstable employee will be very demanding on the office manager's time. This type will be continually returning for either support or new complaints because he has difficulty in adjusting to slight changes. The usual symptoms range over many areas, which include sullenness, generally being miserable, moodiness, outbursts with no explanation, antagonism towards management or another employee, illogical complaints, poor time-keeping and absenteeism. In extreme cases there may be a mental breakdown, long periods of absence on grounds of ill-health, outbursts of physical violence and alcoholism.

With the normal employee, however, a more balanced approach is noticeable. He will usually adjust to change through logical reasoning, provided that he is consulted and he participates in it. Each one may behave in a slightly different manner, but on the whole an acceptable response emerges. Moreover, each employee must be expected to reason along slightly different lines when confronted with a problem or a change. This means that one may demand certain information before accepting the situation, while another may seek other explanations. It is essential to note that both may be behaving normally in spite of the variations in approach. Indeed, it is also unlikely that the approaches will necessarily agree with the office manager's ideas.

The mere mention of any proposed alterations or changes is sufficient to arouse doubts as to management's intentions in

an employee's mind. He must be expected to react from the
selfish point of view because his sense of security may be
threatened. If, however, the change is to his advantage it will
naturally be acceptable and often, provided that there is no
foreseeable disadvantage, changes with no directly favourable
effect are acceptable as long as suitable discussions are undertaken. Even such changes as altering desk positions, changing
staff from one area to another, installing telephones and
carpeting certain areas, although perhaps trivial, are sufficient
to upset people if satisfactory reasons are not given.

Another factor is that people also change their attitudes and
habits. Their ability tends to remain fairly static, but their
capacity to improve can vary. In this connection the office
manager should be on the look-out for change, such as increasing nervousness in an individual, difficulty in concentrating
and odd behaviour, which leads us on to the question of dealing
with staff who are suffering from emotional difficulties.

Emotional problems
Everyone has emotional problems, but some manage to cope
with them easily while others seem to make a tremendous fuss
over them. Normal people adjust readily to these problems,
provided that they receive suitable understanding and sympathy. Remember, however, that even normal healthy people
may contrive to react after the emotional upset has died down
if there is a poor atmosphere in the organisation with no real
sense of belonging or support from management. Grudges may
persist long after the original upheaval and there is always the
possibility that people will change from a stable to unstable
state for one of many reasons. A typical one is a domestic upset,
which can even permanently alter the person's outlook if it is
particularly severe.

An unfortunate fact of present-day life is that many people
feel generally miserable and unhappy. They tend to suffer in
many different ways and the adverse effect on their job

performance is obvious. Coupled with their unhappy relationships with colleagues, these people are generally misunderstood
and deplored, which aggravates the unhealthy situation. The
really bad cases are thankfully few, but if an office manager is
confronted with one his patience will be tried in attempting to
understand the unhappy individual. Generally these people
have difficulty in explaining the problem, they feel persecuted
and their approach to life is often illogical. Others tend to misunderstand them and they are treated as a nuisance.

The main types that can be recognised are those suffering
from insecurity, over-dedication or temperamental problems.
The insecure member of staff is easily recognised because he
constantly needs praising, and if for any reason he is neglected
he will immediately react. Typical signs are ignoring everyone,
generally sulking, picking on any minor detail and exaggerating
it out of all proportion, and making a fuss to draw attention
to himself. Constantly reassuring and praising such an unfortunate individual is wearing and time-consuming, but
essential.

Another difficult employee is the type who is over-dedicated
to his job. The problem generally is that, although he is very
keen to progress at work, his disposition is a distinct disadvantage because of his biased outlook. He soon becomes
frustrated as his demands for promotion and increased responsibility are rejected. The effect of over-dedication is also
extended to his outside activities and domestic life, which are
both neglected generally. Over-dedication at work can also
cause frustration among other staff if the employee is successful
and achieves promotion. He is looked upon as a 'crawler' who
gains favour through working long hours, always being available and generally taking advantage of situations where extra
work is involved. His unbalanced outlook often causes trouble
and eventually the situation rectifies itself when he is forced
to leave through an intolerable relationship with his colleagues.
Occasionally he may be persuaded to become involved in the

social activities in the firm which will then tend to offset his bias.

Finally, there is the temperamental type who often does not feel much obligation towards the firm or his colleagues but who continually finds something to moan about. He gains a reputation for being a pesterer who is always dissatisfied and moaning about trivialities. His emotional problems are openly discussed with other members of staff, who soon become fed-up with the stories and the wrangles they create. Trying to find the causes of the emotional disturbances should be the aim, but this type is difficult to deal with and particularly frustrating for the office manager.

Dealing with the group

An important change, in fact sometimes a drastic change, occurs when an individual becomes a member of a working group. He seems to take on two personalities or roles, one as an individual when he is alone and the other as a group individual when the others are present or when he knows he has their support. The same principle applies to any group, such as a group of supervisors or managers, or any social group.

The reasons for this change are that when separated from a group the person takes on his own personality or individuality and he may feel more insecure, his sense of responsibility may be stronger and he may feel less status and more restricted in his role. As a member of a group, however, he soon loses some of his individuality, but he feels a new form of power through the strength of the whole group. The group influences his outlook and approach to problems, a new form of responsibility is evident and his behaviour is more aligned to the group's behaviour. The tendency for the group to stick together is very strong and is felt by each member, who to some extent influences every other member. The emergence of a group nature probably depends upon the power exerted by certain individuals within the group who may dominate and mould the group's outlook. Thus group spirit, the co-operation of the group and its alignment with objects become critical features in organisational effectiveness and human relations problems.

Group types

Although the various types of group tend to form a complete cluster or merge into each other, the three that certainly distinguish themselves in many situations are the community type, the club type and the crowd type.

The community type of group is ideal for the business situation. A typical description is that of a strong, complicated but stable organisation of people each possessing common interests and motivational potential. *Esprit de Corps* is maintained by the philosophy of the group structuring process, which allows each member to play a part not only in its organisation but also in daily operations and the setting of objectives. Furthermore, the process involves each member in the exercise of self-discipline, self-control and a share of responsibility. There is complete identification of each individual within the group, which means that there is ample opportunity for each person to assert himself and to satisfy his needs and drives.

The formation of such a group should be of vital interest to the office manager. If such groups existed throughout his organisation the dynamism and the results flowing from it would be outstanding. Formation seems to depend upon force of circumstances, which implies that it is created naturally if conditions are right within the firm. Considering the way the community group operates, the conditions required are obvious. The principles to apply when structuring the organisation must be sound and based upon the philosophy of the group described above. Stability of members also appears to be essential, but a low movement level, although desirable, may be difficult to maintain in practice, as people develop and wish to move on for various reasons.

The general climate both within the office and in the concern is also an important feature. Employees should know they are important, really participate in decisions affecting them and possess a genuine pride in being part of a group and in being a member of the company. Obviously most companies have a long, long way to go before such an ideal is reached. Nevertheless, the aims are very clear and they demand long-term programmes. They are expensive in the short term but highly lucrative in the long run.

In passing, the two other types of groups should be mentioned. The club type appears where there is an active participation in social, sporting, welfare or religious work. Members are allocated duties with well-defined objectives. Due to the powerful sentiments associated with the club, the group spirit tends to be strong, otherwise the club would fail. The crowd type is simply a clustering of people brought together at some sporting activity such as a football match or an ice hockey game. In fact, any gathering such as a dance, a public meeting or a theatre performance, fits this description because people with something in common are gathered together. The crowd tends to be impulsive, suffers from hysteria on occasions and is generally guided by events associated with the attraction, whatever it may be. Generally there are no set objectives within the group.

The use of the crowd and club type is naturally limited in the office and undesirable in the case of the crowd type. The club type, however, can be encouraged through the formation of social activities within the concern. Encouragement is essential through the active participation of managers, who can provide reasonable accommodation and financial facilities, and allow employees to suggest and organise the activities.

To summarise the points to be made about group behaviour,

the office manager should be aware that the group is very sensitive about the treatment of each member. The group is much stronger than the sum of its members, but it is equally more emotional. If treated correctly, the group is open to suggestions, it will co-operate extensively, although it may be a little slower to start, and, overriding all else, it possesses a very strong driving force which can overcome most problems. The correlation between group activity and productivity speaks for itself.

Developing appropriate leadership

The two main areas already covered were concerned with the individual and the group. From the point of view of productivity, both depend upon the development of the right type of leadership exerted by the superior and the motivational philosophy of management.

Leadership means influencing people's behaviour so that they will work towards given objectives. Much of the information which is essential to achieve leadership has already been outlined. This knowledge now has to be utilised in such a way that the correct response is achieved from people. Developing this skill must go in tandem with all the other management skills for balance is essential. In reality, leadership is an art because not only must the manager be able to sense the atmosphere that individuals and groups have created but he must also know the many circumstances and conditions surrounding the concern. The situation has to be tackled on a broad front and the art lies in sensing what should be done and how to do it.

Weighing up the situation may indicate that a certain type of leadership is needed, followed by a change later as conditions improve. Getting the feel of the climate is a personal problem; some find it is easy, while others who are more insensitive have great difficulty in even understanding what it is all about.

Furthermore, research into leaders' qualities is very confusing. For example, it is unusual for any two lists of traits and characteristics of good leadership to agree. There is an obvious danger in laying down any essential characteristics because invariably the exception will be quoted as disproving the point. Certain characteristics suit certain situations, which is a safe, true, but useless statement. The type of leadership exerted is probably a better approach to consider.

Types of leadership

Basically there are four types of leaders: the dictatorial, the autocratic, the democratic and the *laissez-faire*.

The dominant feature of dictatorial leadership is fear through threats of penalties, disgrace and dismissal. The philosophy is based upon the individual's inability to satisfy the basic needs of himself and his family if he is thrown out of work. In other words, employment means survival, unemployment means deprivation and near starvation. No doubt this negative approach is successful in the short term where such situations apply, but only up to a point because the disgruntled background which limits the efforts of most people will always be present. Needless to say, this inhuman approach is deplorable.

The autocratic approach, relying upon people looking for guidance and support, is made possible by centralising authority and power in the leader, who makes decisions without consultation or participation from others. This type of leadership is very demanding on the manager, who must be strong and effective as he takes full responsibility for his decisions. Although it may be successful with the right man, the approach must be sustained and there is always the possibility that utilising the staff in a participative way may be more effective if bright people are employed.

Next, the more modern approach to leadership is through the use of democracy. The staff function as a social unit, which in theory uses the capabilities of each member to the full. This is achieved by decentralising authority and decision-making. Consultation and participation are the key words which produce belongingness, recognition, satisfaction and group spirit, all of which result in higher motivation. This approach is not simply a matter of consulting and allowing participation. Unfortunately it is equally, if not more, demanding on managerial qualities. The quality of leadership is highly sophisticated and many other conditions have to be right before this approach can be applied successfully, desirable though it is.

Finally, the most misguided of the four is probably *laissez-faire* leadership. The false assumption is that people are sufficiently educated and trained to be self-disciplined and self-controlled to a high degree when they are given the opportunity to set their own objectives and make their own decisions. The obvious result is that people are mostly in conflict with each other, pulling in different directions and generally creating chaos. The leader is really not in control at all; he is only consulted if information is required, he can make only a small contribution and he probably uses the approach in an attempt to avoid his responsibilities.

Leadership style

The importance of being able to change leadership style has been mentioned and it is worth while considering the fluctuations involved. At the outset the leader will assess the situation and himself, and decide upon a style which he feels will suit the occasión. Whether he carries out this exercise consciously or unthinkingly is by the way. His behaviour as a leader will decidedly be influenced by these features unless he is so insensitive that he does not realise what he is doing. As he influences the staff the situation will naturally change, it is hoped, for the better. In influencing others he will automatically be influenced himself, which means that his style will hopefully change in sympathy with the new situation. These changes in leadership style should be significant to the leader, who may now assess its effectiveness and adjust accordingly. Thus some form of control, although very crude, is being applied and with due sensitiveness he will achieve success.

Naturally much depends upon the leader recognising the subtle changes and making full use of the results. Also, his ability to be flexible in his approach, to understand himself and the effect he has on people, and to recognise capabilities of staff are all essential.

A planned approach to leadership

Although the whole question of leadership is highly complex in the present industrial climate, some salient points do emerge which can be utilised as part of a working plan. The vast amount of literature published on leadership often includes relevant concepts and the findings of many research studies. There should be no need to stress that reading this material will help to clarify many points, but eventually the office manager must reach the stage where he will experiment. He should accept that there will be rebuffs, failures and some successes.

Guidance on the approach should not be rigid. Every situation is different and the list given below is simply a guide—a very flexible guide—to the main features demanding attention. They are not necessarily in the right order and are probably incomplete. Nevertheless, some form of plan is highly desirable:

1   Continue reading on psychology, sociology and motivation concepts, keeping up to date.
2   Develop the skill (or art) by experimenting and noting results. Remember that the tangible side of leadership—the knowledge and technique areas—can be acquired, but the intangible side—personality, drive, character and approach—demands honest self-analysis and adjustment for high flexibility.

3 Place due allowance on other external pressures or factors that will influence and even override all efforts. Try to assess them and see if they are consistent or whether they vary and subside with other approaches.

4 Learn as much about the individuals and the groups as possible. Get to know the way they think and keep in constant touch with the supervisors.

5 Know management's policy and the general philosophy that is applied in practice. Check to see whether there is any misinterpretation.

6 Keep a personal check on yourself and your moods, and note any tendency to be unfair in particular circumstances when you are affected by the situation.

7 Try to improve your sensitivity to the situation and to feel the atmosphere.

8 Leadership is hard work and frustrating, but most important because control is lost without it. Perseverance is the essential element.

9 Bear in mind that leadership in isolation may fail, but if it is ignored there is a marked effect on other motivation techniques. Leadership is part of the broad-front approach.

10 Follow up employee development programmes and change tactics as each individual reaches new goals and shows improvements in capability. Be sure to give each employee the opportunity to stretch his mental powers at appropriate stages.

Motivation

Most of the behavioural scientists' theories on motivation are based on the concept that behaviour tends to lead to attitude, rather than on the usually accepted concept that attitude leads to behaviour. This distinction is fundamental because so often when employees do not perform well the blame is attributed to their poor attitude. If the new philosophy is acceptable the causes of poor performance must be located elsewhere.

Human behaviour seems to hinge upon many aspects associated with the job, the company and external pressures such as domestic life and social activities. In total these tend to override the attitudes of employees if applied correctly. There is ample evidence, however, to show that industry and commerce have concentrated mainly on financial reward in an attempt to influence behaviour and motivate people.

Motivation factors
The main motivational factors to consider are the individual, his domestic life, his social activities, his job and his company. Each factor contains a number of aspects.

Starting with the individual, his particular make-up has already been stressed and discussed. His character, basic needs, mental needs, higher needs, traits, drives, intelligence and general capability mould him into uniqueness. He *does* differ slightly from everyone else and he will demand individual treatment.

His capacity rests on education, training, experience and intelligence. If he is physically and mentally healthy he will want to develop further, take on more responsibility and grow psychologically. His domestic life, however, may easily upset his desire to develop; alternatively, it may increase his desire to grow mentally at too fast a rate. This override factor will abort any motivational philosophy applied by management if the employee should suddenly suffer from an emotional upset at home. Similarly, an upheaval at his social club, a physical injury or mental problem will affect his performance.

Next, the job itself should be considered. The tendency to narrow jobs down to as few tasks as possible seems to conflict with people's mental make-up. The excuse for doing so is that narrow jobs allow people to specialise and to become more adept at performing them. Indeed, the jobs in many instances are so narrow that a child could do them and the outcome seems to be that the adults performing such jobs start to act like children in retaliation. To satisfy human drives the job must be naturally demanding, with due responsibility and with the opportunity to develop further. To make the job more interesting a restructuring of all the tasks within a procedure involving many jobs may often have to be undertaken. This is no mean task in itself, but if the effort is not made the outcome is obvious because people unfortunately cannot switch their drives off when they go to work and on again when they go home to other pursuits.

Finally, there is the company itself to consider. Employees always have a shrewd idea of what management is really like. The true philosophy of the concern is very difficult to hide and this fact is often the undoing of many schemes launched by the concern. Indeed, some senior managers seem to possess a mental blockage over this. They think it is possible to have one secret operating philosophy and another apparent philosophy for the employees' benefit. All they achieve is a downrating of prestige and respect, for no one is fooled.

The standard of all the environmental features offered by the concern directly affects the degree of comfort and the amenities available for the staff. Whether raising their standard, if it is already at a reasonable level, will affect motivation is a debatable point. No doubt comfort, good working conditions, good salaries and ample welfare schemes are important to staff. Being frustrated in comfort is certainly better than in discomfort, but there are other aspects to be considered which lead to the problems associated with overcoming obstacles that impede the satisfaction of drives and the associated aspects of motivation psychology.

Motivation psychology

A study of motives is an essential requirement in the understanding of motivation psychology. Motives may be grouped in many different ways, but this survey will be restricted to the divisions of basic and higher needs, internal and external motives, and known and unknown motives. These three groups are probably the dominant factors in studying behaviour.

The first division of needs is straightforward and consists of one group of *basic* or physiological needs such as the desire to eat, drink and work. The other group is termed *higher* or mental needs and consists of such aspects as safety, esteem, self-fulfilment or creativeness.

The second division is associated with *internal* motives, which are similar to basic needs such as hunger, thirst and higher needs, and *external* motives, which are dominated by outside factors such as temperature changes, other climatic conditions, dangerous elements like fire, water in connection with drowning and so on. An external motive forces an individual to take action, such as running away from an approaching flood or putting on extra clothing if the temperature drops.

The third division is more complex and often difficult to analyse. The group of *known* motives is relatively easy to distinguish, such as ceasing to write through cramp, sitting down when the legs ache and removing a coat if the temperature rises. The group of *unknown* motives, however, is very troublesome. Sudden inexplicable actions are confusing to all who are involved, including the one who, for example, is acting in an illogical way. In the extreme such actions are violent, while other symptoms may be non-cooperation and sullenness. Often the real reason for this conduct is obscured by the surface reasons.

There is also a favourable side of action resulting from *unknown* motives. A sudden upsurge of enthusiasm and willingness to co-operate are typical examples where a change has induced the individual to act in a different way. The vital point to note is that in both favourable and adverse actions the driving force has emerged from within the person, but although an internal cause has motivated him to take a line of action the reason may remain obscure. Sometimes it is difficult to assess whether the motive is known or unknown.

Certainly the reason will be connected with satisfying the needs already outlined and the strength of these needs varies with each individual. Indeed, some needs are easily satisfied with certain individuals, but in others there is great difficulty in satisfying them. When needs are not easily satisfied the barriers or obstacles, if not overcome, cause disappointment or frustration. This results in various patterns of behaviour. To understand this reaction the obstacles are first examined by dividing them into two groups: internal and external.

Internal obstacles

An impressive array of internal barriers restrict a person from achieving the aims and needs he feels are desirable. A self-assessment of his capabilities may mislead him into believing that his limitations are much higher than the true ones. His traits might cause inner conflicts when associated with both physical and mental restrictions. He may lack the right degree of confidence and inhibitions could restrict his desires. Often the way people see themselves is very different to the way other people see them. This situation is misleading and faults are not readily accepted even when they are pointed out to people. This inability to self-analyse accurately causes internal conflicts which confuse and generally upset the individual's stability, producing mental exhaustion and other symptoms such as apathy and an unco-operative outlook.

External obstacles

The main groups of external obstacles are people, society and objective restrictions. The barriers people raise may be direct and indirect in intention. Where enmity or clashing interests are involved there is often a direct restriction which is obvious, but occasionally this may not be known through devious means of raising barriers. Such devious treatment is bewildering as well as frustrating and unfortunately some people are very fond of this technique.

The indirect effect happens through people satisfying their own desires, thus inadvertently stopping or restricting some-one else's efforts. The natural tendency for people to compete in an insensitive manner savours of jungle law which is mainly completely impersonal and often depends upon being in a certain situation at a certain time. Another factor is the effect of family and friends. In some circumstances they can apply restrictions which are very difficult to overcome without bringing about an upheaval in domestic affairs.

Closely associated with this factor are the restrictions applied by the type of society within which the person has to live. Society pressurises the person to conform to certain codes of conduct which, if broken, result in sanctions being applied. The codes are learned through upbringing and education, but if they are unacceptable the resulting conflict may cause change, the erection of insurmountable barriers or eventual adjustment.

Finally, the obstacles associated with objective factors include changes in the economic situation, international problems, governmental policies and even changes in the weather. All these aspects, plus many others not mentioned, cause people to react in various ways which are now described.

Patterns of reaction to obstacles

The office manager should recognise that reaction to obstacles takes many different forms and combinations of forms. These frustration symptoms may be grouped into characteristics. When the characteristic is recognised it should be remembered that the type of obstacle is an important feature in determining the course of action. The main characteristics are direct, introverted and transferred aggression, rationalisation, regression, direct and indirect compensation, rejection, flight and daydreaming.

Direct aggression. The usual symptoms which precede direct aggression are depression, sourness, sullenness and displeasure, which is expressed at every opportunity. These tendencies are caused through some weakness which blocks needs and may suddenly express itself in physical violence and emotional outbursts. This primitive reaction is often seen in children and animals, although more refined versions are displayed by adults who may shout, swear violently, display sarcasm and generally act in an over-excitable fashion. Calmness, judgement and logical thought are thus affected and whenever possible it is better to fight against the tendency and attempt to control it. When dealing with a person who is suffering in this way it is advisable to give him time to 'cool off' before reasoning with him.

Transferred aggression. When aggression is transferred to a false barrier it is generally because the true barrier is unknown or because it would be dangerous to use direct aggression against the barrier. In one sense the irritation is controlled compared with direct aggression, and it may be recognised through symptoms indicating peevishness and pedantry and through constant complaints, criticisms and a negative outlook. The false barrier is generally of a weak nature, which gives the person the opportunity to bully or vent his feelings freely, often with disregard for the harm he might cause. The office manager should be aware of this possibility when dealing with complaints concerning the person's colleagues.

Introverted aggression. Poor energy level, depression, poor initiative and self-accusation are the usual symptoms indicating some failure or sense of failure. This failure results in self-punishment, the anger being diverted inwards and causing introverted aggression. Such a failure may be through failing an examination, not being selected for promotion or through rejection by the opposite sex. Self-denial of this kind normally rights itself in time, but in some abnormal cases it may even result in suicide.

Rationalisation. When a person has acted in a silly way or finds himself in a humiliating situation he may unconsciously twist his motives. For example, if he fails to operate a duplicating machine properly after instruction he may comment that he does not care whether he can operate it or not. In another case he may blame his mistake on someone else by stating that it is not his responsibility to check for errors.

When someone's self-respect is hurt this emotional reaction must be expected: he rationalises to justify his behaviour. It becomes more difficult for him to solve problems logically because the real causes are not acceptable at the time. Later he may admit the fault when his self-respect and esteem have recovered. Admission is not the aim, however, and it is better to help the individual by not dwelling on the mistake and by advising him on how to avoid a similar recurrence.

Regression. When behaviour becomes less practical than may be considered normal it may well be that the individual is retiring into earlier primitive habits and at the same time appears to be forgetting later-acquired, more adaptive habits. This regression tendency is noticeable when, for example, a person insists that he is incapable of performing a task, but it is perfectly obvious that he can.

Initial symptoms are the inability to use knowledge, techniques or skills, along with signs of vague thinking, slovenly dress and the tendency to lose control easily. Gradually the normal workload becomes more and more difficult to cope with because interest wanes and concentration becomes increasingly difficult. Often there is great difficulty in locating the barrier before help is possible.

Direct compensation. When all the person's efforts are concentrated on trying to defeat the obstacle, it is known as direct compensation. The barrier is generally internal, caused by a weakness or lack of some requirement. Good adjustment is possible if his efforts succeed and are socially acceptable, but if he assumes an arrogant and over self-confident manner to cloak his shyness and inferiority feeling he is over-compensating.

Exaggerating and stiffness in behaviour are general symptoms. *Fixation* is another form, which means that the person's energies are too strongly concentrated, resulting in a continual return to the same lines of thought or narrow thought patterns. Such patterns are illustrated by stubbornness, unresponsiveness to logical reasoning and a tendency to argue with no firm foundation. Uncertainty underlies this form of behaviour, which is a desperate attempt to protect self-esteem.

Indirect compensation. If a substitute goal replaces the original one which is unachievable, an obsession to reach the substitute often occurs, which means that all the person's efforts are aimed in that direction.

Although this is a form of frustration, high performance often results in cases where a family upset has occurred and this forces the individual into over-emphasis on his employment. The unbalanced situation is unhealthy, and other signs are wearing unsuitable clothing in keeping with the job and expressing absurd opinions.

Rejection. Casting aside past unsuccessful efforts and trying to forget the problem as if it never existed are known as rejection or repression. To protect self-esteem and self-respect unpleasant memories are forced into the back of a person's mind, thus making his conscience clear and uncluttered with humiliating thoughts.

In the subconscious mind these memories persist and affect behaviour and dreams. The symptoms are very little courage, poor energy and projection. Projection means possessing a fault but refusing to admit it. Alternatively, the person finds that the fault is very noticeable in others and continual attention is drawn to it by the individual who is himself suffering from it. The reason for this strange behaviour is that his own desires and failures are projected onto other people's behaviour, resulting in a feeling that if his weakness is seen in others he will be more secure.

Flight. As the term implies, a person may retreat from an external obstacle, for example, by leaving a job if there is no prospect of promotion, or by transferring to another department to avoid a supervisor's criticism. Flight may be considered a good adjustment if the change is successful. If the change worsens the individual's position, then bad adjustment applies.

Internal obstacles may be subjected to a form of flight such as resorting to alcohol or drugs which only provide temporary relief from the frustration. Persistent absenteeism and lateness are also symptoms of partial flight. A more potent form of flight is recognised when a person 'gives up' or shows resignation in the working situation. His condition unfortunately is contagious, his colleagues may be quickly affected and low morale results.

Day-dreaming. Closely associated with flight is someone's resorting to fantasy when he is frustrated by petty irritations and what seem to be insurmountable problems. Day-dreaming is a blessed release because immediate removal from the ob-

stacle is made possible and time is available to regain control
and drive. Provided that day-dreaming is not preferred continually to reality, there is very little maladjustment; many
people day-dream. Maladjustment is noticeable when continual clerical errors occur for no logical reason and there is
no drive to develop further. When questioned the individual
tends to lapse into blank expressions, staring out of the window,
and in extreme cases seems unable to find words to express
himself.

Solving frustration problems
The probable conclusions from the above brief survey of
frustration caused by needs being blocked either internally or
externally are:

1 Considerable attention is required to ensure that
   employees are placed in suitable jobs appropriate to their
   capabilities.
2 A careful check is essential to monitor progress so that
   the employee does not become frustrated if he cannot
   cope with the job.
3 Continuous assessment is needed because people change
   through various internal and external circumstances.
4 The opportunity to develop further should be open to
   everyone.
5 Employees need considerable help, not only in their jobs
   but also in the social aspects of employment.
6 Restructuring jobs to avoid frustration through boredom
   must be considered.
7 There are many needs to satisfy. Concentrating on one
   group alone will not avoid frustration.
8 Employees are subjected to a wide range of pressures
   that can easily upset performance and their way of life
   indicates that continuously sustained high performance
   should not be expected. It is perfectly natural for people

to be affected at work by external upsets and internal problems.

9   Suitable organisation arrangements are necessary to cope with these human problems. Everyone has off-days, there are no exceptions, and a manager must be very insensitive not to recognise this if he looks at himself occasionally and conducts a little self-diagnosis.

10 The study of human beings is just as important as the technical aspects of an office manager's job if he is to be successful.

Motivation theories

Since World War II behavioural scientists in the United States of America have undertaken many practical studies in motivation resulting in the establishment of various theories. All the theories tend to rest on the new philosophy outlined in the introduction to motivation. Research continues as many questions remain unanswered and undoubtedly new theories will continue to emerge for many years to come.

The most well-known behavioural scientists are Argyris, Gellerman, McClelland, Likert, McGregor, Maslow and Herzberg. A short survey of each one's main idea is now given, followed by further considerations in conclusion.

Executive behaviour patterns
Chris Argyris feels that, although most people are naturally motivated to be responsible, self-reliant and independent, the typical organisation does not provide appropriate opportunity in these directions. Thus normal, healthy people tend to react against an unhealthy company environment, resulting in apathy and lack of effort.

He feels that many jobs do not make demands on employees' abilities and the result is a child-like role for the employee who is frustrated through lack of opportunity and is forced to display indifference and contempt as a defensive measure to maintain his self-respect. Important factors in preventing this are a sense of pride and accomplishment at work, and stimulation and dignity in work, rather than emphasis on financial reward, job security and fringe benefits.

Another feature is that employers are often confused between happiness and motivation. Making an employee happy does not necessarily motivate him, neither does a motivated employee necessarily feel happy. A motivated employee, however, will certainly gain an increased sense of personal value and significance from his work, thus achieving high satisfaction.

Another behaviour pattern observed by Argyris is the nature of interpersonal relationships: the way managers perceive each other. Its significance is that managers tend to filter information given to them and that they have difficulty in saying what is on their minds when they converse with each other. These faults produce delayed reactions and poor decisions. If the pattern could be reversed, Argyris claims that the changes would mean that each employee would make his own unique contribution, on which he would be judged. There would be trust and confidence between organisation members and personal involvement would bring about more commitment to organisation objectives.

Psychological advantage
Saul W. Gellerman claims that some generalisations are possible through the research findings on motivation:

(a) Many motivation problems stem from the method of managing rather than the reluctance of employees to work hard.

(b) There is a tendency to over-manage, which results in too many decisions at too high a level and a narrowing of jobs below reasonable limits.

(*c*) The reasons for employees' behaviour can be located by studying their environment at work.

Gellerman's principle of psychological advantage states that employees are motivated by a desire to get by in the best possible way in the kind of world they think they live in. This involves the demands made on them and the strength of their drives, which are partly governed by their educational standards and their degree of independence. These drives strongly influence behaviour and tend to exert more pressure on the employee compared with the influence of other people. Concentrating on satisfying these drives through uplifting individual roles would be more effective than the use of financial reward alone.

Three recommended approaches are:

1 'Stretch' the employee mentally by allocating more demanding duties.
2 Apply management by objectives principles.
3 Encourage participation by seeking opinions before making decisions affecting his work.

Achievement motive

According to David C. McClelland the achievement motive (AM) is present in most people. In the USA, however, research findings show that only about 10% of the population is strongly motivated for achievement. Before considering this feature it is essential to know McClelland's definition of achievement motive: an individual's tendency, when he is not required to think about anything in particular, to think about ways to accomplish something difficult and significant. This characteristic is important to management because a person possessing a strong AM may perform better than a less strongly motivated individual in jobs associated with selling and marketing, and in all managerial jobs.

Four characteristics of the self-motivated achiever have emerged:

1 He sets his own goals.
2 He prefers moderate goals.
3 He wants immediate feedback on progress.
4 He has a high opinion of his value in cash terms, but it is debatable whether high financial reward affects his performance as he is already working at peak efficiency.

McClelland emphasises that AM is only one source of high achievement and that monetary incentives are more effective on weak achievement drives. AM reserves may be drawn out by increasing personal responsibility, encouraging individual participation in selecting productivity targets, applying moderate goals and ensuring rapid feedback of results.

Leadership style

The background to leadership style in Rensis Likert's work is concerned with his thoughts on the management of human assets. The outcome of his Institute's research on behavioural studies indicated that when a concern found itself in financial difficulties the usual approach was to reduce expenses and to pressurise employees to work harder and spend less. Intensive cost-cutting and a take-it-or-leave-it attitude by management certainly indicated more money being generated than before, but the effect on human assets was ignored.

Such treatment damages relationships and the reaction is seen in three clear phases:

1 Employees become resentful, hostile and distrustful.
2 They tend to complain more than usual, work carelessly and wastefully, apply various restrictions on production and, in the case of competent employees, terminate their employment.
3 This reduction in the effectiveness of employees as a whole and the remainder's reaction to work leads to a

further deterioration in efficiency and, most probably, another financial problem.

The outcome of these findings was the development by Likert of methods to assess various forms of leadership and the stressing of his viewpoint that the style of leadership that gains sustained high productivity, good relations with employees and high profitability is strongly coupled with participation.

The styles are classified into four groups based on the characteristic of the company in terms of the degree of freedom which employees feel about communicating with managers and the amount of confidence and trust they feel the managers have in them. Briefly, the ratings (groups) are system 1—exploitative, authoritarian leadership; system 2—benevolent authoritarian leadership; system 3—consultative leadership; and system 4—participative leadership. The research findings indicated a strong connection between system 4, which is based on teamwork or participation which demands mutual confidence and trust, and the companies with sustained high productivity.

Likert stresses that system 1 often produces short-term gains but long-term disadvantages and that system 4 is difficult and demanding on re-education but is successful in the long term. His way of extracting the productive power of human assets firstly assumes that managers are highly trained both in behavioural science and in the technical field, and secondly relies upon the application of three principles:

1 Full use of the concepts and techniques of motivation.
2 The development of a tightly knit organisation of work groups committed to achieving organisational objectives. These groups should be linked by employees who possess overlapping membership in two groups.
3 The establishment of high aims for managers and employees and clarification with them that the aims are expected to be achieved.

The needs hierarchy

Abraham Maslow's main contribution appeared in a paper written by him in 1943 called *A Theory on Human Motivation*. He classified human needs into groups which form a hierarchy of importance to the individual, who reacts by tending to forget about the group once it is satisfied. Thus implying that effective motivation is only possible by appealing to the group (or groups) of needs in the hierarchy that require satisfaction at the time.

Maslow listed these groups, starting from the lowest, as physiological needs: hunger, thirst, shelter and sex; safety needs: protection from danger and threat; belongingness and love needs: acceptance, affection and identification; esteem needs: success, self-respect and recognition; and self-actualisation needs: desire to be creative, the satisfaction of potentialities and self-fulfilment.

Important aspects to note are that the hierarchy collapses when all needs have been developed and a lower need reasserts itself if it is in jeopardy at any time. Although all the needs remain, the energy spent on satisfying them is constantly altering as attempts are made to find the correct balance; and the needs cannot be switched on and off at will: they stay with the individual all the time.

The significance of his work is in the philosophy that there will be low motivation if a need is appealed to that is already satisfied and effective motivation if a higher need is appealed to which is not already satisfied.

Theory X and Theory Y

The work of Douglas McGregor, who died in 1964, was based upon his interpretations of research findings which indicated to him that effective leadership rested on a manager's assumptions. These assumptions are concerned with the nature of management and the behaviour of human beings.

McGregor's interpretations are best illustrated through an

account of his well-known contributions known as Theory X
and Theory Y. He established two groups of assumptions
about human behaviour. Firstly, Theory X can be described
as a philosophy where employees are viewed as inherently dis-
liking work, unwilling to improve, having to be coerced, directed, controlled and punished, not seeking responsibility and
generally displaying lack of ambition. Secondly, Theory Y
opposes Theory X by assuming the philosophy that employees
naturally work well, seek the opportunity to exercise self-
discipline and self-control, have great potential and wish to
develop in the right circumstances.

A manager tends to adopt one theory or the other in his
dealings with people: the philosophy he chooses has a direct
influence on the behaviour of his subordinates. McGregor
stresses, however, that both theories accept that productive
work is an unnatural form of behaviour and that it is essential
to exercise some pressure to achieve results. Therefore if a
manager adopts Theory Y he will have to coax and structure
jobs in such a way that employees seek further achievement and
personal growth. Many interpretations have been placed on
McGregor's work. Some people even see Theory Y as an
abandonment of discipline and control, thus creating a situation where employees are at liberty to please themselves at
work with no restrictions imposed. Such a view really amounts
to fostering anarchy and certainly this was not McGregor's
intention.

If a manager adopts the Theory X approach he fails to
recognise human talent and treats employees accordingly. Jobs
are kept narrow and a tough, rigid, disciplinarian outlook
underlies the manager's philosophy which is easily recognised
by all employees, thus generating antagonism and unhealthy
behaviour.

This brief description of McGregor's work clearly shows
his belief in the establishment of faith in people, mutual trust
and the urgent need to restructure jobs. His findings were well

in advance of other behavioural scientists' concepts and they have formed the basis for modern thought on job enrichment.

The motivation-hygiene theory

Frederick Herzberg has become the most well-known behavioural scientist in recent years as a result of the breakthrough achieved through his concepts on motivation based on job enrichment. Bearing in mind the needs outlined by Maslow, people possess two different sets of needs according to Herzberg. One set is associated with satisfaction and the other with dissatisfaction. He considers that the satisfaction set of needs are the high motivators whereas the dissatisfaction set (hygiene) has to be catered for, but only a fair day's work should be expected if management concentrates on this alone.

The satisfying experiences at work (the motivators) are directly associated with the job itself, in other words what employees do. The satisfaction needs, therefore, are achievement in the job, recognition, the job itself, the amount of responsibility and the opportunity for the individual to develop or improve his position.

The dissatisfying experiences at work (the hygiene factors) are associated with the job environment or surround, such as company policies, administration aspects, supervision, colleagues, working conditions, salaries, status, job security and fringe benefits. These factors are important and they have to be continually catered for to keep dissatisfaction to a minimum. Employees' demands for hygiene factors are never reduced for very long, thus causing a cycle effect. As soon as a dissatisfaction is reduced it tends to build up again and demands further treatment as the cycle completes itself. Unfortunately the cycle escalates at the same time, therefore, demands continually increase in strength each time round.

Herzberg's answer to this phenomenon is to provide continually for hygiene, forget about it and concentrate on the job enrichment aspects. This approach seems to provide more

satisfaction to the employee whose productivity improves and
is sustained for a much longer period.

Further considerations

The M factor

From the foregoing motivation theories propounded by behavioural scientists there appears to be emphasis on the following factors:

1 Executive behaviour including leadership style.
2 Mutual trust.
3 Company environment.
4 The job itself.
5 Human characteristics.

Taking these points into consideration, there could be four
main areas that directly affect individual performance or motivation: base factors, drive factors, reaction pressures and
opportunity pressures.

Probably each one of these areas contains a number of
aspects:

(a) *Base factors.* Physical capability, mental health, intelligence, knowledge and skills.
(b) *Drive factors.* Achievement motive, background, traits
and temperament.
(c) *Reaction pressures.* Company environment, general environment (national level), the close situation (group
activity) and the domestic situation.
(d) *Opportunity pressures.* The job itself, achievement, recognition, responsibility and personal development.

The assumptions are that dependent upon each individual
there is, firstly, a certain weighting for each factor *and* for each
aspect within each factor; secondly, the factors and aspects
interlock and are interdependent; thirdly, the first three fac-

tors, (*a*), (*b*) and (*c*), may possess an overriding power which defeats the other factors if motivational conflicts occur; and fourthly, on the basis that motivation is a science, there might be a resultant formula to indicate the degree of motivation (M factor) that can be expected from an individual in a given situation.

The usefulness of such a formula would not lie in its ability to portray an individual's M factor because there is doubt as to whether it is possible to gather sufficient information on all the aspects involved to arrive at a satisfactory conclusion. Just as important is the unlikeliness of being able to weight the factors other than roughly, accuracy being completely out of the question.

Its usefulness would lie in indicating the breadth of the problem and in assuring managers that, although they might be on the right track as regards improving motivation, they should not give up for the wrong reasons if setbacks occur. A further use would be to show the overall picture. So often there is the feeling of being 'left up in the air' after reading about motivation and a feeling of being cheated at the end because no real answers are given. Presumably this is the price paid for studying new and developing sciences.

A formula illustrating the magnitude of the problem could be devised along the following lines:

$$\text{M factor} = d\left\{\frac{a+b}{c}\right\}$$

Key: a = Base factors
b = Drive factors
c = Reaction pressures
d = Opportunity pressures

In the formula the make-up of the individual is represented by factors $a + b$; the override characteristics possess high capability for reducing the effects of $(a + b)$ in adverse situations, therefore the reaction pressures (c) are placed as a divisor; finally, the resultant of these three factors is multiplied by the opportunity pressures (d), which are mainly dependent upon the establishment of a suitable job structure. The values for factors a to d could be estimated from suitable scales by the assessor.

A flexible working life

The foregoing discussion assumes that a job has the capability of being enriched either through expanding the breadth of tasks by introducing parallel working or by restructuring a procedure to enrich the job. Unfortunately some menial jobs cannot be enriched, and although ideally they should be mechanised out of existence the associated technology is often not sufficiently advanced for this purpose. The situation is also aggravated because the individual performing the tasks is often educated well above the educational requirement for the job.

In these circumstances one answer is to adopt the concept of a flexible working life. The aim is to enrich the individual's life generally by introducing such features as working in teams if possible rather than working in isolation; allowing the person to work at his own pace and, as soon as the job is completed for the day, to release him with full payment rather than keeping him to a set hour; and offering free educational schemes to enrich his leisure pursuits, for which he will now have more time.

Another possible answer is to adopt job rotation if a number of menial jobs can be grouped together for this purpose. Each employee may change round, say, every four months and, of course, the concept encourages more versatile staff at the same time.

4 Data processing

Introduction

To achieve the objectives of administrative management the office manager has so far had the opportunity to assess the importance and the part the function plays in a concern, and to examine the various methods and skills that are essential to organise and motivate staff. In this chapter the tools and material used to achieve the aims of the function are now examined.

The tools consist of all the office machines and peripheral equipment that can be used to improve efficiency in the processes, while the material covers all information that is available for processing. The data may be known or unknown at any point in time, thus initially there could be a case for an individual to seek out unknown data or for each manager to accept this task as part of his job.

A brief breakdown of data in a manufacturing concern is given below to indicate the vast range:

1. *Production*: information on processes, machines, tools, raw materials, sub-assemblies, finished goods, output, quality, inspection, maintenance, layout, range of products, degree of standardisation, production and material control, and plant management.
2. *Marketing*: packaging, transportation, stocks, advertising, sales promotion, representatives, showrooms, selling prices and the export market.
3. *Personnel*: records, wages and salaries, holidays, pension schemes, job specifications, interviews, training, safety, medical, rehabilitation and conditions of employment.

4 *Finance:* legal documents, credit, financial statements, valuation of assets, books of account, cash position, costing and estimating, and control of expenditure.

5 *Company secretarial:* share registration, company formation documents, dividends and legal aspects.

6 *Research and development:* research information, market research, forecasting, design, prototypes and modifications.

7 *Administration:* systems, procedures, records, office services, O & M, OR, office machines and equipment, office layout, working conditions, information teams, forms control, information retrieval, communications, control of work and organisation.

The need in modern business for effective data processing (DP) has already been stressed in Chapter 1. The information component which is the basic material for DP conveniently divides into two groups: internal and external information. The ongoing side of the business caters for all the internal information, whereas the activities outside the business which are also relevant to its overall effectiveness are covered under external information.

Choosing which external information should be processed is fundamental, very difficult and critical considering the high cost of DP, the importance of data and the effect on the concern if a vital piece of information is not known. Similarly, the free flow of data between each of the main functions—say, marketing, production and finance—encourages co-ordination as everyone has more opportunity to appreciate the others' difficulties. Unfortunately there is not always sufficient time to assimilate all the information and the importance of concise summaries becomes clear. Indeed, an essential requirement for all presentation of information to management is that it must be useful. There is a tendency, however, to ask for or to give information with the idea that it might be needed or it should not be excluded 'just in case'. Such extravagance cannot be permitted in modern competitive business firms, but avoiding this waste is time-consuming in itself and involves many techniques, including clerical work study, planning, costing, budgetary control and the employment of a highly effective managerial team.

The criteria are that useful information must be relevant to the ongoing business or its future, pending information must undergo rigorous regular checks for validity and useless information, such as late information for immediate use, incomplete or inaccurate information, must be either destroyed or rectified.

Processing data in the most economical way involves the study of problems associated with obtaining, classifying, storing and giving information. Although these problems have existed for many years, in recent times they have accelerated well beyond the dreams of most people who lived a century ago. Today the tremendous advance in information technology caused by the insatiable demand for information has revolutionised DP. The general or all-purpose clerk is largely disappearing and being replaced by the specialist clerk, who is needing more technical knowledge, skill in operating machines and know-how to cope with narrower, specialised activities, such as typewriting, filing, duplicating, posting accounts to ledgers and involved calculating.

This change has caused many problems. On the mechanical side the range of office machines available is now extensive in an attempt to overcome difficulties such as the high information recording time found at various levels of analysis and presentation, transporting data in terms of cost of time and the increasingly complex tasks of processing data.

On the human side there is considerable apprehension as this so-called dehumanised technology forges ahead at speeds in excess of human adjustment time. Thus the introduction of the computer and computer technology demands considerable attention to the education and training needs of employees if full advantage of changes is to be taken. The effectiveness of machines still rests on the level of human development and capability to use them. A machine's value depends on people rather than on technological capability and, although no doubt the situation may eventually reverse itself, the outcome is still debatable.

DP offers many choices to the office manager. Bearing the human and technical aspects in mind, processing may be done manually, mechanically or electronically. The choice is not always an easy one. Similarly, who should decide on the information to be given to management is debatable. The argument hinges on whether an information specialist should decide or whether each manager should know his job sufficiently well to decide for himself. Possibly a combination of the two is the answer, assuming of course that all managers and the specialist are sufficiently educated, trained and experienced to say accurately what their true requirements are. This problem is very near to the question of who should control DP. Fundamentally it should be the office manager at, say, departmental level, although it should be the wider responsibility of the administrative manager at senior level. There is a tendency, however, for line managers to take part, probably because they feel the DP results are not at a really effective stage so far.

The costs of DP have escalated in recent years, involving senior management in critical decisions associated with allocation of capital investment in machines, materials and space. These decisions have often been disappointing and projects may have failed not necessarily because of poor choice of equipment but probably because of poor expertise in using the equipment. Priorities in the use of equipment involve high-level decisions that are exceptionally complex, as each functional manager will naturally feel his needs are greater and more urgent than others.

Changes in DP unfortunately involve employees in upheavals, which may mean breaking up groups, retraining and the operation of new techniques. For success, the human aspect has to be given a considerable amount of thought.

Finally, the emphasis on DP in recent years has not come about through increasing costs in this area and the general demand for more information alone. More noticeable has been the continual stream of company disasters, including those involving large well-known concerns, which have highlighted the critical features of DP. Investigation has often proved that poor assimilation of information caused the chaos and eventual downfall. Insufficient attention to these aspects and managers' lack of training in knowing what data is needed and how to use it are contributory factors. Lack of information should not be made the scapegoat when in fact the *cause* of lack of information is the key to solving the problem.

Elements of data processing

Although the term DP is self-explanatory the broad area covered under this heading has to be considered. The office function, it will be remembered, includes dealing with inward information flow, recording appropriate information, processing information, the retrieval of information and administrative control. DP cannot be excluded from any of these elements because it forms the base material in each case. The function of office management in turn relies upon DP efficiency in fulfilling the administrative requirements of other functions in the concern.

The dilemma faced by the office manager is knowing that, on the one hand, comprehensive data is essential to the smooth running of all other functions but, on the other hand, the cost of providing such data could be excessive and uneconomic for the company as a whole. A degree of compromise is necessary and this can only be worked out by studying the choices available in terms of cost, time and value of data. Each element is now discussed.

Inward information flow
A logical point to start is the stage at which information enters the office. Initially the information may be received in a number of different ways: mechanically printed, written, or in verbal or electronic form. If it is verbally received a separate recording operation is necessary, should the data be considered worth processing.

Alternatively, a positive action may be needed to obtain the information, meaning that two aspects have to be considered. Firstly, there is data that arrives voluntarily and, secondly, data that has to be collected or requested. The distinction lies in the fact that often a progressing activity is essential for collection of data as the first attempt may fail. Important decisions are also needed, firstly, as to whether or not information should be sought; secondly, whether it should be circulated or recorded within the business; and, thirdly, who should receive the data after processing.

This reception element in the broad form described partially governs the degree of generation of data within the organisation. Thus a control feature at these entry points is essential.

Recording appropriate information
The reception element is concerned with the actual physical recording of data. Initially the data appear either in mental or physical forms, for example, telephone conversations and correspondence. It is possible that the information may not be converted from mental to physical form for various reasons, such as forgetfulness, unimportance and ignorance of the need to convert it.

Where conversion or physical form change occurs another

control point is needed. Recording is costly, recording and re-recording is costlier, and so on progressively in terms of cost. Ideally, the data should be recorded once only and utilised in such a way that all requirements are satisfied without further re-recording. In other words, the cheapest way is to record once and use the data from that basic source without having to record again for processing purposes. In practice this is often exceptionally difficult to achieve. The concept is known as integrated data processing (IDP) and it should be one of the basic objectives of any system.

Another costly problem involves the length of time the data should remain recorded before destruction. Both legal and business requirements have to be considered.

Processing information

Unfortunately information is seldom initially recorded in the most suitable form for use in procedures and for managerial purposes. The main difficulties are that matching with other data is necessary, the sequence is often wrong, the data are incomplete, calculations are necessary and comparisons are warranted for control purposes. Arrangements to cope with these problems can be expensive. To achieve a good service at minimum cost is very demanding and it involves consider-able knowledge and expertise to arrive at the right answer. Failure may cost the concern large sums of money and con-siderable disruption in operating efficiency.

Information retrieval

The transmission element involves the movement of data from a record such as a file, magnetic tape or other form of storage to the user. This movement may take many forms such as speech, written words or figures and the use of mechanical or electronic recording and transmission devices. Movement can be requested by the user or it can be part of a routine built into a procedure. If a special information service is operating there is a discriminating element which decides whether the information should be passed, held or destroyed.

Timing is most important. The need to provide data within time scales is fundamental and if a failure occurs the outcome could be disastrous. So often late data will be useless data. A typical simple example is when a consumer telephones to say that she cannot keep an appointment for the service engineer to call this afternoon to repair her washing machine. If he does not receive the message the result will be a wasted journey. A more complex example is when budgetary control figures are received by a departmental manager six weeks late. Remedial action for the six-week period is lost, perhaps resulting in considerable avoidable expense in many sectors.

The degree of comprehensiveness of data must also be examined. Naturally the most expensive way is to provide fully comprehensive data, but often it is not necessary and abbreviated forms can be just as effective. For example, if costs are within an acceptable range it may be pointless to notify the responsible manager. Only costs that are deviating sharply need be brought to his attention, thus applying the economic principle of exceptions.

Speed is another factor that can affect overall costs. An examination of the choices of transmitting data on the basis of cost and time as well as other aspects should indicate the most appropriate method.

Administrative control

Finally, the element associated with control is often overlooked. Records of transactions, acquisition of various assets, cash movement and legal documents must be used intelligently. Considering the importance of physical resources in the survival of the company suitable processing of this data to include follow-up and general control features is essential.

Main aspects of data processing

Bearing in mind the elements already described the main aspects of data processing are:

1   The administration of DP to ensure that the most effective service is offered.
2   The use of machines and equipment must be examined relative to the cost and service required.
3   The use of human resources in relation to manual processes, mechanisation and automation problems.
4   The use of appropriate paperwork and techniques associated with DP.

Each of these aspects embraces many complex areas of study involving the use of specialists in practice who often have great difficulty in coping with a constantly changing technology in high cost areas. A survey is now given.

The administration of data processing
This aspect is concerned with making the best possible use of DP resources at the disposal of the office manager. In many situations the most suitable machines and equipment are not available for various reasons, therefore the effectiveness of DP rests heavily on staff and the way they are administered.

Discounting the improvement of procedures, forms and paperwork generally, the need for appropriate control features becomes very important. How to minimise human error without over-elaborate control is a fundamental problem. The cost of mistakes has to be equated somehow with the control cost and unfortunately the equation is not limited to quantitative terms, as the qualitative element also has to be considered. A mistake on an invoice sent to a customer could be interpreted as genuine, but in the case of some customers an inflated figure may make them feel that the concern is trying to exploit them, which could result in loss of business. There are no hard-and-fast rules to apply in control features. The broad picture has to be envisaged and decisions should be based on this approach.

The more that the insatiable demand for data becomes more obvious to top management, along with the increasing risks of disaster if the demand is ignored, the more likelihood there is of expenditure being channelled towards mechanisation and eventually towards electronic data processing. Although the office manager should indicate the critical situation whenever possible, it finally rests with the board or managing director to recognise the problem and agree to the capital expenditure.

The main features that may affect the office manager during the period of negotiations, the purchase of equipment and changeover periods are now studied after examining the range of machines.

Mechanisation

The decision to mechanise a task demands far more thought than simply considering whether the cash to buy the machine is available. Unfortunately not every task benefits from using a machine instead of a mental or physical process: many machines and equipment are bought which end up in a cupboard.

The main aspects that must be considered may be conveniently listed:

Volume of work.
The time factor, if any saving is effected.
Bottlenecks.
Training the operator.
Resistance to the changeover.
Cost of the machine.
Maintenance and service costs.
Speed of maintenance and availability of spares.
Running costs.

Special paperwork required.
Space available.
Accuracy and quality required.
Relief (or creation) of boredom and monotony.
Less risk of fraud if checking built in.
Obsolescence factor.
Reaction from other staff and the staff association.
Fear of redundancy and lowering of morale.
Output of machine.
Lower fatigue factor.
Degree of supervision.
Information requirements of management.

Many of these aspects may appear to be common sense approaches, but there are many more than those listed. The above is only a representative sample: the office manager must look carefully at each situation, which is bound to be unique in some respects. A sound method is to list as many aspects as possible for the particular situation. Some aspects need a careful examination of work flow and load factors at various points. A logical approach is essential, together with some sensitivity towards the staff who are involved.

Choosing the right machine

Bearing in mind the main aspects of choosing the right machine which have already been mentioned, there are some factors that are difficult to assess. For example, the list below gives some indication of areas that demand forecasting as well as up-to-date knowledge:

1 Expansion (or contraction) of programmes.
2 Probability of achieving expansion.
3 Risk of machine becoming obsolescent.
4 Rejection of machine by managers or staff.
5 Stability of manufacturer.

6 Possibility of more versatile or general-purpose machines being marketed.
7 Whether to rent or buy.
8 Matching up with machines already purchased or likely to be bought later.
9 Comparative costs of similar machines.
10 Comparative speeds of similar machines.
11 Flexibility of machines.
12 Ease of operation over long periods.

Some disadvantages of machines

(a) Machines do not dispense with the human factor. In some ways they create more human problems than before.
(b) Specialists remain essential; in fact, with more sophisticated machines the range of specialists required increases.
(c) Machines do not operate themselves except in isolated cases. Trained operators are essential otherwise more mistakes and much wasted time can result. The cost of training must be accounted for.
(d) Machines need servicing regularly; they generally break down at the most inopportune moments and prompt maintenance is essential.
(e) The office manager will be exceptionally lucky if he manages to foresee all the possible problems associated with mechanisation.
(f) Often the machine desired and the cash available do not match. A compromise is difficult and there is some degree of frustration at the beginning which is not a very healthy situation.
(g) The continual upsurge in the range and types of machines guarantees rapid obsolescence.
(h) Being restricted to the manufacturer's stationery can be costly.

(*i*) The balancing and flexibility of all clerical operations in a procedure may be difficult if one area is mechanised,

(*j*) A degree of distraction may be introduced through increased noise or vibration.

Installation problems

Unfortunately the difficulties of installation compared with the favourable features of a machine are not always stressed strongly by sales representatives. The cold facts are that the office manager should not trust the salesman whose job is to sell his company's machine, which he must sincerely believe in otherwise he would never convince anyone that it is worth buying. The salesman is not going to deliberately point out the bad features of the machine from the installation point of view and there are bound to be some. Indeed, if he does point some out, they are not going to be the ones that are likely to put the office manager off the sale. The need for a demonstration in the proposed working situation is essential, not forgetting the importance of asking nearby staff for any comments. Even this precaution is not a certain way of finding out whether there are any snags. Machines develop odd irritating noises and faults after a while which are hardly noticeable at the time of purchase.

The features to note are the size of the machine, its weight, the availability of a suitable power point, any problems of trailing cable between the machine and the power point, vibration, the need to dampen the resonance with a rubber or felt pad, excessive noise demanding shrouding or a separate room to avoid distraction, correct position of arms for operating purposes when the machine is mounted on a desk, lighting difficulties for viewing visual panels or paper, any special requirements such as a certain humidity, temperature or extractor device for fume removal, space for holding associated equipment, servicing tools and feed or storage facilities.

The range of office machines

The office manager cannot hope to possess a detailed knowledge of all the machines available—in fact, it would be pointless to attempt this in view of the amount of work involved in keeping up to date. A more reasonable approach is to aim for a wide general knowledge and to know the functions of the various classes of machine. It is important to note that objectives must first be clarified before considering the selection of suitable machines to fit the procedure.

There are many sources of information on office machines:

(a) Manufacturers and agents who can be located in telephone and trade directories.
(b) Institutes and professional associations directly connected with office management.
(c) Government offices which generally issue publications on office machines.
(d) Various technical journals.
(e) Business directories and exhibitions.

One way of examining machines is to classify them under the basic clerical activities which are listed below:

1 Transmitting information.
2 Recording information.
3 Sorting information.
4 Copying information.
5 Checking information.
6 Calculating.
7 Storing information.
8 Various combinations of the above activities.

All these activities initially demand perception because they rely upon someone to see or hear the information before it is fed into a machine; thus each activity involves a mental and a physical process.

The machines within each clerical activity are now described to give a superficial indication only of the range available. Finally, punched card installations and the computer are mentioned to complete the range. There should be no need to stress that the easiest and quickest way to gain knowledge of machines is to see them, handle them and talk to specialists on their capabilities. More can be learned in a few hours at an exhibition than from many hours of studying a mass of details in a book.

1 Transmitting information

The machines involved in transmitting information include all the communications equipment and machines transporting and handling information between all points in the organisation. A good starting point is mail-handling operations, which involve machines for letter opening and sealing, collators, folding and inserting correspondence in envelopes and franking.

For conversion from speech to speech reproduction at a later stage there are dictating machines of many types using principles such as magnetic, disc and electronic means. From speech to written words or ciphers there are stenographic machines, palantype machines and typewriters.

The transmission of written work may be undertaken by teleprinters and facsimile transmitters. The physical movement of information in the form of paperwork includes initially simple sorting equipment such as pockets, flap-sorters and many different types of files. The actual transportation may utilise pneumatic tubes, document lifts, band conveyors and overhead wire systems. Speech transmission may be arranged through conventional telephone and audio systems.

2 Recording information

The writing or recording of information may be considered under three main groups: new information, existing information and a combination of the two. The creation or appearance of new information can be undertaken by a wide range of typewriters that can cope with completely variable data. If existing information is used a plate may be prepared for repeated application in addressing machines. If a combination of the two is necessary, as in the case of cheque preparation, receipts and standing production orders, there are various imprinting machines for cheque writing, perforating, franking and duplicating standard information on job tickets, and many other dockets used for production control purposes. A spirit duplicating machine with a line selection device may also be used for this purpose.

3 Sorting information
The physical sorting of paperwork such as correspondence and invoices is very difficult to mechanise and is generally done by hand. Sorting by machine demands some means of sensing the information and so far this is restricted to various mechanical and electronic sensing devices associated with punched card installations and computer equipment. Collators are available which assist with sorting and these are gradually becoming more efficient.

4 Copying information
This activity includes reproduction and duplicating. The three main duplicating processes which involve the preparation of a master to run off a large number of copies are called the spirit process, the stencil and the offset litho process. Choosing the correct one for a job is straightforward. The main critical points are: cost per copy, length of run, prestige factor, number of colours, cost of master, maintenance, usage, simplicity of operation and cost of machine. Once these points are clarified the choice is obvious.

When only a few copies are required the choice is restricted to a photocopier. The process is similar to contact printing where light-sensitive paper is exposed against the original. In some processes heat-sensitive paper is used. The main methods are: direct positive, dyeline, gelatine transfer, electrostatic, reflex, thermal process and transfer diffusion. There is a wide range of machines available, varying in price, size of reproduction, quality of image, speed of reproduction, cost per copy and servicing costs. The main points to consider are the capital cost of the equipment, hire charges, servicing costs, risk of breakdowns, quality of reproduction, permanent or temporary copies, type of process (liquid or dry), number of copies required, the maximum size of originals, the type of original (opaque or translucent), effect of colour and ball-point pen on reproduction, simplicity of operation, availability of spares, and servicing speed and cost.

5 Checking information

Comments similar to those expressed under the heading of sorting information apply here. Invariably staff have to undertake this activity except when expensive, sophisticated equipment is employed.

6 Calculating

This activity covers all forms of calculating, including adding, subtraction, multiplication, division and other more involved calculations. There are three main classes:

(a) Calculating machines with visual dials, which means that a transferring operation is necessary from the dial into written form unless a checking activity only is involved.
(b) Machines with paper printouts of the results and other information.
(c) Machines with registers or memories that hold information until required later.

The range runs from very simple adding machines to increasingly complex machines, including adding–listing machines; adding machines with storage facilities; calculating machines with dials, printouts or storage facilities, or with a capability to calculate complex formulae; and accounting machines with posting facilities made possible by the inclusion of a typewriter keyboard, multi-register devices and complex analysis capability.

Purchase of the more sophisticated machines demands careful consideration of their effect on procedures and systems which are discussed in Chapter 5. On the accounting side these machines, if properly utilised, can increase efficiency by producing more accurate, legible entries which provide easier control features.

7 Storing information

Storage problems conveniently divide into two main groups: how to keep original documents which will be needed for future use and how to transfer information from original documents into storage for future reference and use in ongoing procedures.

The first group includes a communication aspect which is associated with information retrieval and a filing aspect to locate the documents in suitable storage equipment. Both of these aspects are discussed in Chapter 6, which deals with communication. The second group includes such equipment as microfilming devices, which are also considered in Chapter 6, and it forms an essential part of installations associated with punched cards and computers which are now discussed.

Punched card installations

A comprehensive punched card installation combines all the clerical activities already mentioned into mechanised form. Its versatility is only superseded by the computer, therefore it could be referred to as the halfway stage between manual clerical work and electronic data processing (EDP). Many installations are gradually being replaced by a small computer, but the peripheral equipment for punching and sorting often remains to act as input devices for computers.

The principle of punched cards is that numerical or alphabetical information can be recorded by punching holes in cards at precise predetermined positions. These can later be sensed at high speed for the purpose of performing many clerical activities such as calculating, sorting, checking and so on. The cards are rectangular with a number of vertical columns, each divided into numbers from 0 to 9 with appropriate descriptive headings. The number of columns varies according to the size of the equipment, but eighty columns is typical. Punching a hole in the second position down, for example, will record the digit 1. If alphabetical punching is desired the use of extra punching positions at the top of the card allows for a coding system to coincide with a letter.

Two main types of equipment can still be seen; these are mechanically operated, where holes are sensed by rods, and electrically operated, where holes are sensed by means of brush contacts.

Important factors to consider are that the cards are costly to produce but that once the information is recorded it can be used repeatedly, quickly and with a minimum amount of human effort. The criterion, therefore, is to be sure that each piece of information is worth recording on the basis of the number of times it will be utilised.

The equipment provides data quickly at reasonable cost, which means that more control information can be provided by adopting various forms of analysis which would be too costly if attempted manually. There are limiting factors to consider, however, such as the size of the card (which also determines machine size), the possibility of breakdowns and the correct balancing of each item of equipment to avoid bottlenecks at certain stages in the processing.

The main classes of machine utilised are as follows.

Punching machines
These are normally electric, although manual machines may be seen occasionally. The operator is provided with information which is generally numerically coded. The punching operation simply involves depressing the appropriate key on a small keyboard and with practice the operator can develop high speeds.

The verifier
To ensure accuracy the same operation is repeated using the cards that have just been punched and a sensing device which detects any errors as the verifier operator depresses the keys which correspond to the information already recorded. Any mistake is recorded automatically and errors may then be corrected later.

The sorter
The sorting machine will rearrange a batch of cards into any desired sequence, but there is a restriction of only one column at a time with each run. The machine operates at high speed, therefore analysis time is reduced to a minimum.

The interpreter
If the punched information needs to be read for any reason, the card may be fed into the interpreter, which senses the holes and prints the details in plain language on the card face. Some interpreters will also print the information on a plain card.

The collator
This machine is also known as an interpolator. It will merge two sets of cards into one pack in the correct sequence and, if desired, one set of cards may be verified with another set, any error being automatically rejected.

The reproducer
As its name implies, this machine will produce a duplicate set

of cards and, in addition, will punch information from a
master card onto other groups of cards.

The calculator
Any calculations required on a card may be undertaken by
this class of machine. The results are punched on the card.

Summary card punch
If cumulative totals are required this machine will store and
print or punch the results on summary cards.

Mark sensor
This device senses graphite pencil markings in any position on
the card and automatically punches a hole, thus saving the
punching process normally undertaken by an operator.

The tabulator
This device is sometimes known as an accounting machine. It
reads the punched cards, summarises and prints the information on concertina-style paper. The tabulator is not very often
seen now as it has been largely replaced by the small computer.

With the exception of the puncher and verifier, the machines
mentioned are automatic once the packs of cards are inserted.
The cards are easily stored, are compact and can be used
repeatedly, although eventually they become ragged at the
edges and cause blockages in the machines. A new set of cards
has to be duplicated to avoid repeated hold-ups. The cards
are particularly useful for large-volume work associated with
such procedures as the payroll, invoicing and stock control.

The computer

Data processing has been revolutionised through the introduction of the electronic computer. This equipment has
brought about a major change by performing all the processing

activities through the employment of complex electronic circuitry which dispenses with all the mechanical features of previous machines. The use of certain mechanical devices remains, however, to place the data at an appropriate input point and to print out information as required in plain language form. The processing activities are performed at such exceptionally high speeds that the limiting factors governing throughput are located at the input and output points. Once the information ha s been introduced, however, continuous processing fo llows at a high level of accuracy.

The equipment is very expensive, but it has compactness, versatility and high capacity. Continuous progress in design is ensuring the introduction of more sophisticated computers every year. The early 1950s produced the first generation, which consisted of vacuum tubes in the circuitry. The second generation appeared in the mid 1950s with the use of solid-state devices which replaced the out-dated vacuum tubes. Finally, the third-generation machines appeared in 1964 with the introduction of micro-miniaturised components. The significance of these generations is that each advancement has resulted in smaller machines with vastly increased capacity, speed, flexibility and operating efficiency. At the same time the peripheral equipment and programming have also advanced considerably. These terms are explained later.

Basic units

To provide sufficient flexibility of operation the computer is divided into a number of units, often called hardware. The units when grouped together must provide appropriate input and output facilities; be automatic; have the capability to store, rearrange, calculate, summarise and obey programmed instructions at electronic speed; and allow for overall control by an operator. These facilities are made possible by dividing the computer into the following sections: input, output, control, storage, auxiliary storage and arithmetic logical units.

Input

Information is fed into the computer at the input stage. The choice of input device depends upon various factors associated with the systems in operation. Typical input devices are punched card readers, punched paper-tape readers, magnetic-tape units, magnetic ink character readers, optical character readers, printer keyboard terminals, transaction recorders and voice response systems.

If the information is fed directly (electrically) into the computer, the term 'on-line' is used. If the information has to be connected to a converter device first, as in the case of transaction recorders, the term 'off-line' applies. On-line processing applies to input and output facilities, the advantage being that data may be fed in and printed out during the internal processing so that alterations and updating of information may immediately be placed at the output point if it is required. This arrangement allows for real-time processing: the computer automatically processes information to a set programme as it enters and the results immediately appear at the output stage. A typical application is for airline bookings, which may be taken at many different agencies but are all immediately updated at a central computer point. The computer is programmed to process other information as soon as each flight is up to capacity.

Output

This is a convenient point at which to consider output because many similar devices are used in the input stage with appropriate modifications. Naturally their function is reversed to cope with information produced by the computer in various forms such as punched cards, magnetic tape, punched paper tape and so on.

These input–output devices do not necessarily have to be physically located very near to the computer. Keyboard terminals may be located many miles apart, the connecting link being a telephone line. Whenever possible, however, all the devices are grouped together because control is much easier. One outcome of this facility is that computer time may be hired by installing an input–output terminal in a concern's premises. This arrangement is known as a computer bureau.

If permanent visual records are needed there are various printing devices which work at high speed. Another visual device is known as a display station because it utilises a cathode ray tube for showing the information on its screen. Even graphs, tables and drawings can be displayed on the face.

The console
The console monitors the whole process externally from the input point through to the output point. It is operated by the controller, who is responsible for all its functions including testing and locating failure points. The control panel houses a number of indicator lamps which show the state of the circuitry at various critical stages and the loading of storage devices. A switchboard and often a typewriter are incorporated, providing the facility for starting and stopping the computer, selecting various input and output units, manually inserting instructions and controlling the computer if a fault occurs.

Storage
Data may be stored internally, which is often known as main or primary storage, as an integral part of the computer. In addition, data can be accommodated in auxiliary stores and external stores.

Internal storage is based upon recording data in the form of electronic signals. In common with all electronic devices there are two states in a circuit: either current is flowing or it is not. In other words, the current is on or off; therefore storage must be based upon a two-digit system only. As the decimal system —using values 0 to 9—is unsuitable, the binary scale is ideal as it employs only two values: 0 and 1. The two popular forms of internal storage are magnetic core and magnetic thin film. These devices allow for immediate random access to information, which still remains stored after it has been used. In other words, it is not erased after use unless specifically desired.

There is generally a need for auxiliary storage to supplement the main store. The devices available for this purpose, in addition to those mentioned under internal storage, are discs, drums, cards, strips and tape, all of which are magnetic. All data from an auxiliary source are fed through the main storage device, therefore they are not immediately accessible or quite so rapid compared with internal storage.

Finally, external storage is used to hold information before or after processing. There has to be a physical switching over of this equipment to connect it with the computer as generally it does not form an integral part, nor does it come under the electrical control of the computer until coupled. The devices often used are punched cards, paper tape, magnetic tape, magnetic discs and magnetic cards.

The central processing unit

The CPU controls and monitors the process automatically by referring to the stored programme and informing the various units on the required operations to complete the task. Overall control is exercised by the console, which has already been described. To perform efficiently the CPU has facilities for the logical addressing of information in the main store and auxiliary stores, for retrieving the information as required, referring to the programmed instructions in the correct sequence, for arranging any calculations and analysis, for receiving information from input devices and for utilising output units when desired. These facilities are made possible through the use of various internal units, the main ones being registers, decoders and adders. Also, the control unit within the CPU directs and co-ordinates the input and output units, reception and retrieval of information from the store facilities, the routing of data between the various units for directing calculations, and analysis.

Arithmetic unit

The unit, often called the arithmetic-logic unit, provides the facility for calculations and logical activities. Logic refers to any relationships between numbers, such as comparing them to see whether they are equal, whether one is smaller than the other or whether they differ substantially. The unit is directly controlled by the CPU, which arranges for the operations, caters for the input and utilises the results.

Further considerations

In conclusion, there are certain aspects associated with electronic data processing that should be examined. Those directly connected with the computer are programming and the feasibility study; integrated data processing, data transmission, information retrieval and source data automation are also discussed. Incidentally, an alternative term to EDP is automatic data processing (ADP), which is usually defined as a system that minimises the manual tasks in processing data.

Programming

Although computers are automatic they still require detailed instructions on the operations to be performed with the data available. The routing of information to the correct points and the processes involved at these points is governed in its entirety by the stored programme, thus the correct sequence is essential. Writing the programme for storage in the computer is very involved. To prepare the complete series of instructions the programmer must first study the problem, prepare flow charts, write the instructions in strict sequence, test it and finally, if it is correct, prepare the programme for production by ensuring that all documentation and the run manual are complete.

The cost of producing a programme is very expensive and often packaged programmes at a reduced cost are available from the computer manufacturer as part of the customer service. This service indicates a change in emphasis from the hardware aspect to more consideration for software, which involves systems and preparation of programmes to suit individual needs.

The feasibility study

In common with any costly project contemplated by management, the feasibility of introducing a computer must be carefully considered on a cost-benefit basis. Generally a senior executive committee or a group of administration specialists is formed initially to consider whether the project is worth while. The obvious points to raise are the present service offered, the total expense incurred in providing the service and such aspects as the time-saving of the service, its quality, degree of completeness, comprehensiveness and conciseness. Opinions should be sought from all departments in the organisation.

If agreement is reached on the justification of the installation the next stage is to conduct a study in depth. Finally, the questions of suitable equipment, operating costs and installation time and changeover have to be determined, and decisions agreed by senior management. The entire feasibility study is often very protracted because of the tremendous amount of work and investigation time involved. The high expenditure incurred in a computer installation warrants careful analysis and serious study before embarking on this major step in data processing.

Integrated data processing

As already discussed, the IDP concept means integrating the clerical processes by connecting up all the units of equipment to form a comprehensive system so that the data is recorded initially and can be used as required without further recording. This intercoupling process is possible with equipment other than the computer so long as the above requirements are satisfied, which means that punched card installations would comply. The need to transmit the information in recognisable form to various units is fundamental and this step is the first move towards total systems, which are discussed later.

The advantages of IDP, in addition to the greatly reduced recording costs, are that a higher degree of co-ordination is made possible between systems and that faster processing speeds, higher accuracy and a more sophisticated information service are achieved.

Data transmission

The sources of data and the demand points for information can be very remote as concerns diversify, relocate factories in various parts of the country and overseas and establish branches in many areas. The bringing together of data and retransmitting results poses many problems which are gradually being overcome now by the use of revolutionary transmission means such as space satellites, microwave transmitters and voice-grade circuitry.

Telephone land lines are already in common use between sites. These lines connect terminals with the computer so that machine language can flow freely in both directions, thus providing an information service at any point in a concern's diverse organisation. These computer terminals may be located anywhere so long as a line is made available.

Information retrieval

The need to have access to vast amounts of information is becoming more apparent to senior executives. Recording, storing and even retrieving information can be measured easily in terms of cost, but measurement of the benefits is very difficult. There is a tendency, therefore, to ignore its importance, although there are many classic examples of chaos created through lack of information.

Efficient Information Retrieval (IR) is possible now through the use of the computer storage devices and other means such as microfilming. Technical data may be stored and retrieved rapidly, and many control features such as running balances of expense items, and daily profit and loss summaries may now become a reality. Such sensitive control provides management with ample opportunity to make more logical decisions and to solve problems more easily. The efficient control of IR often depends on the employment of specialists who can successfully index and locate the information quickly and on the effectiveness of managers, who must be able to describe their requirements accurately and in suitable language which identifies the requirement easily.

Source data automation
More attention has recently been paid to devices that will automatically feed data into the computer. This interest has arisen because there are always hold-ups in locating the data for input and in changing it into a suitable form for computer usage, both of which increase the cost. Conventional devices are much too slow relative to computer performance and the acquisition of data also presents a problem as it is often the responsibility of line managers to provide data, which means that complex planning and co-ordination are necessary for successful input control.

Two main devices are now appearing to cope with these problems: magnetic ink character recognition units and optical scanners. Both may be employed as a direct input unit and their names indicate fairly clearly the mode of operation. MICR may be seen on many cheques, the principle being that sensing of a figure is possible by assessing the amount of iron oxide on its surface. This sensing is immediately changed into a common language which is fed directly into the computer. OS (Optical Scanners) actually read a document and automatically transfer the data into a language directly acceptable to the computer.

Ergonomic aspects

The successful use of machines still lies in the hands of the operator. To reduce his fatigue while operating machines, attention must be given to the mental stresses and strains associated with the job. These are grouped into psychological, physiological and anatomical aspects, which merge together to form the basis of the operator's behaviour and reactions at work.

The breadth of disciplines involved in ergonomics has brought into consideration many topics, such as a study of the way the human body works and the body's physical dimensions, which must be taken into account when designing equipment like seats, desks and machines. The surrounding working environment, such as air freshness, draughts, light, noise, humidity and temperature, affects performance from the physiological angle. Applied psychology also affects the operator's performance. The reception, processing and reaction to various forms of transmitting information are critical features in improving efficiency.

Many of the topics mentioned are discussed in Chapter 8, 'The office environment'. The relationship between the operator and his machine will be considered at this point. As has already been stressed, the machine relies upon the operator, and therefore the machine should be designed—at points where contact is made—to suit human requirements.

The office manager will immediately become aware of any awkward feelings of bad posture, difficulties in reading dials and operating controls if he takes the bother to give the equipment a trial run. With no knowledge of ergonomics just a little common sense is needed to see and feel immediately whether good design has been employed. The use of controls should be easy, with very little effort required and risk of error minimised. Similarly, visual displays should indicate the situation clearly with no ambiguity, the changing situation should be demonstrated visually if possible and the setting of values should be straightforward, with minimum risk of incorrect settings. To satisfy these needs a great deal of research has been undertaken, and many volumes have been published on the results and on ways to provide the necessary requirements in machine design.

5 Systems and procedures

Introduction

The need for administrative management has so far been examined in conjunction with the way the organisation may be planned to accommodate departmental office managers who achieve results through the correct treatment of staff. In the previous chapter the first stages of considering the work involved were considered by isolating the various clerical activities and studying the means available for processing the data.

The achievement of objectives associated with clerical work also rests on the analysis and design of suitable systems and procedures. The philosophy of design remains unchanged regardless of the particular field in mind. Effective product design, for example, pays attention to the requirement, the price bracket, integration of all features, stress and strain factors, special demands, durability, utility, and many other aspects that may be easily thought of if a motor car is considered.

Similarly, successful system design depends upon broad thinking which integrates all the desirable features. This does not necessarily mean aiming for the best but rather for the optimum requirement for each feature based upon the overall aim. Thinking in terms of a car again, the main aim may be a low price range, in which case the best of everything need not apply, but the optimum within the price bracket becomes essential for competitive purposes and economic viability.

System design is just as important as product design; they are interdependent for successful marketing operations. Unfortunately systems and procedures often do not receive sufficient attention at the design stage and this deficiency may contribute to the failure of a very well-designed product. The design problem also would be easier to solve if managers knew exactly what information they required for correct skill utilisation, but often they do not.

It is not unusual for the burden of judging what information is needed and attempting improvements in procedures to fall upon the office manager. The following study therefore looks at the part procedures play, the analysis of systems, and their functional and structural aspects. The importance of management information is then discussed, along with documentation problems. In conclusion, procedures are examined more closely and some examples are drawn from a selection of systems.

The need for systems

Unless all the activities of the business are carefully analysed and divided into suitable systems and procedures, the requirements of the ongoing business—production, selling and financial operations—will not be satisfied. Furthermore, information for projects and new concepts will not be continually presented unless the systems are also designed for this purpose. Thus survival partly depends upon this aspect—but only partly, because solving problems and making the right decisions for company survival still depends upon the expertise of management.

Systems can help considerably, however, by providing retentive *memories* of information (records), analysing the information into more meaningful forms, providing substantial control information and maintaining continuity of information availability despite staff changes. All these aids must be provided at minimum cost in the most effective way.

With these features in mind, a system may be described as a cluster of procedures closely relating to each other and each consisting of a number of operations which collectively provide adequate information in various suitable forms for staff to work efficiently and for managers to control and direct effectively.

To provide an indication of the use of systems and procedures a simplified list is given below.

System		*Procedure*
A	Sales	1 Customer's enquiry
		2 Customer's order
		3 Sales statistics
		4 After-sales service
B	Production	5 Operator utilisation
		6 Materials utilisation
		7 Plant utilisation
		8 Progressing
		9 Maintenance
		10 Inspection
C	Accounting	11 Bought ledger
		12 Sales ledger
		13 Payroll
		14 Cash book
		15 Share register
		16 Fixed assets
D	Purchasing	17 Purchase order
		18 Goods received
		19 Stock control
		20 Purchase invoices
E	Distribution	21 Warehousing
		22 Despatch
		23 Transport

Systems analysis and integration

From the previous remarks it would seem that systems analysis is directly concerned with the exceptionally complicated task of unravelling the data and information at all points in the organisation and reassembling them in the best form so that the right information constantly reaches the right people at the right time and in the correct meaningful sequence.

Even that description, if viewed as a systems analyst's job, is a gross oversimplification considering the vast areas of knowledge required to identify managers' requirements, to assess data, to rearrange it effectively, to present it in various forms and to know sufficient about the particular business to think intelligently in terms of the possible problems and decisions that will arise. Whether such specialists actually exist and operate in the manner described is debatable. Probably it is essential to have a collective effort, forming catalysts of specialists in various fields who actually decide on the system's requirements.

In practice the office manager will often find a complete lack of forethought and very little attempt by senior managers to integrate systems. The tendency is for systems and procedures to grow in a haphazard fashion, which produces ineffectiveness, much duplication of effort and unnecessary paperwork. The true costs of this uneconomic method of operating are easily lost among other expenses unless a system of costing is in operation which isolates real administration costs. The office manager will also find very few managers who really appreciate the subject and most will be somewhat puzzled over what all the fuss is about; but times are gradually changing.

The functional aspect

Although it is clear that a business can be organised into its main functions—such as in a manufacturing concern: selling, production and finance; or in a commercial concern: say, agents, insurance and finance—the analysis of any system soon reveals that the functional borders of activity tend to disappear. All functions are dependent and interdependent on each other, therefore activities and paper flow cut across the so-called boundaries and a system can only really be analysed and designed by ignoring these restrictive functional lines. If this point is ignored there is bound to be unnecessary duplication of records and a more expensive administration set-up.

This aspect becomes clearer when procedures are considered later and the concept of total systems is explained. If design is left to functional specialists and individual office managers there is a tendency to build up procedures within the organisation boundaries, as might be expected, because of self-interests and jealously guarded areas of functional responsibility. Managers are generally not sufficiently co-operative to provide access for true analysis and integration of paper flow, thus procedures tend to develop artificial costly barriers which hamper smooth working.

If the opportunity occurs the office manager should attempt to remove these hazards by discussing with colleagues in other departments ways of improving the flow, thus indicating his willingness to lower any barriers for the sake of improving the systems. If the administrative management function is well established this problem is lessened considerably.

Systems investigation

More detail of the systems analyst's job is necessary because the office manager may have to liaise with him and it helps if the scope of the job is understood.

A logical sequence of investigation which the analyst undertakes could be:

1 Overall assessment
The analyst gathers as much information as possible on the
sector being investigated by considering many aspects such as
the company background, operating conditions, the particular
industry or trade, the financial situation and the philosophy of
the concern. Thus a complete familiarisation should lead to a
comprehensive picture and evaluation of the information
requirements.

2 Activity analysis
The complete requirements for each clerical activity are
studied and divided into sequential groups which consist of a
number of tasks, thus indicating work that has to be undertaken to ensure continuity. As already explained, these activities will cut through functional lines between, say, sales and
production. A considerable amount of documentation is involved and various techniques are employed, including information interface diagramming.

3 The system model
From all the information gathered it is now possible to
establish a suitable model by analysing and reanalysing all the
tasks that involve data processing. This form must satisfy all
the system requirements and is often called the prototype
stage.

4 The operational model
The prototype is now developed into operational form, which
includes the processing steps, their sequence and much detail
on input, output, means of processing, records, reports and
other control features. Thus a complete plan is assembled which
is often called the operational plan.

5 Documentation of the system
Complete documentation, including a detailed description of
the system, the hardware and software requirements, and the

operational plan mentioned above, are now assembled for submission to management. After appropriate discussion with everyone concerned and various changes have been incorporated, official approval is given.

6 Introducing the system

The final step is to implement the scheme and to ensure that the proposed control features actually satisfy the requirements. Invariably there are teething problems and some managers, if not completely sold on the new system, will take full advantage of these faults unless there is carefully controlled implementation.

Structural aspects

The complete structure of systems and procedures is now examined to classify the introductory remarks and to ensure that the office manager clearly sees the particular role he should play, which is dependent upon the system or number of procedures for which he is responsible.

The office manager should understand that the efficient operation of a procedure does not necessarily provide the most effective operational value or give sufficient relevant information to management. He must be involved in providing not only routine reports but also special reports, which fill the inevitable gaps in any information matrix. This wider role awareness is often overlooked or swamped in the daily problems associated with the ongoing business, but in view of its critical company survival feature a determined attempt must be made not to become over-involved in day-to-day activities up to a point where the wider role aspects are neglected. The correct operational outlook thus hinges on the way the office manager organises his department (which was stressed in Chapter 2), the strict allocation of his time to various tasks and the expertise he develops. Expertise is essential because, without it, he

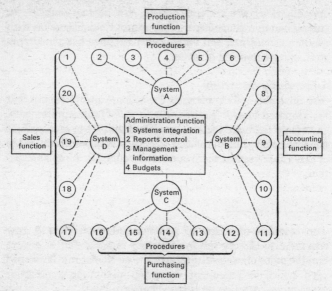

Fig. 15   A simplified systems structure

will tend to concentrate on detail and on easy tasks instead of thinking in broader terms about improving the procedures and providing more comprehensive management information.

A simplified structure of systems and procedures is shown in Fig. 15 to illustrate the make-up of a scheme with systems integration in mind. This concept is aligned with the philosophy of systems analysis, the view of administrative management as a function and the objective of providing an improved management information system.

There should be no doubt of the part that information plays in the provision of a real awareness of the situation relating to all the resources available in the concern. Obviously the resources themselves are of prime importance: the employees, plant and machinery, buildings and land, furniture, equipment, materials, financial resources and so on. Nevertheless a variety of information on these resources is essential for managers to apply their skills. The diagram should be studied with this fact in mind and with the idea that all office managers must see clearly the goals they must achieve if management's overall objectives are to be reached.

The diagram is oversimplified intentionally with the procedures represented by numbers and the systems by letters. System control within each sector has a two-fold purpose of integrating the procedures within the sector and of ensuring adequate information flow to integration centres within the administration function which provides the more sophisticated and condensed information requirements for senior management.

Normally the office supervisors are responsible for control adjustments at procedural level while middle managers are responsible for decisions affecting more than one procedure, and incorporated in these decisions are the financial aspects, including operating expenses. Middle managers generally coordinate the procedures and recommend changes based upon information received from office supervisors.

Management information

As already indicated, the bulk of information is flowing and being utilised at the base level of the organisation where the actual work is done. As the levels above are approached the tendency is for the information to be sifted, condensed and presented in new forms appropriate to its use. Considering the pyramid nature of the organisation, the sifting process becomes more drastic as the top is approached. The process therefore depends on whether someone is actually doing the work (clerical activities) or seeing that it is done, or on whether policy-making and adjusting are involved.

In addition, the rapid availability of information at higher
levels and the use of specialist advice are paramount, together
with sound bases for comparison and closer relationships with
other relevant information. Thus the indications of trends,
percentages and ratios in presentable form greatly assist
management. Typical examples are sales turnover; production
and expenditure for each month and comparisons with previous
years; stock levels; employee productivity; ratios between sales
turnover and gross profit; cash in hand and creditors; and net
profit and dividend.

Management information system

Although each function in a concern is highly specialised there
is a strong need for all functions to be integrated from the
viewpoint of decision-making, which should be interrelated so
that overall objectives are aimed for, not functional aims alone.

A sound management information system (MIS), it is
claimed, can be so designed that a degree of influence is
exerted on each functional specialist. Company objectives are
more likely to be reached through this higher co-ordination of
the main functions. The development of such an integrated
systems concept is very tedious and slow, but many concerns
are now aiming for this approach, which is often called total
systems.

Documentation

Any piece of paper containing, or intended to contain, data or
information may be called a document. Thus the main documents seen in procedures are letters from customers, suppliers
and others; notes containing details of a telephone call or a
personal call; memoranda; various forms that are filled in
externally by customers, suppliers, state departments, legal
offices and local authorities; internal forms completed by employees for such purposes as requisitioning stationery, ordering

materials, applications for staff, claiming petty cash and providing data or information; routine reports, special reports; charts and graphs.

The tendency for the number of these documents to grow at an alarming rate is well known and there is a need for careful control. Part of this control feature is to consider the use of the documents:

1 For reference: filed, copied or recorded.
2 For processing: details and results entered in other forms and reports.
3 For control: records of output, quality, timeliness and cost sent to supervisors and some managers.
4 For reporting: to supervisors and managers on information requirements.
5 For communicating: to other employees for operational purposes.

Location of documents

During the usage of documents the location points may vary considerably, thus rapid retrieval can become a problem if a particular document is suddenly required. Some indication of the likely places is given below:

(*a*) In a wide variety of files throughout the concern.
(*b*) In transit—in- and out-trays, messengers, internal and external transport systems, the mail.
(*c*) Waste and eventual destruction—waste-paper baskets, dustbins and incinerators.
(*d*) Mislaid—back of a drawer or cabinet, on a typist's chair, under a table leg, misfiled, among miscellaneous piles of papers or in someone's pocket.
(*e*) Processing stages—on a desk, in a drawer, on a machine, with equipment, in the stores, in a representative's car, in a van, at reception or on benches in the factory.
(*f*) Query stages—with a manager or supervisor.

To operate a control scheme where every document's location is known at any time is exceptionally difficult and grossly uneconomic. There must always be reliance on staff interest and the application of common trust. These factors really make the procedure work well, but there should also be a written procedure indicating clearly, among other things, the movement of documents in the correct sequence. This leads on to the next topic.

Procedure manuals

To ensure that each member of staff knows exactly what his role is and the extent to which it impinges on that of others, a well-designed procedure manual can help considerably. This should contain a detailed plan of each procedure, indicating the sequential flow of documents, the processes involved at each stage, the aims and subsidiary aims, the make-up of each job and the method to be used. In fact, all essential details of the work at operational level should be included. Thus the manual should show—provided that it is kept up to date—the work plan, the communication network, the documents in use, the control points and the aims. An extract from a procedure manual is given below:

Procedure: payroll preparation   page 7

Job   *Task*

Payroll clerk B   1   Calculate total hours worked and enter in column 1 on the clock card.
    2   Locate personnel record card, tally with appropriate clock card and enter basic rate in column 2.
    3   If over 37 hours worked, enter overtime rate in column 3.
    4   Pass batch to clerk C.

Job	*Task*	
Payroll clerk C	5	Calculate basic pay in column 4.
	6	Calculate any overtime pay in column 5.
	7	Total columns 4 and 5 in column 6.
	8	Pass to supervisor.
Supervisor	9	Check batch of clock cards with tally roll.
	10	Pass to machine operator for payroll preparation.

Aims of a procedure

Whether a procedure ever actually achieves all its aims is doubtful. The office manager should therefore continually strive to improve the procedures under his control by testing and attempting to find better ways of operating. A composite list of aims that could apply to most procedures is now given:

1 To ensure the smooth flow of information in correct sequence.
2 To prevent any possibilities of fraud.
3 To provide appropriate control points.
4 To allow for insertion of missing information according to the requirements of the system.
5 To adjust any inaccurate information.
6 To insert any additional information as considered necessary.
7 To conform to legal requirements.
8 To provide appropriate information to supervisors and managers on time.
9 To integrate with other procedures and systems.
10 To be economically viable.
11 To satisfy quickly any queries from staff, customers, suppliers and others.

12 To be designed in such a way that staff interest in the work and performance are maintained at their highest levels.

13 To present all information on time and in its most suitable form for the purpose.

14 To indicate the accuracy of the information from its source, such as factual, second-hand and opinion.

Achieving the aims

Knowing how to achieve the aims of a procedure first involves the question of how well it works already. The usual feedback includes complaints (or praise) from customers, suppliers and other departments. The problem of operating within the budget also arises. The true situation is not always clear. Staff cover up for each other, errors are amended without being highlighted, employees do not always complain directly and, unless the office manager knows what he is looking for, there is no hope of making a genuine assessment.

In a sense, every procedure has something to sell. Whether other departments 'buy' it is fundamental, and if they do not they will find other less efficient ways to satisfy their requirements, more expense is incurred and poor relationships are apparent. They may go through the motions of conforming to the procedure but, operationally speaking, other means are employed. It may take an office manager a long time to find out the causes for this, as people are generally reluctant to disclose not only the true way they operate but also the reasons for not adhering to the laid-down procedure.

The considerations affecting the achievement of aims are:

Primary considerations. These consist of:

(*a*) Careful and detailed systems analysis and design.
(*b*) Constant attention to all motivational aspects of staff.

(c) Good supervision and office management.
(d) Effective operation of the senior executive function of administrative management.
(e) Correct selection of employees and managers throughout the organisation.

Secondary considerations. Through the satisfactory application of the primary considerations a number of techniques and skills will be utilised. Typical examples are:

(a) Continuing training schemes for all employees and managers.
(b) The use of clerical work study.
(c) Regular assessments of staff and promotional programmes.
(d) Revision of personnel policy as required.
(e) Adequate internal and external research on various information aspects.
(f) The use of budgetary control and modern costing schemes that indicate clearly the real costs of information production.
(g) Regular assessments of systems and procedures performance both for the ongoing business and for management information.

The validity of documented information

Considering the high cost of documenting information and passing it through the system, there should be a measure of control over this process. The aggravating situation exists, however, where it is practically impossible—except in a very small firm—for everyone to be familiar with all the information passing in and out of the concern. There are bound to be overlaps and duplication; nevertheless, an attempt to overcome this inherent fault must be made.

A questioning approach is worth while, bearing in mind the following main areas involving validity of documentation:

1 Information should not be duplicated in other documents without a good reason.
2 Information must be of use, not superfluous.
3 The cost of producing the information should be weighed against the benefit derived from it.
4 The continued existence of information must be justified, otherwise it should be destroyed.
5 Keeping information just in case it is needed is costly. Whenever possible the time and cost of relocating such information should be considered first.
6 Management information is difficult to assess. Certainly it must be produced quickly, accurately and wholly when specially required. Situations change very rapidly, therefore it is often impossible to say with accuracy whether certain recorded information will be required again. The high cost of storage inevitably forces arbitrary decisions to be made.

Procedure examples

To conclude this chapter some procedures are examined to show their main aims, the documents that are often seen in use, the stages that are easily distinguishable and, in certain cases, the precautions that are essential. The selection includes procedures usually encountered in most companies. Within the purchasing system the purchasing order procedure is considered, followed by the payroll as part of the accounting system. An example of a procedure in the production system is covered by stock control, sales invoicing is dealt with as part of a sales system and, finally, the main precautions to bear in mind with cash control are given.

Purchase order procedure

Within the purchasing system there could be four procedures: the purchase order, purchase invoicing, goods received and stock control.

The first procedure, the purchase order, would deal with the initial raising of a requisition through to the receipt of goods; the second with the receipt of invoice through to the payment of the account; the third with receipt of goods through to storage; and the fourth with issuing the goods from the stores and charging the amount to the department concerned.

The aim of the purchase order procedure is to ensure that the most appropriate arrangement is made between the con-

Forms	Requisition	Quotation	Purchase order	Goods received note
Production: Department	(1) Write requisition, copy to purchasing department			
Purchasing department:	(2) Check details	(4) Write for quotations	(7) Write order, copy to stores	
	(3) Locate suppliers	(5) Receive quotations	(8) Check acknowledged	
		(6) Choose quotation	(9) Progress order	
Stores:				(10) Receive goods
				(11) Write GR note, copies to: Inspection Purchasing Production departments

Fig. 16   Purchase order procedure

cern and the supplier to deliver specified items at the right price, in the right quantity and quality, at the right time.

The four documents used in the procedure could be the requisition, quotation, purchase order and goods received note. The requisition is raised by the department requiring the goods; the quotations are sent in by various suppliers who are contacted by the purchasing department; the purchase order is raised by the purchasing department when a quotation has been chosen; and the goods received note is raised when the goods are delivered to the stores. The eleven stages involved in this procedure are illustrated in Fig. 16.

The payroll

A payroll procedure generally forms part of the accounting system. In a manufacturing concern there may be two payrolls, one for operators and one for staff.

In a large concern the procedure may be split into three separate procedures:

1 Clock card procedure—initial preparation, distribution and collection at end of period, and calculation of basic pay, overtime and any bonus.

2 Payroll preparation—transferring information from the clock cards on to the payroll, together with additional information from personnel record cards and final totals of all pay which are allocated to various cost accounts and accounts.

3 Paying-out procedure—cash dissection, collection of cash from the bank, making up individual pay, inserting in pay envelopes together with pay slips, and issuing to employees.

The aims of the procedure are to allocate the correct wages with appropriate deductions to employees, to prevent any risk of fraud during preparation, to abide by any legal requirements, to allocate portions of the payroll to appropriate cost centres and to maintain up-to-date personnel records on wages.

A wide variety of forms may be seen in operation. Typical forms that are generally used are the employee record card, which gives the wages agreed; clock cards, which record actual hours worked; the payroll, which lists in detail each employee and all the details of pay, deductions, tax, etc.; earnings records for each employee; the pay slip, giving full details of gross and net pay and all deductions; the pay packet for inserting the cash; and a payment list of employees to sign when they receive their pay packets.

Stock control

As the name of the procedure implies, the aim is to ensure efficient control of all goods from the time they enter the stores until they are booked out. Such control includes minimising the risk of pilfering and fraud, drawing attention to slow-moving stocks, keeping the stock in good condition and providing a quick stores service.

To achieve these aims a reliable procedure must be employed which provides accurate reports on balances, items booked in and out, and any discrepancies. Much reliance is placed upon the storekeepers who physically handle the goods and who deal with the paperwork too.

The usual documents that can often be seen in a stock control procedure are the delivery note that arrives with the goods from the supplier; the goods received note that is raised by the stores after the goods have been checked in; the inspection note raised by the inspection department which states whether the goods are passed or rejected; the bin card, which is located where the goods are stored and provides an up-to-date balance of the number of goods in stock; the stock record, which usually provides the value as well as amount of stock and the reordering level; the stores requisition that is raised by a department to withdraw goods from the stores; and, finally, the goods returned note for those unused items returned to the stores.

Dependent upon the size of the stores there could be a stores clerk who maintains the stock record, a number of storekeepers who book the items in and out, perhaps assisted by labourers if heavy goods are handled, and a chief storekeeper who controls the whole procedure.

Sales invoicing procedure

A sales system generally covers activities that commence with the original contact with a customer and go on through to the eventual payment of the amount outstanding for the goods delivered or services rendered. One of the procedures within the system is concerned with sales invoicing and it is an important one because it often forms the basis for triggering-off a number of other procedures in various functions.

An example illustrates this point: on receipt of a customer's order a number of departments are affected and plans have to be adjusted. If the required items are in stock the warehouse is notified and the paperwork involved could be the despatch note and advice note. The accounts department will then be notified of the amount charged from a copy of the invoice and an entry is made in the sales ledger to show the amount owing by the customer, which will eventually be cleared by a corresponding entry when he pays. The sales department will also need the information for analysis in the form of sales statistics for management and, finally, the customer will need the invoice to notify him of the amount he owes. The procedure would be even more complex if the item had to be produced. In this case a copy of the invoice is sent to the factory or production department indicating the customer's requirements.

Such a situation where similar information is demanded by many sections in a concern indicates the obvious choice of duplicating the information in the form of an invoice set, within which each duplicated sheet would have its own title

Systems and procedures 165

clearly indicating its use and destination. A typical set would
therefore consist of: the invoice, accounts copy invoice, production order, delivery note, despatch note, advice note and
sales department copy.

Some of the main aspects of the procedure that may develop
into additional complicated activities are the reception of
customers' orders and acknowledgements, the checking processes for determining credit facilities, terms such as a discount, quantity discounts and monthly discount arrangements.

In simple flow form the procedure would appear as:

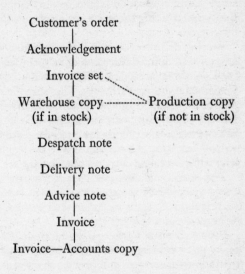

Customer's order
|
Acknowledgement
|
Invoice set
|
Warehouse copy ············> Production copy
(if in stock)   (if not in stock)
|
Despatch note
|
Delivery note
|
Advice note
|
Invoice
|
Invoice—Accounts copy

Cash control

Particular care is essential in designing a cash control procedure
within the accounting system because of the high risk of em-
bezzlement and the responsibility of the concern to reduce
temptation to a minimum and safeguard the finances of the
company.

Except perhaps in the small firm it is usual to appoint a cashier who is responsible, firstly, for all movements of money, which would include cheques and various bills as well as cash, and, secondly, for accurate recording of the transactions.

The ingenuity of people in managing to find loopholes in the most elaborately designed control schemes is well known, but it is often astonishing to see very slack controls applied in many concerns. The social responsibility of management is clear. Every attempt must be made to avoid placing any employee in a situation where he may easily remove cash in the knowledge that there is a strong chance that he will not be discovered.

Bearing this point in mind, the following outline of a cash control system indicates some of its main features. The forms used in these procedures vary considerably, but some are fundamental in most schemes. These are the cash book, which may be drawn up in many different ways ranging from straightforward debit and credit entries for cash in hand and at the bank to elaborate rulings for analysis, discounts and various control features; the cheque book; the paying-in book; the tally roll or receipts list; and the receipt.

The main points for receiving money are at showrooms or shops operated by the concern, through customer contact by representatives, at the reception desk in the firm's main offices or branches and through the mail.

Payments made by the concern include wages and salaries; many petty cash items such as travelling expenses, hotel bills, subsistence allowances and postage stamps; and the settlement of purchase invoices, normally by cheque. The essential facilities for these payments are a bank account, cash in hand, and the drawing and signing of cheques.

The main control features are now given as an indication only of some important points, many of which should contain ancillary controls unique to the particular situation:

1   A signature from the recipient for any cash payment.
2   The use of a cash register with tally roll for all cash received whenever feasible.
3   Control of all documents, which should be designed with sufficient complexity to avoid easy reproduction.
4   No cash should be left unsecured or unattended during processing.
5   Cash should be banked as soon as possible.
6   Whenever possible the activities within the procedure should be divided among clerical staff in such a way that the risk of fraud or collusion is reduced to a minimum.
7   All cash movements should be accompanied by a tally roll or suitable document that provides adequate information for control purposes.
8   Money received through the mail demands special precautions, such as two employees being present when letters are opened; an immediate recording on a document, tally roll or receipts book; and the totalling, coding and checking of the batch with the money. In addition, all cheques should be crossed; the time of arrival and the date may be considered a necessary feature to record on the accompanying correspondence; and the documents and money should be transferred to the cashier as soon as the batch is completed.
9   The issuing of receipts should be done only by those with appropriate authority.
10   Payments made by the company are generally restricted to two managers, such as the cashier and financial director, who sign each cheque jointly.
11   Petty cash procedures normally require a receipt for any item or expense incurred; a petty cash voucher, which is signed by the recipient and the payer; and a petty cash float operating the imprest system.
12   Large sums of money should not be left in the premises

overnight if there is no suitable provision for keeping them safe. The use of a banker's night deposit box is generally available.

13   The cash book should be balanced regularly and reconciled with the bank statements.

14   Any cash discrepancies should be immediately reported to the cashier.

6 Business communication

Introduction

The aim of communication in modern management thought is to achieve a closer understanding between all employees (including managers) so that a complete awareness of aims, up-to-date information and job responsibility will enable each member of staff to be fully productive when he is effectively motivated.

Communication theory is highly complex as it embraces not only the basic ideas of communication, which involve the mechanics of making information available and understood by everyone, but also the question of how to place employees in a situation where unfavourable reaction can be reduced to a minimum. The breadth of communication in this sense includes solving organisation problems, the correct treatment of employees, diagnosing individual problems, improving the climate within the concern, the development of employees and adopting a modern management philosophy.

The management skill of taking action described in Chapter I means something far more than simply communicating the information to the people concerned. The skill lies in creating a favourable response in the individual as well as ensuring that he fully understands the message. As already pointed out, however, this favourable impulse does not mean that the individual will be motivated into actually doing something. The office manager's motivating skill decides this factor.

The absence of a favourable response in an employee or placing him in an intolerable situation could lead to a communication blockage. He may attempt to withdraw from his operational role as a provider of information, or he may not fully co-operate by withdrawing some information, often the vital pieces. Seen from this point of view, the whole concept of communication relies heavily upon people getting on well together in situations which reduce antagonism to the minimum.

Failures in the communication network tend to negate all the efforts of specialists associated with information technology in the concern. Lack of information reduces the degree of understanding at all levels in the organisation. In these circumstances people become unsure of the reasons for carrying out the tasks, they are suspicious of changes and they do not provide appropriate feedback to higher levels.

There is emphasis today on ensuring that employees really become involved as part of a team in which everyone contributes and participates in the decisions that affect them. This philosophy certainly goes a long way towards creating a higher degree of understanding, which is one of the main aims of communication. One example of lack of understanding is that about one-third of strikes are attributed to communication failure.

The office manager has to allocate time regularly for dealing with communication problems because many of them unfortunately are of a recurring nature. Often the problems are associated with human characteristics, such as jealousy, personality clashes, secretiveness and status. People withhold information for a variety of reasons. They may plead that they are too busy or that they did not realise they were doing so. Others are practically the opposite and they spread rumours rapidly through the 'grapevine'. Communication problems increase in relation to the size of the organisation and unless due attention is given to this phenomenon chaos inevitably develops, leading to communication failures that can be very costly and even disastrous.

To summarise, the main purposes of communication are to

develop mutual trust between all employees including managers and supervisors, to reduce the number of mistakes, to minimise misunderstandings, to encourage teamwork and to instil in each employee a favourable impulse for motivational purposes.

The four main approaches to achieving these communication objectives are:

1 Improve the mechanics of communication by concentrating on the message itself, the channel along which it will run and the means of passing on the information.

2 Improve personal contact by studying such aspects as order giving, discipline, reprimanding, absenteeism, lateness, errors, slacking, grievances, group discussion, committees and casual meetings.

3 Develop the informative approach by:

  (*a*) Improving personal performance in reading speed, public speaking, the art of listening, thinking logically, problem-solving, decision-making and report-writing;

  (*b*) improving information aspects such as records, reproduction services, the typing pool, dictation and general office services.

4 Adopt a psychological approach by concentrating on the personal development of employees and the active participation by employees in all matters affecting them, ensuring that they have the opportunity to maximise their contribution through full use of their intelligence and experience.

The mechanics of communication

The mechanics approach to improving communication is as important as other approaches because without due attention the others will fail.

Basically, the approach is concentrated on three main fronts:

1 Ensure that the message itself is as simple as possible and clear, giving any reasons for action required and stating any aims.
2 Choose the right channel, bearing in mind such factors as economy, speed, efficiency, accuracy, time available, the importance of the message and acknowledgement.
3 Choose the most appropriate way of passing the message, such as face-to-face contact, a telephone call or a letter. The choice should take into account the reaction of the recipient, the response and the likely effect of the overall situation on the individual.

Main aims

The mechanical approach aims to ensure that the receiver of the information knows exactly what the sender has in mind. A further aim is to gain support, which means that the communication must be acceptable. Furthermore, every attempt should be made to remove any doubts or suspicions about intentions which could be detrimental to the receiver. Finally, a two-way technique can be adopted to assess the receiver's viewpoint and the possibility of some positive action being undertaken.

The message

The easiest and most common fault in communication is being misunderstood. The reasons for this are, firstly, that people do misunderstand, both intentionally and unintentionally. A plea of misunderstanding is difficult to break down if someone is at fault and so people often deliberately use this excuse when they are at fault. Secondly, clear, concise messages are exceptionally difficult to achieve in situations that are anything but clear and concise.

There are many causes of misunderstanding. Typical ones often quoted are: poor educational level, inexperience, poor IQ, the use of abstract terms, technical jargon, gobbledygook, past environment, inferiority feelings, confusing facts, false inferences, value judgements and even heredity differences. These and many others obviously cannot be put right in the short term. However, much can be done by simple checking to ensure that the person has understood. There are still many dangers though, even after checks have been made. For ex-example, if an employee is asked if he understands and he nods his head in agreement, it is quite likely that he does not. Simple checks cannot be that simple if they are to be effective. A positive indication from the receiver, such as giving an example, is an essential requirement.

In practice there are many other factors to consider. The sender may be under pressure at the time; he may not have sufficient time to 'tune-in' to the receiver; he may misjudge the situation completely in his haste or inability to size it up; or he may employ the wrong approach to a certain individual. Poor expression, incomplete messages, poor listening to feed-back and the use of the wrong channel are a few other common faults. Similarly, the receiver may misunderstand for such reasons as dislike of the sender, suspicion about the motive of the message, trying to size up the situation and listen at the same time, lack of training, being a misfit in the group, having a poor attitude, suffering from a poor memory or being emo-tionally upset at the time.

These examples indicate the magnitude of the problem and there are many famous cases of misunderstandings by eminent people that make interesting reading.

The importance of checking is fundamental in any com-munication between two people because of the six-fold inter-play that actually exists: the sender *thinks* he gives a message, which probably differs from what he *actually* gives and differs again from what the receiver *thinks* he says; the receiver then *thinks* he gives a particular reply, which probably differs from what he *actually* gives and differs again from what the sender *thinks* he gives.

Some rules to reduce misunderstandings are:

(*a*) Use simple, clear and concise words.
(*b*) Avoid elaborate explanations that may confuse.
(*c*) Develop precise, clear speech and writing.
(*d*) Do not rush if understanding is essential.
(*e*) Be sensitive to the receiver's feelings.
(*f*) Weigh up the receiver's ability to comprehend.
(*g*) Check carefully to be sure he understands.
(*h*) Try to reduce any suspicions of your intentions which may adversely affect the receiver.

Channels of communication

The establishment of suitable channels for communication depends upon the desired communication network, the problems of communication that normally exist and the facilities that are offered.

The two main networks are known as one-way and two-way. The one-way network operates on the assumption that the communication is passed downward and that no opportunity is given for consultation or participation in deciding on the action desired. The assumption is that the receiver will understand and is ready to take action. It is also assumed that the communication will be quicker and more effective if the routines involved are well established and acceptable, and if employees know exactly what is required of them in given situations. If a group operates under this system the group leader will get satisfaction, but there will be very little satisfaction for the group members and no co-ordination.

The two-way network is much slower because there is ample opportunity given for consultation and participation between the leader and the group, and between group members. Thus everyone gets more satisfaction and in theory becomes more adaptable to proposed changes. There should be fewer misunderstandings and each member will be far more aware of the others' performance and opinions, meaning that better coordination can be achieved.

Both types of network have their particular uses. There is no point in having a long discussion in an emergency or in routine situations, but there is a need to discuss complex problems and human situations which demand ideas and agreement before workable solutions can emerge.

Before considering the actual channels of communication, the question of the communication patterns which are recognisable in most concerns should be borne in mind. Firstly, there is the vertical pattern which was illustrated in networks; this is normally considered in two parts, upward and downward. Next there is the horizontal pattern which consists of a number of layers, one at each level in the organisation structure. Finally, there is the complex external communication pattern which is linked to many points in the structure. Thinking in terms of a matrix pattern there are also many diagonal links between the vertical and horizontal lines. Within this matrix there may exist a number of formal and informal channels. The formal channels consist of the recognised lines of command, various management committees, project discussion groups, formal discussions with trade union and staff representatives, personnel interviews, works and staff committees, and various publications such as the company periodical, posters, notices, literature on specific topics, personnel policy publications and general policy publications.

The informal channels are the 'grapevine'; unofficial discussions with trade union and staff representatives; informal talks between members of staff, supervisors and managers; external contacts with friends, relatives and various news services; and informal approaches on such topics as promotion, disputes and complaints.

The grapevine probably causes more anxiety than other informal channels because it works so well. Gossip and scandal are circulated at astonishing speed throughout the organisation and, if managers use the grapevine, accurate information can also be passed in the same way. Many managers unintentionally provide so-called confidential information through carelessness, but these scraps of information are often incomplete and the gaps are filled in by bright individuals who are usually very good at making intelligent guesses.

The office manager should make full use of the grapevine by injecting any information that he knows is missing; by constantly checking to see that information is not distorted and that he is up to date; by counteracting any dangerous rumours by providing factual information whenever possible; and by locating any malicious member of the staff who is using the grapevine to slander individuals. The person to use for the purpose of feeding the grapevine is not difficult to find as he generally has a reputation for being 'in-the-know'.

To summarise the mains points about channels of communication:

(a) Use two-way communication whenever possible.
(b) Only use one-way communication in emergencies and for routine purposes.
(c) Encourage the diagonal pattern of communication as it is the shortest distance between two points generally and it also avoids going through too many people.
(d) Choose the channels carefully by developing a sensitivity towards individuals and finding out which channel—often an informal one—suits them best.
(e) Make full use of the grapevine.

The means of communication
The last factor to consider under the mechanics approach is the actual means of communication to employ, such as speech,

writing, actions, signs, gestures, silence and even facial expressions.

Face-to-face oral communication is undoubtedly the best means, but this should not exclude the foregoing precautions. Very few people really master a language and the probability of two people conversing with complete mastery is therefore low. Similar problems apply to written communication with the additional snag of no face-to-face contact. People tend to make assumptions—invariably the wrong ones—which add to the risk of misunderstanding.

As a 'back-up' means of communication the use of signs and various types of indicators is commonplace, but their impact is soon lost. The classic example is a 'No Smoking' sign. People either forget the sign, intentionally ignore it or become unaware of it after a while.

A very effective physical approach is to give a positive demonstration: actions speak louder than words. Unfortunately, in many situations this is not possible. An extreme means is to maintain silence, which can be effective in particular circumstances but can also be dangerous because there are many ways of interpreting this message. Silence can be used to express disgust, boredom, disagreement, agreement, disassociation, displeasure, indifference and amusement. If the person maintaining the silence can keep a straight face there is bound to be confusion, and no doubt if the aim is to confuse the means is successful.

Finally, gestures that emphasise a point or have a particular meaning, along with a variety of facial expressions, are effective reinforcement approaches.

In brief, the points to remember are:

(*a*) Speak clearly, concisely and slowly.
(*b*) Use an appropriate volume of speech based upon the surroundings: extreme cases are the quiet private office and the factory floor.

(c) Use face-to-face means whenever feasible.
(d) Use back-up means.
(e) Beware of ambiguity.

Conclusion

The mechanics approach to communication always pays off because invariably people think that communication is much better than it actually is, but in fact improvements are always possible. The casual technique of the 'ever-open door' is not generally successful because unless the climate is right employees will not come in to discuss problems. Similarly, the grapevine should only be used for back-up purposes. The media technique includes notices, circulars, personal letters, handbooks, manuals and audio systems, but the snag is that one-way communication does not allow for questions and there is no check on comprehension.

The committee technique is very useful to management as the opinions of employees are directly communicated, provided that there are frank discussions. As a means of developing mutual trust, consultative committees, advisory committees and staff meetings should help, provided that managers always demonstrate sincerity.

The line of command technique is an essential requirement. Full flow of information up and down the line is not easy to achieve. Briefing sessions and regular contact with each employee must be part of the office manager's routine work. Although it sounds like a drudgery, the pay-off is definite in terms of less time being spent on queries, complaints, misunderstandings and general problems.

The personal contact approach

The aim of the personal contact approach is to develop better relationships through making full use of the opportunities that occur daily when the office manager contacts members of staff

under his control. The contact points are mainly associated
with topics such as order-giving, discipline, reprimanding,
absenteeism, lateness, errors, slacking, grievances, group discussion, committees and casual meetings.

Order-giving

A sound philosophy of order-giving is: do not give an order
if it can possibly be avoided. This philosophy is based upon
the premise that most people will feel an antagonistic response
if direct orders or commands are given to them. A better
approach is to ensure that they know their job well and simply
give them information that concerns their job. They should
then respond favourably.

The employee's response, of course, depends upon many
factors already discussed in the section on motivation, but the
office manager has an excellent opportunity to assess performance if he adopts the information-passing approach and checks
after applying his motivating skill. In this way the main purposes of order-giving may be achieved: the provision of
information that demands attention, the indication to the
individual that it is his responsibility to do something about
a situation, the opportunity to contact the individual personally and the creation of two-way communication where the
person may be consulted and may participate.

The main types of order practised in business are the
command, such as 'Do this . . .'; the request, a mild approach
such as 'I wonder if you could do . . .'; the implied order,
mentioning that some action is necessary in view of the
situation without being specific; the open order, giving an
opportunity for personal interpretation and timing; and the
passing of information, which has already been discussed.

Although the information approach may be ideal, the choice
may well depend on how well the office manager knows his
staff and on his relationships with them. Each individual
demands a slightly different approach which will be a variation

or combination of the types of orders listed. Each situation is also critical. Some examples are: bringing attention to an error; allocating a new task; drawing attention to a responsibility, an emergency or a disagreeable task; and a task involving a confidential reason.

Discipline

In a modern society there are certain rules, codes of conduct and safety precautions that are generally acceptable in both business and social life. This system to some extent safeguards the individual, creates a civilised way of living and working, and benefits everyone. Most normal people are prepared to accept these standards, although there are some who practise totally different ones. Because of their upbringing people tend to accept that some form of reaction is necessary if they break the rules. Apart from parasites and fanatics, organised society develops with this concept of rules and reprimands in mind, and makes allowances for the aforementioned types.

A highly sophisticated society goes a step further and attempts to induce self-discipline by raising educational standards, developing new technologies and encouraging a concept of employment in which people can fully develop their capabilities in a decent working environment. This idea of self-control and self-discipline is exceptionally difficult to achieve in industrial and commercial situations, where not only are there many adverse pressures working against its implementation but where there may also be a minority of employees who take full advantage of the situation. Thus managers are often forced to rely upon rebukes and penalties to survive the day. It should be remembered, however, that fair-minded people accept discipline if the reasons justify it. They will also respond to fair treatment to such a degree that fear, as a measure of control, may be practically abandoned and be replaced by more conscientious feelings that induce self-discipline.

This sophisticated approach is very demanding on management time. It is essentially a long-term project, setbacks are part of the scheme and there will be times when the temptation to abandon it is overwhelming. The approach has to be tackled on a broad front: concentrating on one or two factors alone will fail. The philosophy of self-discipline relies on the maintenance of high morale, a group spirit aligned with common aims, a sincere belief in people and their high capabilities and, most important of all, on a sincere, straightforward and incorruptible management team. Establishing such a management team is a tall order and is probably more difficult to achieve than all the other factors put together; nevertheless it is essential because employees are hypersensitive towards management and one false move is sufficient to destroy morale.

Disregarding the overall situation in a concern, the office manager should adopt and maintain this approach because it is the easiest way to improve group morale. No doubt there will be setbacks when his staff see others taking advantage, but at least he will establish a reputation as a good manager.

In addition to the factors already mentioned, which amount to a summary, there are many points to bear in mind which are covered in other chapters. All have to be actively pursued to develop high morale.

Reprimanding

The office manager will inevitably be forced into situations where reprimands have to be undertaken. Although to some extent a reprimand can be considered as a recognition of failure, the justification lies in its impartiality. Everyone must be treated equally: if one person is allowed a misdemeanour the others will surely feel offended and regard the treatment as unfair if they are conforming.

A well-worn but effective method is:

(*a*) Before reprimanding, be sure that the information is correct and the full picture has been given.

(b) During the reprimand be fair and humane; do not lose your temper; make sure that you are alone with the individual and are not disturbed or overheard; be straight and forthright, say why he is being reprimanded and what the consequences will be; give him a chance to explain; try to find out the cause for his action; avoid sarcasm and threats; and do not be drawn into arguments.

(c) After the reprimand emphasise his strong points, make it obvious that no grudge will be held against him and offer any assistance if he has a problem.

The four main aspects that are particularly troublesome and often involve reprimands are absenteeism, lateness, errors and slacking.

Absenteeism. Regular attendance of staff is becoming an increasing problem and is the subject of research because of the high rate of absenteeism on a national level. The causes often quoted are sickness, domestic problems, sports activities, other forms of pleasure, poor job interest, job problems, antagonistic colleagues, managerial treatment, extra holidays and public duties. Some of the causes are unavoidable, but the habitual absentee who deliberately gives continual excuses makes life very difficult for the office manager and causes dissension among the staff. It is advisable to mete out fair treatment with an appropriate degree of leniency based upon sensing the situation.

Avoidable causes of absenteeism seem to have roots in such factors as the job itself, the degree of responsibility and satisfaction in the work, group spirit and fair treatment, all of which are all too familiar factors in motivation.

Lateness. Probably a very similar story to the one above applies to lateness. The usual causes are transport difficulties, over-sleeping, domestic mishaps or problems, sickness, job problems, boredom, lack of discipline and poor attitude. A good example should be set by managers and there should be work ready for staff when they arrive. Personal interviews for persistent latecomers are essential.

Errors. These generally occur through lack of concentration, poor training or poor selection for the job. Concentration depends upon job interest, lack of distractions, no emotional problems and a sufficient variety of tasks within the job. Most of the causes of errors are due to managerial ineffectiveness. Even emotional problems are not necessarily the individual's fault and a therapy approach is essential. The individual should be helped in as many ways as possible rather than being blamed or reprimanded.

Slacking. When someone slacks he is generally branded as lazy. It has already been stressed that laziness is really a generic term which demands to be broken down into components such as physical incapability, mental incapability, poor attitude, a domestic problem, boredom, incorrect workloading or an erratic supply of work. Unobtrusive investigation and interviews should eventually determine the cause or causes. In many cases specialist advice is advisable and if work problems are the cause the office manager should take the necessary steps to correct the situation.

Grievances

Dealing with grievances provides an excellent opportunity for the office manager to improve relationships because he can demonstrate understanding, fairness and willingness to consult, and take the opportunity to establish a continual follow-up contact with the members of staff.

A grievance may be defined as any business situation or managerial act that appears to be unfair or unjust to an employee. The justification for the grievance is relatively unimportant compared with the feelings of the individual and their effect on his performance. The main causes of grievances are the full story not being known; intentional or unintentional unfair treatment by management; an individual's personal bias, such as believing that he should have been chosen for a promotion; false information from a malicious person; lack of information through a communication failure; or incomprehension.

To detect grievances the office manager should adopt a positive approach by constantly checking for any change in an individual's attitude or performance. A passive role is unlikely to be successful as staff are not generally keen to air a grievance and they tend to be silent until an emotional outburst occurs.

When there are signs of a grievance the employee should be consulted without delay. A private interview should be conducted with a sympathetic approach so that there is ample opportunity for the employee to explain why the change in attitude has occurred. A suggested interview sequence would be to put the employee at ease, ask if there are any work problems or domestic problems; mention the reason for the interview; give the employee ample opportunity to explain; and, finally, propose a solution. At the end of the discussion due praise (if any) should be given and the employee should be told that if there are any further difficulties he should not hesitate to make them known.

Group discussion

The more informal type of meeting, which is often held at short notice to discuss a particular topic, is called a group discussion. This arrangement encourages the participation of all who are directly concerned with the topic and, in theory, ensures that all information is disclosed and opinions are given before a decision is made by the group leader. Success in group discussions still depends largely upon the leader and the climate he has created in the department. If he is weak and constantly changes his mind, dithers or is influenced by other people who may have a say later, then group discussions become futile and, in fact, create more bad feeling than existed before. The leader must possess sufficient strength to make a sensible decision after due participation and stick by it, otherwise the participants will be frustrated.

Fundamental requirements for conducting a group discussion are gathering together all the immediate staff who are affected by the topic but limiting the number to the six or so members who are closest to the situation; establishing a relaxed atmosphere; giving appropriate information and encouraging everyone to offer their points of view; controlling the discussion; and deciding on a course when everyone has fully aired his views.

Committees

The office manager will invariably become involved in committee work at various levels in the organisation. To be an active committee member he should know all the technical terms used at meetings. He should also be sufficiently conscientious to attend each meeting with a prepared brief on any points he may wish to make together with factual information on the topics under discussion.

If the office manager is appointed as chairman he must thoroughly familiarise himself with all the chairmanship duties and be prepared to conduct his meetings in a firm, fair and friendly manner. A weak chairman is always deplored by everyone and there is probably a tendency for all but the toughest characters to be too lenient with committee members. Much can be sensed from looking at members' facial expressions during the meeting and assessing whether firm control has been established.

A few of the important points associated with committees are ensuring that an agenda is provided well before the meeting so that members know when, where and why the meeting is to be held; issuing any documents in time for people to read and digest the contents; properly preparing the room for the meeting; the chairman ensuring that all members are given the opportunity to speak; and not allowing the meeting to become too protracted.

Casual meetings

The office manager should never miss the opportunity of contacting staff through casual meetings in the general offices, corridors, cloakrooms, dining room and so on. Passing the time of day and a few friendly words pay big dividends. If the opportunity to have a chat about any topic occurs, full advantage should be taken to establish a better relationship.

Establishing a reputation for being 'snooty' must be avoided and this can only be overcome by making sure that friendliness and openness are demonstrated at every opportunity. There is nothing to lose and a tremendous amount to be gained by taking the initiative and making the opening remark in a conversation with members of staff.

The informative approach

The informative approach concentrates on two main areas:

1   Improving personal performance by studying quicker reading, public speaking, thinking effectively, logical methods, the art of listening and report writing.
2   Improving information aspects such as records, reproduction services, the typing pool and general office services.

Each factor within the areas mentioned is very involved and in the space available only a sketch is possible.

Improving personal performance

A sustained programme is essential to improve personal performance and some of the factors can be covered by attending appropriate courses. For the office manager, attention to these factors is a distinct advantage because eventually much time will be saved and communication should improve.

Quicker reading. The conscientious individual will find that more and more time has to be spent on reading the mass of literature that circulates if he is to remain up to date. This time can be drastically reduced by adopting particular quicker reading techniques. Many courses are available and, in view of the high cost of time, full advantage should be taken of these opportunities.

Effective speaking. The ability to speak in public is extremely useful and essential in the modern business world. This is a basic requirement for practically every manager, who will inevitably find himself confronted with an audience and will be judged by his ability to speak well. In addition to learning many rules and hints about public speaking, practice and appropriate criticisms on performance are essential. Suitable courses are offered by many institutions.

Closely allied to effective speaking is the use of the telephone, a simple, cheap technique which is often neglected. A concise and logical approach is, firstly, to determine the right person to speak with, ascertain the number and extension, decide what to say—jotting down the main points and having any papers ready for reference during the conversation; secondly, to contact the person by telephone, give your name, discuss the question and ensure comprehension; thirdly, if there is a query unanswerable immediately, to arrange to telephone back at a set time or, if everything has been settled, thank the individual.

The art of listening. An unfortunate fact of life is that most people prefer to talk rather than to listen. Coupled with the fact that generally people only learn when they listen, the whole question of listening becomes relevant. The problem with listening is that unless the topic is interesting there is a tendency to think of other things. Concentration is often difficult, but although the topic may be boring to the listener the sender probably feels it is very important to him, otherwise he would not be discussing it.

People get very annoyed if they see that they are not receiving due attention when they are speaking and this is the easiest way to upset them and create poor relationships. Concentration must be developed, and to achieve this the following points should be remembered:

(a) The mind should be cleared and tuned to the receiver.

(b) Thought is faster than speech, so use the spare time to assess the communication. For example, are facts being presented? Is the speaker sincere? Are there gaps in the presentation? Is there a personal bias?

(c) Try to anticipate the possible questions and weigh the evidence as it appears, making mental summaries whenever possible.

(d) Display interest by indicating your sole attention to the speaker.

(e) If there are faults, make a mental note and ask at an appropriate time rather than interrupting, otherwise the speaker's train of thought is lost.

(f) Fight against distractions and do not create them.

(g) If you have difficulty in remembering, write down the salient points and questions.

(h) Try to avoid criticising the delivery, but concentrate on the message.

(i) If the topic is complex or distasteful there is a tendency to 'switch-off', therefore try to fight against giving up.

(j) Try not to be over-irritated by mannerisms and words that may be objectionable.

Logical thought. The ability to solve problems, make decisions, and create clear messages depends on clear thinking and the use of appropriate techniques. Logical thought is based on imagination, judgement and precise reasoning which determine the degree of success in a managerial job. Being able to think clearly and objectively is a great asset considering the barriers that have to be overcome, such as emotional bias, indifference, laziness, rationalisation, prejudiced ideas, previous environment and previous experience which may tend to give a distorted outlook, jealousy and indoctrination.

The thinking process should use logic, which means the careful analysis of rules or guides which are employed to decide whether statements are related and, by viewing them as a whole, to produce new statements. This form of deductive thinking reasons from the general to the particular and in its common form is known as syllogism. Great care is needed when using syllogism, which consists of a major premise, a minor premise and a conclusion. If one term is not common to both premises a false statement will emerge:

All aircraft have wings,
A bird has wings,
Therefore a bird is an aircraft.

The correct use of syllogism is:

All birds have wings,
A swan has wings,
Therefore a swan is a bird.

Another approach to clear thinking is through inductive thought, which reasons from the particular to the general, analysing many observations and arriving at a conclusion that fits all the findings. This conclusion is often a generalisation because the number of observations is insufficient to arrive at a factual answer. A teacher may, for example, arrive at the conclusion that girls are brighter than boys because they always come nearer the top in examinations set by him, but unless a large survey is undertaken he would not know whether a school 50 miles away produces different results. On the other hand, continual observation of the sun rising and setting over a very long period leads to the factual conclusions that the sun rises in the east and sets in the west.

Problem-solving. In recent years the use of logical method in problem-solving has received much attention. Textbooks are published dealing specifically with this topic and some approaches are very involved.

The basis for solving problems is determined by the definition of a problem. A generally accepted definition is that a problem is an unacceptable deviation from a plan which has a given objective. This negative or adverse deviation is caused by an unanticipated event (or events) which has created an unacceptable condition and will have to be corrected by management.

This definition assumes that a plan is used indicating paths to objectives, that variations from the planned path are known and that every attempt is made to achieve the original objective by finding out the cause of the deviation. When the cause is known the problem is solved and the next step is to make a decision to correct the adverse trend. A simple example is where a payroll procedure is scheduled to pay wages at a set time based on estimated times for each stage. If stage two, clock card analysis, should be finished by 1.00 a.m. on Wednesday and by 4.00 p.m. the analysis is still not complete, obviously an unanticipated event has occurred which is unacceptable to management.

An 'unacceptable' deviation is sometimes acceptable if there is only a small, acceptable change. Similarly, unacceptable conditions are those that management feels must be corrected. If a manager feels that the condition is acceptable, then a situation exists rather than a problem.

A method for solving problems is the four-step approach which is a form of inductive problem-solving. Each step contains a number of aspects, each of which demands consideration and attention in practice. This introductory outline is intended to show the scope of problem-solving only:

(a) Define the problem
(b) Expand the definition
(c) Process the elements
(d) Trace the cause

Although there are many short cuts derived through experience, the habit of approaching a problem in four separate steps avoids wasted time in the long term.

(a) *Define the problem.* Two main factors are involved; firstly, being able to recognise problems and, secondly, separating them from the jumbled mass of everyday activities. Some problems pass unnoticed because deviations are not recognised. Recognition mainly depends upon measurement, setting standards and checking to see whether the standards are met.

Separating the problem means continually analysing the information. There is a tendency for problems to adhere to each other in such a way that the overall picture becomes confusing. Each deviation may affect many sectors and careful analysis is essential.

(b) *Expand the definition.* When the deviation is isolated and defined a more detailed description will indicate the right line of investigation. The description should include the identity of the subject, the time of occurrence if known, a concise description of the fault in the procedure and any other relevant information. As the evidence is accumulated the picture should become clearer.

(c) *Process the elements.* A detailed examination is undertaken by drawing up an analysis of the elements that affect all the sectors, ignoring at this stage whether or not they seem relevant or important. These elements are located by using the old technique: where, when, why, how, whom, degree and so on. Each element is examined to see if there is any common link or uncommon feature which might lead to the cause or produce an idea that could be followed through.

(d) *Trace the cause*. The final step is a deductive process which eliminates the blind alleys and eventually leads to the cause.

Decision-making. The opening remarks on problem-solving also apply to the decision-making skill. Decisions may be divided into two groups, immediate and calculated decisions. Both should be followed by continued anticipation in view of the likely effects that may be overlooked at the time, especially after immediate decisions where the probability of error is high.

Although immediate decisions or on-the-spot decisions may be considered basically unsound, they are often unavoidable and essential in preventing trouble-spots developing into major problems. Considerable sensitivity towards situations, experience and quick, accurate thinking are needed, along with hunches or intuition, for successful decisions of this nature.

Calculated decision-making is possible when there is a time-lag between locating the cause of a problem and deciding on what to do about it. The usual approach is to gather relevant information, consult all who are involved, consider the choices available and arrive at a conclusion. Another modern approach is participative decisions, where the immediate staff involved actually take part in deciding what should be done. Calculated decisions also use decision-making theory, which includes utility and subjective probability, riskless choice, and various mathematical and statistical models of an advanced nature.

Decisions may also be divided into long and short term. The

office manager will often find himself in a situation where a stop-gap measure is needed for various reasons, such as to prevent a further deterioration in a crisis, to wait for information or to conform to a policy issued by senior management.

Report-writing. A typical method for writing reports is:

(a) *Clarify the aim of the report.* Establish the terms of reference and ensure that the topic of the investigation is clearly stated, that any limitations are recorded and its purpose is stated.

(b) *Prepare a suitable framework.* A suitable plan should be prepared before starting the investigation. Difficulties should be anticipated, such as the time factor, detail required, any secrecy, investigating the facts, degree of co-operation and any special features.

(c) *Collect the information.* Observation, discussion and searching are the main procedures for determining the sources of information and obtaining the detail for analysis and presentation.

(d) *Collate the report.* The first draft should be written under the following headings in this sequence: the subject or title, introduction, findings, conclusions, recommendations, references and summary.

(e) *Revise the report.* The revision should be undertaken after a suitable time-lag of a few hours. The draft should be read critically with the object of cutting out superfluous words or any repetition.

Reports are needed on time and they should be concise, tactful, logical, comprehensive and contain appropriate conclusions and recommendations.

The written word. Many of the comments on report-writing apply to all written communications. When writing is essential the purpose should be clear, the message planned and concise language should be used, but not to a point where courtesy may be abused. A friendly and straightforward approach is ideal. In the case of documents involving legal matters and company records of meetings, ambiguity must be avoided and great care should be taken to include only the agreed or determined points.

Inproving information aspects

To complete the informative approach to communication the back-up services must receive attention, otherwise severe frustration will ruin the work already undertaken. The topics discussed form critical communication links, but often they are neglected through lack of vision and ignorance of their true function.

Records. The purpose of records is to provide efficient information retrieval from all points in the organisation at minimum cost. To achieve this aim the main features to be considered are easy and rapid access, compact storage, safety and simplicity, an economic retrieval procedure, flexibility to allow for expansion and contraction, and the most suitable equipment for the situation. Some of these features were discussed in Chapter 4 under the heading of information retrieval.

Filing, magnetic taping and microfilming are now briefly mentioned as most information is stored under one of these three headings. Because of its high cost the recording of every piece of information should be justified and, once filed, it should be easily and quickly identifiable otherwise it is virtually useless. Thus classification and indexing are key features in the system.

Before investigating any filing system, knowledge should be acquired in the following sectors: filing equipment, methods of filing, classification schemes, indexing and cross-referencing, records retention periods, centralisation and decentralisation of filing, and information retrieval schemes. The high cost of storage and, in some cases, the desperate lack of storage space have encouraged suppliers to market more compact and efficient recording equipment so that documents may be safely destroyed after being recorded. Microfilming, microfiche, micro-dot, magnetic tape and video-tape are some of the methods.

Microfilming is worth considering because of its space-saving characteristics. Documents are sorted and then photographed in miniature on a reel of film which is developed and stored for future reference. A special reader quickly locates a frame on the film and displays the enlarged image on a screen. Various installation methods are available which vary in cost and suitability according to the volume of documents and usage. Other advantages are that legal and other important documents may be photographed and stored in a safe place; the film is durable; there is rapid access; transportation costs are reduced; and the film may be built into existing procedures such as sales invoicing with very little difficulty.

Finally, the use of magnetic tape, mainly associated with computer installations, is becoming well known because of its rapid retrieval capability and its versatility for transferring to visual displays and to microfilm. The question of cost again has to be considered as magnetic tape is still expensive, but there are many possibilities for its use in the future.

Reproduction services. Although one of the aims of office management is to keep paperwork to a minimum, the effective operation of procedures and the flow of information to management often depends upon the rapid reproduction of documents and the duplication of large numbers of copies.

The vast range of photocopiers and duplicators on the market serves to indicate the insatiable demand for these machines in offices. Growth continues as clerical activities increase to provide a better service to management, customers and various Government departments. The machines are justified mainly on the grounds of savings in time and money compared with, say, retyping a letter or typing many copies of a document. Also, many machines are versatile, they help to ensure the smooth flow of work and they are generally cheaper to run if used economically, compared with using the services of an outside printing concern.

Determining suitable equipment means analysing work flow and procedures to see where and how many copies of documents are required. An allowance must be made for managers who will take advantage of asking for more information when they know it is more easily available. Briefly, the market is divided into duplicating and photocopying machines, both of which were discussed in Chapter 4, under the heading of copying information.

Inevitably the question of whether to centralise reproduction services will be raised in a firm. There are advantages and disadvantages, and often a combination of centralising some services, such as duplicating long runs, and decentralising others, to allow for making a few copies on cheap machines distributed at various points in the organisation, is a satisfactory answer. Each case should be investigated and decided on its own merits.

Centralised services certainly offer advantages, such as increased supervision, specialisation, minimum capital outlay, maximum machine utilisation and skilled operators. There are other factors to remember, however, such as staff time spent in co-ordination between the departments and the central point, delay and lack of continuity.

Addressing machines should also be mentioned here as they provide a useful service if a limited amount of standard information is repeatedly required, such as names and addresses for envelopes or sales invoices. The main types of machine are classified according to the master used: embossed metal plates, silk screen or stencil frames and hectographic carbon paper. They are used extensively for such purposes as printing standard information on dividend warrants, payroll slips and envelopes, production control documents, credit control papers and advertising literature.

The typing pool. Typewriters are used extensively in offices to produce memoranda, reports, letters and legal documents on the grounds that appearance and output are greatly improved. The process is costly considering the employment of typists, managerial time in dictating either to the shorthand typist or to a dictating machine, capital outlay for machines and all the fringe expenses such as paper, maintenance of equipment and space.

Many surveys have indicated under-utilisation of typists and equipment and there is often a good case for centralising typing. The advantages usually claimed for this are: better supervision, even work distribution, better use of specialist typists, improved training schemes, improved service to managers, better working conditions and increased machine utilisation. There are difficulties that tend to override the advantages, however, such as the loss of personal contact with executives, who rely on their secretaries for many other duties. Loss of interest is also likely, delays may occur, the risk of documents going astray is increased and typists may feel their status is lowered.

The justification for typing is often queried and it is true that handwriting is becoming more acceptable. Unfortunately some handwriting is deplorable and the risk of misinterpretation is probably high. There are signs that more people are learning to type, but the problem of providing sufficient typewriters if everyone could type would mean that this would not really help. No doubt rapidly advancing technologies will eventually provide an answer, perhaps in the form of more sophisticated closed-circuit television communication systems.

Dictating machines. The efficient use of dictating machines saves considerable secretarial time. The enormous demand for these machines in recent years has resulted in considerable design improvements. The most popular types employ the magnetic recording principle and they are much cheaper now.

The machines may be used for many purposes, such as dictating all forms of correspondence and recording meetings, interviews and group discussions. Many machines are portable and so recordings may be made in a car or anywhere when travelling around. The main features to remember are weight, ease of operating, quality and length of recording, means of marking points, as well as cost and maintenance charges.

A little practice with recording will soon indicate faults in speech or technique. A simple procedure to assist the typist is to prepare the framework of the message before commencing, give all instructions at the beginning of each message, develop a technique for thinking in terms of sentences and paragraphs so that the work flows easily, speak slowly and clearly, remember to mention all punctuation, indicate any corrections as soon as possible after a mistake is located and mention them on the marking sheet or on a separate instruction sheet.

Centralisation should be mentioned here as there is ample equipment available for this purpose, which is naturally economic in the medium-sized and large concern. Usually the system is worked in conjunction with a typing pool.

General office services. Important information points under the general office services heading are mail handling, reception, the telephone switchboard and the messenger service. The degree to which mailing staff are relied on is often overlooked. Although much of the work is monotonous, it forms a critical link in the communication chain. The use of modern machines and equipment, procedure design and possible centralisation are features to consider, likely conclusions depending mainly upon the volume of work and the handling points.

The reception of visitors and customers often moulds their

impressions of the concern. These impressions may make a considerable difference to the company and every attempt should be made to employ the right type of individual for this job. The reception area should be pleasing and comfortable; magazines should be available and perhaps the company's products could be on view. People should be received courteously and the receptionist must be efficient in dealing with the individual's requirements. She must also be able to deal with awkward people who will not take no for an answer, persistent sales representatives, and occasionally those who are downright rude and antagonistic. She has to be firm, fair and friendly.

Very similar characteristics are required in the switchboard operator, another company ambassador who is often the first contact that an individual makes with the firm. A first-class switchboard service saves staff a considerable amount of time, but a poor one causes much frustration. There is no doubt that operating a switchboard is a tiresome job. The right type of board is essential, taking into account the amount of traffic involved, and the operator needs a flair for this work.

Finally, the messenger service has to be considered as another vital link in the communication chain. If individuals are employed solely to deliver and collect all the messages they must be efficient. Leaving messages at the wrong destination points and mislaying them can cause major problems. This soul-destroying job is often undertaken by the young or the elderly, who may suffer from inexperience or senility respectively. Transmission devices, such as pneumatic tubes and paper conveyor systems, offer an alternative.

The psychological approach

The three approaches already considered—the mechanics, personal contact and informative methods—rely heavily upon improving each individual's capability in communicating and in improving personal contact and information flow. They assume that the degree of receptiveness and response will be more favourable if personal performance and stronger information flow are improved. There is still no guarantee, unfortunately, that these concepts will be of benefit, although it would be difficult to argue that they have no effect. The reluctance to give such a guarantee is based upon the realisation that, unless certain psychological efforts are made, the effect of other approaches is minimised through adverse receptive conditions. The most important of these, previously mentioned in the introduction, are concentrating on personal development, active participation, maximising each employee's contribution and making full use of everyone's intelligence and experience.

Research in this field shows that poor communication indicates symptoms of organisation faults, poor line managers, inappropriate personnel policy and an inadequate managerial philosophy. Thus the foundation of the psychological approach consists of a basic knowledge of human beings and their reactions in different situations.

The main point to note is that if an individual is suspicious of another person's intentions through, say, the display of little sincerity, the outcome is that he dislikes him and has no trust in him. In these circumstances it is unlikely that the individual will be favourably receptive to what the other person says; furthermore, he will tend to distort any messages passed.

Another important point is that people are constantly sizing-up each other: listening to what is said, noting their actions, taking heed of information on the grapevine and continually changing their opinions. Any information that is not available automatically creates gaps in the overall perception of each individual. When these occur the mind's chief function is to fill the gaps, often with material which is not necessarily accurate but which fits conveniently into the pattern.

The psychological approach to counteract these tendencies is fairly obvious, but rather difficult to achieve in practice because it tends to move against not only the traditional pattern of management but also the considerable intrigue and conflict that some people say are essential in a dynamic business.

Firstly, to reduce dislike and suspicion, managers must be sincere and genuinely believe in people and their capabilities. Secondly, to create the right image managers have to be likeable and they must adopt the right approach, manners and disposition that go with a favourable sizing-up process. They should also display confidence and avoid unnecessary emphasis on their superiority or higher status. Thirdly, the gaps in information should be minimised, thus avoiding any misconceptions.

In general this approach concentrates on the following features which are of paramount importance: the psychological use of line managers; careful analysis of job requirements so as to encourage personal development; a realistic personnel policy that provides ample opportunity for staff to continue with their education and training; complete openness in negotiations between staff and management; active participation by staff in all matters affecting them; and development of a climate where friendliness, fair-dealing, alignment of interests and complete trust are paramount.

7   Personnel aspects

The personnel function

Part of the skill of establishing suitable conditions to activate the plan—as outlined in Chapter 1—is to staff the organisation properly. Appropriate staffing involves a number of techniques which are discussed throughout this chapter and these, in view of their importance, have created a new function in many concerns, the personnel function.

The personnel function in recent years has continued to grow in strength and often not only includes the selection and placement of staff but also attempts to improve relationships between management and employees by promoting the general well-being of the employee. The office manager may, however, find himself in a situation where no personnel manager is employed in the firm, especially in the small company. At the other extreme he may find in the larger concern a very powerful personnel function, some of whose activities may puzzle him a little, especially if the firm has a paternal background. For example, if Personnel (as the department is often known) evaluate the jobs regularly and decide to upgrade one, in effect giving an increase in pay to the person in the job whose performance happens to be very low, the logic seems to be at fault. Personnel will argue, however, that the job is being upgraded, not the person. Theoretically sound, perhaps, but disastrous in practice in its effect on other members of staff.

This and many other instances involve the office manager, who should possess a reasonable working knowledge of personnel techniques so that he may converse intelligently with personnel staff.

In the absence of a personnel department the office manager will, of course, be directly involved and may have to practise many of the techniques himself.

The main aspects of the personnel function are:

1 Personnel policy
2 Job specification and evaluation
3 Job grading
4 Salaries, merit rating and financial incentives
5 Staff associations
6 Suggestion schemes
7 Welfare and safety
8 Recruitment and interviewing
9 Induction and training
10 Staff appraisal and records
11 Promotions and transfers
12 Termination interviews

To summarise the above aspects, the personnel function is involved with assessing all the jobs, locating suitable staff, providing them with sufficient information, developing them, and arranging a safe and attractive working environment. Each aspect is now considered.

Personnel policy

The adoption of a personnel policy is within the province of senior management, who must agree with it and be prepared to operate within its boundaries. There is a fundamental need for the policy to be in writing and any divergence should be the subject of a recognised procedure which all concerned can use. Unless all managers are prepared to abide by the policy, it becomes a farce and an object of ridicule.

The main features of a sound personnel policy are:

(*a*) Fair and just treatment of all staff.

(*b*) A realistic salary structure and compensation for high performance.

(*c*) Genuine scientific selection of staff.

(*d*) Ample opportunity for staff to continue with their education and training.

(*e*) A reasonable working environment consistent with good health and safety requirements.

(*f*) The provision of modern welfare and social activities.

(*g*) Sympathetic help in times of domestic and other difficulties.

(*h*) The encouragement of a friendly atmosphere.

The job requirements

Before advertising and interviewing prospective staff, the requirements of the job must be accurately known, together with other details such as salary, working conditions and the qualifications required. The approach—considering the above requirements—should be coupled with any readjustment programmes, mentioned in Chapter 2 in the section on organisation, which may involve the restructuring of jobs as opportunities occur.

Four phases cover all contingencies:

1 Activity analysis
2 Job specification
3 Job analysis
4 Job evaluation

1 Activity analysis

This technique was explained in Chapter 2 and Fig. 12 on page 55 shows a typical example. As a reminder, all the activities in a section or department are listed, together with the time spent on each by members of staff; series and parallel working should be borne in mind in view of the importance of job enrichment; and in the event of a transfer or termination there may be an opportunity to restructure. This phase naturally must be successfully resolved before passing to the job specification phase.

2 *Job specification*

Writing a job specification or job description means noting what *should* be done, not necessarily what *is* being done. Asking the member of staff who is doing the job about it is not sufficient. It is essential to study the job role in the procedure and to ask others who are associated with it. The purpose is to study and describe the job, not the person who is undertaking it.

The main features of a clerical job are:

(*a*) Job title and department.
(*b*) Responsible to . . .
(*c*) Responsible for . . . (tasks should be listed).
(*d*) The purpose of each task.
(*e*) The frequency of occurrence for each task.
(*f*) Degree of accuracy required in each task.
(*g*) Any special responsibilities.
(*h*) Working conditions.
(*i*) Degree of supervision.
(*j*) Contacts with other departments or sections.
(*k*) The location of the job in the procedure.
(*l*) Summary of the job.

The job specification may be expanded or contracted to suit the requirements by introducing additional features such as responsibility for cash, maximum complexity in the job and any critical aspects of decisions taken, or removing features such as special responsibilities. A typical job description layout is given in Fig. 17.

3 *Job analysis*

This phase decides the qualities required from the individual

Job specification   Ref. no..............

Job title _____   Date_____

Department _____   Signature_____

Section _____

Responsible to _____

Main duties
(1)
(2)
(3)
(4)
(5)
(6)
(7)
(8)
(9)
(10)
Special responsibilities
(1)
(2)
(3)
(4)

Skill requirements:

Mental requirements:

Physical requirements:

Working conditions:

Fig. 17   Simplified job specification layout

to perform the job satisfactorily. Each task must be examined
to establish a number of factors such as:

(*a*) Degree of skill required.
(*b*) Any manual dexterity required, including operating
machines.
(*c*) Capacity for taking an appropriate degree of responsibility.
(*d*) Accuracy in figures, copying and so on.
(*e*) Degree of concentration and manual effort.
(*f*) Ability to work in conditions surrounding the job.
(*g*) An appropriate educational standard.
(*h*) Any particular experience required.
(*i*) Special requirements such as trustworthiness if there is
cash handling and a pleasing personality if customer
contact is part of the job.
(*j*) Capacity for working without supervision.

4 Job evaluation
The final phase determines the value of the job relative to
other jobs. Many members of staff instinctively know this and
they are often right, thus care is needed in evaluating to avoid
general dissatisfaction.

The four main ways of evaluating jobs are:

(*a*) *Points rating.* Each factor within a job is rated by
appropriating a certain number of points—within a
range of, say, o to 10 points—through subjective assessment based upon a close inspection of each factor and
its degree of weighting. All the allocated points are
casted and compared with a salary/points table to locate
the appropriate salary. An example is shown in Fig. 18.
(*b*) *Factor comparison.* This variation of points rating uses
only five factors in the job: mental level, degree of skill,
physical requirements, responsibility and working conditions. The subjective aspect is that key jobs have to be

	Maximum points	Award
Job evaluation Ref. no...............		
Job title _____ Date _____		
Department _____ Signature _____		
Section _____		
Skill	10	
Experience	10	
Special aptitude	10	
Responsibility	25	
Mathematical accuracy	10	
Grammatical accuracy	10	
Educational standard	10	
Mental effort	15	
Manual effort	5	
Trustworthiness – information	5	
Trustworthiness – cash	10	
Trustworthiness – customer relations	10	
Working conditions	20	
Supervision exercised	35	
Checking work	15	
	200	

Fig. 18   Simplified job evaluation form

selected to form standards of salary levels within the range and the salary for each job is divided into the five factors, each one being allocated a proportion of the salary dependent upon its weighting. A greater degree of accuracy is possible by using this technique, which is more complex and more difficult for staff to understand.

(c) *Ranking*. If the job is judged as a whole and compared with other jobs as a whole, this simple device is called ranking. Surprising accuracy is possible when a limited number of jobs is involved, as in the small firm, but in the large concern so many factors are involved that it becomes impossible to achieve any degree of accuracy.

(d) *Classification*. Before the jobs are ranked this scheme determines the grades and salaries within which prepared job specifications are fitted. The jobs are then grouped and ranked accordingly. Personal judgement is again called for, as it is in working out ranking.

As already stressed, the four ways of evaluating jobs each involve a certain amount of personal judgement, although these evaluations or attempts at job grading are often called scientific methods of assessing work content in a job. An example of a job grading scheme offered by the Institute of Administrative Management groups jobs into six grades. Information on typical jobs that fall into these categories is available from the Institute:

Grade A   Simple or closely directed tasks requiring no previous experience to perform them.

      B   Simple tasks requiring only a few weeks' training, closely directed, carried out within a small number of well-defined rules, checked and following a daily routine.

      C   Routine tasks following well-defined rules, requiring a reasonable degree of experience (or

a special aptitude), amounting to a daily routine
and subject to short period control.

D   Tasks requiring considerable experience, some
initiative, predetermined procedure and a
slightly varying daily routine.

E   Tasks requiring a significant amount of discretion and initiative (or a specialised knowledge),
and responsibility for the work undertaken.

F   Tasks demanding an extensive amount of responsibility and judgement or the use of a professional technique, such as legal, accounting or
engineering.

More involved studies of clerical work are examined in
Chapter 10. The methods described, however, greatly assist
the office manager in ensuring that a fairer scheme is offered.
Other advantages are that newly created jobs are more easily
assessed, bargaining for salary is reduced to a minimum, transfers are more easily arranged and budgeting is more scientific.

Financial aspects

The establishment of a salary scale for each grade is the next
problem, along with the question of awarding extra sums for
various levels of performance in the job and any other forms
of bonus in times of prosperity in the company. Furthermore,
there are other financial aspects such as payments for overtime
and any special arrangements for nightwork or weekend work.
This section is limited to considering salaries, merit rating,
overtime and flexible working hours.

Payment for work is a touchy subject and every endeavour
should be made to avoid ambiguity, uncertainty and erratic
decisions affecting this area. Obvious as this may appear, it is
surprising to see even large, well-established concerns still

haggling over overtime rates and the like. A little more thought might indicate to management that the amounts of money involved are relatively small compared with the discontent, disgust and general non-cooperation that results from senseless bargaining and indecision.

Salaries

The salary for each grade is decided upon by senior management, sometimes in conjunction with the staff association. The amount depends upon many internal and external economic factors, such as company policy to pay either above or below the going rate, the demand and supply of various classes of employees, and company prosperity. Much depends upon the locality: in depressed areas salaries are often pitched low, but in thriving areas salary spirals occur as companies vie for a limited number of staff.

Should the office manager be involved in drafting proposals for salary scales, he should bear in mind that salaries must be pitched at a level where prospective staff will be attracted to the concern; above-average staff, although more highly motivated, still expect above-average financial recognition; grades should be sufficiently flexible to allow for adequate increases; and some overlapping should be built in to allow for those who are leaving and others who are awaiting promotion.

Equal pay

The Equal Pay Act of 1970 comes into effect in 1975. This could mean considerable adjustments to salaries—about two-thirds of clerical staff being women—but not necessarily so, because some types of jobs are solely performed by women.

The case for equal pay is debatable, considering that many women use employment as a stop-gap measure; they tend to spend shorter periods with each employer; and they are apparently more prone to absenteeism and sickness. Whether their output is lower is another question, but many offices would be dull places without them. Certainly it would be difficult to argue against the concept of equal pay for equal work, so long as this is the maxim.

Merit rating

Staff are usually placed on a particular step within the salary grade depending upon their expected performance. When they are appraised, say every year, their salaries are adjusted to place them on the appropriate step. An alternative arrangement is to pay an annual increment regardless of performance, but its merits are doubtful.

A typical merit rating scheme is submitted by the Institute of Administrative Management.

Merit grade	Classification
1	beginner
2	qualified
3	experienced
4	superior
5	superlative (ready for promotion)

Overtime

During World War II managers soon discovered that constant overtime did not necessarily increase output. The reasons are that employees tend to adjust their output in relation to the time available (Parkinson's Law); sustained performance over very long periods is mentally and physically distressing; there is more likelihood of errors occurring; and there is a possibility of an increased sickness and absenteeism rate. Whenever possible, constant overtime should be avoided, but sometimes —if there is a staff shortage—there is no choice. Steps should be taken to alleviate the situation quickly by, for example, gearing up training schemes and recruiting staff from further afield if possible.

Spasmodic overtime is not unusual as panics occur at peak

periods. This is not to say that overtime is inevitable; in fact, well-organised departments co-operating closely together can easily dispense with the problem through appropriate transfers of versatile staff to ease excess loads as they occur. All peaks in workload do not appear at the same time: troughs in other areas often coincide and with the goodwill of all concerned the problem can often be solved in this way. The overall aim, of course, should be to remove the peaks.

The main ways of compensating staff for overtime are to offer time off in lieu, to pay a flat rate based on salary or to inflate the rate by, say, time-and-a-half or double time. Some concerns do not pay overtime to staff on grades above an arbitrary level, often on the grounds that there is already adequate remuneratory compensation and increased status, and it is expected of senior staff. This arrangement is dangerous as a situation may arise in which staff in the grade immediately below the fixed level could easily earn more in an overtime situation than, say, the supervisor in the grade above. Such an arrangement is not conducive to fostering good relationships between employees and, of course, it is guaranteed to upset those who are placed at a disadvantage. Closely associated with overtime is the question of timekeeping and flexible working hours.

Flexible working hours

Further to the comments on timekeeping contained in the previous chapter, one way of overcoming transport difficulties and domestic problems is to offer flexible working hours. A standard scheme stipulates core hours from 10.00 a.m. to 4.00 p.m. when everyone should be present; on either side of these times individual arrangements are negotiated, for example 8.00 a.m. to 4.00 p.m. or 9.30 a.m. to 5.30 p.m. Variations on this scheme to suit particular circumstances are also seen operating in some European countries.

The advantages claimed are that timekeeping improves,

overtime is greatly reduced and in some cases a more even flow of work is attained. There are disadvantages, however, but these may be overcome by more careful planning. In the case of some employees arriving early, they will no doubt be working on their own until the supervisor arrives; this situation calls for trust, conscientiousness and the provision of a measurable workload arranged last thing every day. Workload planning may become more involved and schedules will have to be adjusted to suit this arrangement so that a more even distribution of work over the longer day is viable.

Staff seem to like flexible working hours for reasons such as finishing earlier in the day or starting later to suit their social programmes, as well as reconciling the difficulties already mentioned.

Welfare

Another well-established sector of personnel work is the provision of various welfare facilities, such as a dining room, savings schemes, pension and superannuation schemes, loans in certain circumstances, social and sports facilities, legal assistance and medical facilities. Members of staff take many of these facilities for granted because most firms now consider that welfare is important and make reasonable provision. For this reason welfare should not be overstressed at interviews, except to mention, of course, the facilities that are offered. Three important aspects associated with welfare are staff associations, suggestion schemes and safety. The first two are discussed now, but safety, because of its strong association with the office environment, is covered in the next chapter.

Staff associations

There is an increasing trend for staff to either form an association within the concern or join a clerical workers' trade union.

The majority of staff, however, are still not represented formally, and although some managers may claim this is an advantage there are also certain disadvantages for staff.

In many ways it is easier for the office manager to deal with a staff representative, and when the right relationship is established an excellent communication network can operate. This does not mean that normal contact with staff is discontinued or slackened, the arrangement simply amplifies and knits closely together the existing network for both formal and informal negotiations.

The slow growth of associations in offices could be due to greater loyalty towards management compared with manual operatives, or perhaps to dislike for the use of collective force, although in view of the number of female clerical staff the reason might be general disinterest. The office manager should note, however, that office employees rapidly become very interested when they see a group in the factory receiving financial awards that are denied to office staff.

Suggestion schemes
There is no doubt that the maximum contribution from staff will be reduced if they do not feel free to offer their ideas on improvements. Whether the ideas should be financially rewarded or considered as part of the job is debatable and it is often the deciding factor when a suggestion scheme is proposed. One way to upset existing relationships is to offer financial reward for suggestions in the factory but to expect office staff to propose ideas as part of their job.

Personnel often has the task of running a suggestion scheme. If it is badly arranged it becomes an object of ridicule and the whole scheme must therefore be taken seriously by management. The essential requirements are to explain fully the reasons for the scheme and the procedure, provide suitable boxes at various points, supply a standard suggestion form, appoint an assessing committee who must meet regularly as long delays are irritating, establish a generous reward system and advertise the scheme periodically.

The assessments must be scrupulously fair and the decision, with reasons if rejected, should be given to the member of staff as soon as possible. Rewards should be well publicised to stimulate further interest.

Recruitment

The recruitment of staff should not be attempted until all the foregoing aspects have been clarified. Vague statements given to prospective employees are psychologically unsound and guaranteed to create misunderstandings later.

Recruitment consists of gathering all the essential information on the vacancy; deciding on the source of recruitment to use; providing the information to the source or sources; short-listing the replies by matching the details given by the applicants with the job specification; interviewing the applicants; checking and writing for references; confirming the appointment, including all terms and conditions of employment; and writing to the successful and unsuccessful applicants. Two important features, sources of recruitment and interviewing, are now discussed.

Sources of recruitment

The main sources are listed below:

(a) Advertising in national or local newspapers and magazines.
(b) Circulars to surrounding estates.
(c) Consultants who specialise in locating appropriate staff to specific requirements.
(d) Employment agencies.
(e) Employment exchanges.
(f) Educational institutions: universities, colleges and schools.

(*g*) Professional institutes.
(*h*) Recommendations from existing employees.
(*i*) Staff notice boards.
(*j*) Youth employment offices.

Interviewing

The concept of interviewing a number of candidates individually and deciding which one is most suitable for the job involves many disciplines, including psychology, sociology and communication. Within these disciplines there are various techniques which greatly assist the interviewer.

Scientific interviewing is a subject that either 'raises the hackles' of an individual or is praised as a successful technique, depending on whether there has been luck or misfortune at an important point in the person's career. The complexity of interviewing is now examined, firstly by making some general observations, followed by a consideration of the aims of the interview, aids to assessment, advance arrangements, the interview itself and, finally, the employment contract.

Out of a group of interviewees—if an appointment is made—one will be happy and the rest disappointed. Some will probably be embittered if they feel the interviews were not conducted fairly and every opportunity was not given for them to state their case fully.

From the interviewer's viewpoint he will probably never know whether he has made the right choice. On the one hand, if the newcomer makes a success of his job, this is no indication that another applicant would not have performed the job even better, although at least the choice was successful. On the other hand, if the newcomer is a failure, who can say whether he would be successful in a different situation or whether he may have suffered a domestic or mental problem since his appointment? There are so many possibilities and imponderables that accurate assessments on the appointment are exceptionally difficult.

There are two main approaches associated with interviewing. Firstly, a person's character and likely performance may be more accurately judged by the interviewer on a purely personal basis. Secondly, scientific selection through the use of a methodical approach and objective testing is a superior way of assessing the applicant.

Evidence against the first approach is based upon psychological factors that indicate a personal bias towards individuals through many disturbing events in childhood years, such as being attacked by a ginger-haired boy which results in a revulsion for ginger-haired people later in life. There is also evidence, however, that shows how remarkably accurate personal assessments can be, even after only a few minutes' contact—especially if the assessor has direct experience of the work involved and has a shrewd idea of the type of person who will be able to cope with the job.

Evidence against the second approach rests on the artificial interview situation: the interviewee is obviously going to be on his best behaviour consistent with what he thinks are the job requirements; he will be under severe stress, which may work for or against him through the way he reacts, which is not necessarily consistent with his normal behaviour; he may not perform well in the tests for many obscure reasons; and he may be less articulate in false conditions which might incorrectly indicate his capabilities.

Evidence in support of scientific selection techniques is that a systematic approach should cut down the risk of errors and that in a well-conducted interview the dangers mentioned above are greatly reduced. Unfortunately the scientific method demands very capable interviewers and if they are not available the method will surely be prone to errors.

Before studying the interview itself the associated features are considered: these are the aims, aids and advance arrangements.

Aims of the interview. The main aims are:

(*a*) To find the right applicant who will fulfil the role most adequately.
(*b*) To assess each candidate so that an accurate picture is built up of his character and capabilities.
(*c*) To complete any missing information on the application form.
(*d*) To reassess any doubtful information on the form.
(*e*) To provide a full description of the vacancy and to answer any relevant queries.
(*f*) To reach complete agreement with the successful applicant and to draw up an acceptable contract of employment, which should be signed by him and the interviewer.

Aids to assessment. Research into ways of measuring individual variation—often termed differential psychology—has produced a number of tests which are split into three groups: questionnaires, achievement tests and projective tests. Some of these tests are complicated and further reading in depth is necessary before embarking on a programme to include them in assessment methods.

Briefly, questionnaires are used to reveal the individuals' likes, dislikes, feelings, hobbies, worries and fears, and by so doing also to assess his truthfulness. Achievement tests are designed to indicate the maximum achievement level in intelligence. A wide variety of tests is available to demonstrate a whole range of individual abilities. Projective tests are designed to see how a person reacts to ambiguous text material so that his perception and expressions of what he sees indicates his whole personality to a psychologist. The ink-blot test is well known and irregular shapes are also used to demonstrate the technique. More mundane aids are the completion of an application form, an interviewing sheet which contains some questions and spaces for further information as the interview progresses, the taking-up of references and a medical examination.

Advance arrangements. The interviewing room should be furnished to provide an informal, friendly atmosphere so that the applicant is encouraged to feel at ease. A timetable should be arranged and adhered to so that long delays are avoided. The waiting room should also provide comfortable chairs with a range of magazines available to help relieve the tension.

The interview. Before calling in the applicant the interviewer should have prepared a plan which includes the information required, the range of topics to be covered and some flexibility to cater for modifications during the interview.

A common mistake is to spend too much time talking rather than listening to the interviewee. When the interviewer is speaking very little is being learned about the interviewee. With this fact in mind, the interviewer should refrain from becoming involved in arguments, giving advice, general conversation or moralising. He should, however, relieve the tension whenever possible or move on to other topics by conversing at appropriate points in the interview. The tactical times to talk are when it is obvious that the applicant is still nervous, when he is stuck and does not know what to say, when a little praise is needed for displaying frankness and when it is time to switch the conversation to new areas. The interviewer should use discretion and tact when he is making notes so that he does not disconcert the interviewee. A casual approach is ideal and it is safer not to interrupt if a point is missed but to wait until a suitable pause and then check.

From the above observations it should be clear that interviewing is an art that demands considerable knowledge and experience. Successful application, however, is a great asset to any manager.

The employment contract. A standard contract is usually adopted for clerical staff which may differ from the one for managers. In the UK the contract must conform to the Contracts of Employment Act 1963, copies of which are available from the Department of Employment. The Act includes rights to minimum periods of notice to terminate employment and main terms of employment which must be in writing.

Induction

The next step after engagement is the introduction of the newcomer into the completely new surroundings he faces when he commences with the company. Most people can recall the experience of starting a new job: nervousness, general apprehension, feelings of strangeness, uncertainty about the work and the firm are just a few of the stresses suffered at such times. Every attempt to alleviate these feelings is fundamental, but some concerns still have not got around to dealing with induction in a comprehensive manner.

The main areas that cause embarrassment to the newcomer are:

1 Lack of knowledge concerning the department and the people he will be contacting.
2 Strange surroundings generally.
3 Uncertainty as to what is expected of him.
4 Poor information on the company and its personnel policy.

The department
The department head should introduce himself and all other members of staff associated with the new employee. Any special departmental arrangements should be discussed along with its work, aims and plans for the future.

The environment

All the facilities should be shown to the newcomer without
waiting for him to ask. He should be made to feel at home,
treated in a friendly manner and immediately accepted into the
department.

The job

To be sure that no misunderstandings have occurred his job
should be outlined again, and every opportunity should be
given for him to query any points. The part the job plays in
the procedure and its effect on his personal contacts should be
made clear. The likely queries that will arise should also be
discussed.

The company

As much general information on the company as possible should
be given to the newcomer. This includes its background,
products, organisation, personnel policy, reputation, terms and
conditions of employment, safety regulations, and social and
welfare activities. Ideally, booklets should be available so that
he may read about the company at his leisure rather than trying
to assimilate masses of detail outlined verbally.

Training

From the narrow viewpoint a company trains staff to achieve
higher performance in the job, which, of course, is very
important. From a broader viewpoint, training is undertaken
to raise the level of development of employees regardless of
whether they stay with the firm or leave and seek employment
elsewhere. Considering that some advantage is taken of
another company's training whenever an employee is engaged
(except in the case of school-leavers) the broad view is both
feasible and morally sound.

Within the concern a certain amount of training is inevitable
to fit a newcomer for a job regardless of his experience. If a

motivation programme is practised there should be facilities for further education and training to develop staff for higher posts. Not every company shares the broad view; in fact, many concerns tend to ignore certain training responsibilities and take advantage of other concerns' schemes by engaging trained staff, but they do not promote further training themselves. It was in an attempt to overcome this poor attitude that the Industrial Training Act 1964 was introduced in the UK.

In addition to social or national responsibilities, there are many advantages attached to a sound training programme:

(a) Morale is raised as employees see a demonstrated interest in their well-being and development.

(b) Motivation should improve as personal development is encouraged.

(c) Staff should become more proficient in a shorter time.

(d) The latest developments in technologies will be known and practised by staff if they are given the opportunity.

(e) Staff may become more versatile and so assist in over-coming the peak-loads that occur in certain sections.

(f) Staff flexibility should improve, which helps consider-ably with staff turnover problems and during staff shortage periods.

Three important areas of training, namely training methods, the learning process and retraining, are now discussed.

Training methods
The need for training has just been explained. How to train employees involves initially the question of interpreting the terms 'education' and 'training'. The difference—if any—between the two is often hotly argued. The usual statements are that education is a revelation whereas training involves repetition. Also, training is regarded as indicating and teaching skills, and thus the educational aspect associated with the skill could be assumed to be part of the training programme.

If training is used as an overall term, the following main methods apply:

On-the-job training. This well-known and well-worn method generally means sitting by the side of the employee doing the work and hoping that he will find sufficient spare time to teach the job. The method is slow, frustrating, bad-habit forming, often incomplete and generally unsatisfactory. This simple method is often called 'sitting by Nellie'; more advanced on-the-job methods include the supervisor undertaking to train the newcomer, who watches the activities, attempts to copy, is corrected as necessary by the supervisor and gradually takes over the work as his performance improves.

More sophisticated methods under this heading include breaking the job down into its component parts and explaining and teaching them individually before bringing them together to form the complete job.

Off-the-job training. This method involves a planned programme of training consisting of assessing the newcomer, deciding on the education and training required, arranging for him to join suitable courses and nursing him through the development stages while he is training. Fostering should be done by the supervisor, who should report regularly on progress. A training centre may be located on site in the large firm.

The learning process

Teaching is another technique that most people instinctively feel they possess the inborn expertise to perform. In fact, good teachers are rare within this realm of flair and natural teaching art, but many people in industry have to undertake teaching and, provided that they possess some knowledge of the learning process, there is considerable benefit. So long as there is the basic mental capability it is probably true to say that people never stop learning: they are continually influenced by their surroundings in all situations, thus adding to their knowledge but not necessarily improving their performance at work.

If an assessment of performance is the gauge, this must be related to the attempt to teach the individual how to be more successful in his job. Measurement alone is not always an accurate indication in the short term as there are often setbacks during the processes which are generally called learning plateaus. These occur when stages are reached where consolidation is needed before proceeding further and they are particularly noticeable in skill development. The causes of plateaus, in addition to consolidation, are setbacks through the adoption of poor methods that must be corrected first; sudden lack of interest partly through poor teaching and partly through becoming discouraged; and changes in procedure that upset the original planned programme.

Claims are often made that the *analytical* method of teaching a job dispenses with the learning plateau. This may be true with some jobs but not with all, as may be judged by briefly examining the technique. The other technique is known as the *traditional* method. In short, the traditional method involves the treatment of the job as a complete unit: the whole job is explained, demonstrated and practised by the trainee until the plateau is reached, progress is consolidated, then he breaks through and increases performance, and so on until proficiency is reached.

The analytical method means dividing the job into suitable component parts, conducting basic exercises, demonstrating each part, practising, gradually combining the parts at appropriate stages, but maintaining the desired speed until the whole job is operating. Where a job can be broken down in this fashion the method is suitable, but some jobs do not lend themselves to this treatment: examples outside the office field are piloting an aircraft and even riding a bicycle.

Needless to say, the description of the learning process can be endlessly elaborated upon. Nevertheless these basic rules may be helpful to any person who finds himself in the unenviable position of having to teach a newcomer a job:

(a) Always encourage and avoid being critical.
(b) Use errors to give further advice, not to reprimand.
(c) Relate performance levels to eventual expected performance as a means of self-evaluation, rather than as a gauge of learning speed.
(d) Avoid learning by rote and aim for a thorough practical understanding of the subject.
(e) Avoid excessive delays between the practice period and notifying the learner of the results achieved.
(f) Remember to summarise the previous session of training, present the material, revise as required and recapitulate at the end. Repetition never does any harm and certainly helps the trainee to retain the knowledge.
(g) Arouse a desire to learn by establishing a good rapport with the trainee and appeal to his own interests, which should coincide if selection has been sound.
(h) Do not avoid praising when it is due.
(i) People learn at different rates, so do not expect identical results from each trainee.
(j) Always simplify and avoid making the work appear to be more complex than it really is.

Retraining
The unfortunate employee who suddenly finds that he is unable to carry out his duties reasonably well needs sympathetic treatment and retraining for a more suitable job. This problem may happen to anyone at any time, and the human approach is to help rather than to ridicule.

The causes of incapability suddenly occurring are a mental difficulty, a physical disability brought on through, say, an illness and technological changes in the job itself. A similar problem occurs when, for example, new office machines are introduced and procedures are changed. Also, the idea of developing a more versatile group of staff involves job rotation and retraining programmes.

Understandably there may be some reluctance on the part of staff to retrain and every form of encouragement must be tried to overcome resistance to change. Most employees tend to form habits in jobs, and these habits are often the real barriers that have to be removed before versatility is possible. In the older employee these habits are particularly strong if he has been with the company for many years in one job, hence the saying 'You can't teach an old dog new tricks'. With correct treatment, however, these habits can be broken successfully, hence the saying 'You're never too old to learn'.

Performance appraisal

As the newcomer progresses in his job and he receives additional training, appraisal should follow in sequence. This will provide information that can be used to indicate to the employee his development rate, to assess the results of training, to provide a gauge of progress for judging merit associated with such factors as salary, promotion and transfers, and to assist in staff planning.

A comprehensive performance appraisal should include an interview by a trained assessor, the opinions of the supervisor and the manager, and feedback from other sections or departments associated with the individual's work. The assessment should take into account the factors outlined in the job specification as well as personal attributes. Some aspects associated with appraisal are now considered.

Promotion

The initial question that arises with any vacancy above the lowest level job is whether to appoint someone from outside or to promote an employee. Each case has its good and bad points and involves personnel policy. The main factors that should be considered are ability, capability, qualifications, age, development record and personality.

Promotion is often seen to be based on considerations such as nepotism, seniority, qualifications, experience, performance in the present job, ability and personality. Various combinations of these aspects are also seen. The constant necessity of ensuring that fairness and justice are amply demonstrated to employees applies again, very forcibly in this instance. Other staff have to associate with the ones who are promoted and with those who are neglected or who feel they have been overlooked. The encouragement and fostering of teamwork and group activity depends largely upon minimising ill-feeling.

Transfers

Inevitably there will be failures in the selection procedure, employees will change and become unsettled in a job, and there will be personality clashes within an office. Many problems of this nature may be solved by transferring people from one job to another as opportunities occur. The practice soon becomes established as staff recognise the pattern. They will take advantage of it by requesting a transfer and the office manager may also suggest it to those who do not apply.

Enforced transfers are not really recommended, although sometimes they are the only way, short of terminating employment. Within the scope of transfers is the pursuance of the aim to establish more versatile groups of staff. Their co-operation cannot necessarily be bought; it is far better to indicate the advantages of personal development through job variety and the invaluable experience gained by spending a period of time in various departments.

Personnel counselling

Within the area of performance appraisal and general well-being of staff, the use of regular personal interviews by trained counsellors is often undertaken in large concerns. The two main approaches are to listen and give direct advice and assistance, or to listen and guide or encourage the interviewee to consider how the problem may be solved. In the absence of an established programme the office manager might consider the use of this effective means of maintaining and improving harmony among staff.

Termination interviews

Finally, the chain of events outlined in this chapter ends at the termination interview or retirement. Terminations occur through the desire of the employee to leave, a hint from management, redundancy or instant dismissal. Before instantly dismissing an employee particular care is needed to be sure that the misconduct justifies dismissal and that company procedure is followed.

In the UK it is advisable to consult the Contracts of Employment Act 1963, the Redundancy Payments Act 1965 and the Industrial Relations Act 1971. Generally dismissal is justified if an employee has stolen company property, or because of immorality, habitual drunkenness or drug-taking which results in an incapability to perform the job properly, or as a result of disclosure of business secrets. Other reasons, such as disobedience, gross negligence and wilful misconduct, are not very easy to prove if the case reaches court. Usually a set company procedure is laid down that conforms to any Acts in force. The office manager must familiarise himself with the details as soon as possible after taking up an appointment.

When the employee leaves at his own request it is customary in some firms to conduct a termination interview in an attempt to find out the true reason for leaving. Unfortunately not many people are prepared to divulge this information and instead give a reasoned answer that they feel will be acceptable. This cover-up is quite natural as no one is going to deliberately disclose information that may be used against him if references are requested later. At the interview, however, an experienced interviewer may be able to judge the real reason through consideration of reports from management, the tone of discussion and other indications that may emerge without necessarily amounting to a direct admission from the individual.

If the office manager should be involved it is worth mentioning that every endeavour should be made to end the relationship in a friendly and genuine manner. Wishing the individual good luck and success in his new job is courteous, costs nothing and shows some feeling for him.

Staff turnover

The assessment of turnover for control purposes is usually calculated for each month or year by adopting the following formula:

$$\frac{\text{No. of staff leaving} \times 100}{\text{average no. of staff on payroll}} = \% \text{ staff turnover}$$

Trends may be plotted annually and an attempt should be made to explain the variations.

8 The office environment

So far the composite skill of establishing suitable conditions in the office has been examined in two sectors: creating the right type of organisation structure (Chapter 2) and selecting suitable staff to man the organisation (Chapter 7). The third and final sector involves the creation of a suitable office environment within which staff can operate effectively. This skill is directly associated with the dynamic aspect of the environment: the atmosphere established through the interpretation of company policies; the style of supervision; the philosophy of management; encouragement of suitable relationships conducive to high morale; and many personnel aspects already discussed in the previous chapter, especially salaries, job security and welfare facilities.

The knowledge required to create a suitable office environment covers the static aspect which is not directly associated with staff. Locating a suitable office site, selecting suitable accommodation and the provision of appropriate and safe physical working conditions are the main areas. Skill development in the office environment sector is governed by experience and the use of techniques and knowledge acquired in the psychological and sociological aspects outlined in Chapter 3.

The main physical aspects of office environment are now considered, but it should constantly be borne in mind that the way staff are treated as regards attention to the office environment generally is still a motivating factor, though less effective (it is often claimed) than job enrichment programmes. Although the neglect of the office environment may be compensated by considerable attention to factors affecting the job itself and successful motivation achieved, it is probably a safer policy to balance both approaches because invariably the situation will change. When this happens good employees may be lost if they see that another concern offers both and, in addition, they can think of no good reason why the environment sector should be ignored in their present company. In the UK particular attention is drawn to the Offices, Shops and Railway Premises Act 1963, which makes provision for the safety, health and welfare of people employed in these premises.

As the standard of living increases, so the physical office environment must improve if a concern is to achieve or maintain a good name. The two features are inseparable, although many managers do not see this point, to the eventual cost of the companies for whom they work.

Any policy that does not seem logical to employees is designed for eventual disaster. The extremes between the senior executives' elaborate suites extending to ornate corridors and palatial reception areas and the dirty, cramped accommodation of the clerk are often still vast. All the arguments for this arrangement are fallacious considering the importance and high cost of staff today. There is little doubt that if people are treated like cattle they will tend to act like cattle. Due attention to all the aspects shown in Fig. 19 is essential.

Location of office site

Although it is unlikely that the office manager will become directly involved in locating a suitable office site, it is useful to be able to answer questions from staff on the factors involved and to contribute to the task if the opportunity does occur.

The main considerations are:

1   Local costs: including purchase price or rental, rates and other local expenses.

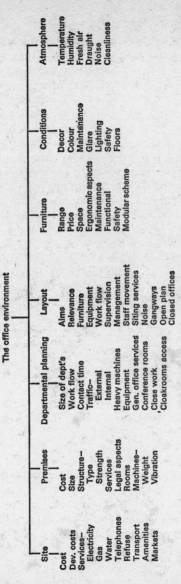

Fig. 19 The main aspects of office environment

The office environment

Site
Cost
Dev. costs
Services—
Electricity
Gas
Water
Telephones
Refuse
Transport
Amenities
Markets

Premises
Cost
Size
Structure—
Type
Strength
Services
Legal aspects
Rooms
Machines—
Weight
Vibration

Departmental planning
Size of dept's
Work flow
Contact time
Traffic—
External
Internal
Heavy machines
Equipment
Gen. office services
Conference rooms
Close work
Cloakrooms access

Layout
Aims
Relevance
Furniture
Equipment
Work flow
Supervision
Management
Staff movement
Siting services
Noise
Gangways
Open plan
Closed offices

Furniture
Range
Price
Space
Ergonomic aspects
Maintenance
Functional
Safety
Modular scheme

Conditions
Decor
Colour
Maintenance
Glare
Lighting
Safety
Floors

Atmosphere
Temperature
Humidity
Fresh air
Draught
Noise
Cleanliness

2 Local development costs: electricity, gas and water charges.
3 Proximity of services: electricity, gas, water, telephone cables and refuse disposal.
4 Transport facilities: parking, roads, trains and buses.
5 Local amenities: banks, shops, post office and restaurants.
6 Proximity of markets: customer convenience.

Generally the choice depends upon the advantages associated with siting the office in, or on the outskirts of, a large town, a small country town or an isolated location. In addition to the points already mentioned, there is the question of clean air, health of employees, houses for staff, space for expansion, the importance of nearness to market, company prestige and availability of suitable staff in the area.

The office premises

When a suitable general site is located the next step is either to find existing premises or to build a new office block.
The main features to be considered are:

1 Size, depending on present staffing and envisaged expansion.
2 Type of building, depending on the capital available or the amount of rent that can be afforded, and prestige.
3 Facilities required: electricity, water, etc.
4 Legal aspects: true ownership, rates, fire risk, lease and other charges.
5 Rooms: based upon the type of layout envisaged.
6 Furniture and equipment: the building design must be able to cope with the size and weight of these items.
7 Physical facilities: cloakrooms, lifts, window area and emergency staircases.

Departmental planning

Some of the above features are governed by departmental planning, which can contribute greatly to office efficiency if given sufficient time and care.

The main features to bear in mind are:

(*a*) Size of each department, also taking into consideration the number of sections and the work flow within them.

(*b*) Work flow and contact time between departments.

(*c*) External traffic to departments.

(*d*) Siting of heavy machines and equipment.

(*e*) Siting of general office services such as mailing, filing and the typing pool.

(*f*) Location of conference rooms and private offices in quieter surroundings.

(*g*) Need for natural light for close work.

(*h*) Ease of access to toilets, cloakrooms and dining room.

Generally it is impracticable to satisfy all these requirements and a compromise is inevitable.

Office layout

When office layout is considered the office manager is often directly involved, not only in designing or redesigning the layout but also in attempting to resolve the differences between individuals over their location in the office. Staff positioning is a delicate operation: there are often favourite spots, draughty areas, noisy parts and detestable situations, coupled with the problem of clashing personalities. Sometimes a strong personality will attempt to dominate the arrangement and after the office has been designed around him he will probably promptly leave.

Although individuals have to be considered, there are many other important factors that will strongly influence the layout.

Firstly, the main aims of layout should be stated and, secondly, all the relevant factors listed in order of priority before proceeding further.

In addition to the various forms of charting work flow and procedures mentioned in Chapter 10, a practical method of designing the layout when the plan is completed is, firstly, to draw a scale outline of the office on graph paper; secondly, to cut out from cardboard the scaled-down sizes of each item of office furniture and equipment; thirdly, to try the templates in various positions on the graph paper to arrive at the best layout in view of the plan; and, fourthly, to discuss the layout with supervisors and staff to get their opinions and ideas before finally deciding.

Particular attention should be paid to any legal requirements. The aims should be to provide the most suitable layout consistent with economy, good working conditions, efficient operation of the procedures, and overall effectiveness of supervision and management.

To achieve these aims the office manager should bear in mind such aspects as any possible resistance to change by staff; work flow, including staff movement during routine operations and queries with other people; overhead expenses such as use of telephones, heating, lighting, etc.; achieving co-ordination through supervision; health of staff; degree of flexibility envisaged through possible expansion programmes; location of machines, equipment and furniture; possible distraction through noise; outlook from windows and staff movement; and the general atmosphere that will be created by the design. Other features to be borne in mind are the location of doors, windows, safes, gangways and existing services, such as pipes and lights, that are fixed and probably costly to resite if they happen to foul tall equipment in the revised layout.

An interesting feature that now seems to be running in a cycle is the use of the open-plan office in its various forms, which is now discussed.

The open-plan office

Whether the open office (landscaped or panoramic) is more effective than the closed office is a subject for dispute. Effectiveness is governed by the features already mentioned and these do not necessarily fall easily into one category. The open office is certainly cheaper to run because the capital outlay is lower, maintenance and redecoration are easier, and more space is available for scientific layout design. Furthermore, supervision should improve, flexibility is easier to achieve, heating and lighting should be cheaper, and communication and work flow should improve in open surroundings.

Unfortunately there are several disadvantages that some specialists claim outweigh the advantages. The general atmosphere changes drastically: somehow it feels more impersonal; new forms of noise are noticeable and distracting; there is a general dislike for working in a large open area and morale seems to suffer; effective grouping of staff is more difficult to achieve; feelings of insecurity are sometimes mentioned; and there appears to be a tendency towards strained relationships. Other disadvantages often quoted are the rapid spreading of colds, the problems of setting ventilation and heating to suit everyone, and status problems for supervisors and managers.

The answer to many of these problems is a compromise achieved by erecting movable partitions at head height to provide some privacy, allocating distinctive areas to each group by using low partitions, widening gangways and deploying office furniture such as filing cabinets to define the lines, or landscaping the office. It is often argued that the whole exercise is wasted if more equipment is introduced that takes up valuable space. Some concerns are actually reconsidering after introducing the open-plan concept and are proposing to revert to closed offices.

Some companies specialise in gutting closed offices and refurnishing to open or panoramic office standards. The panoramic or landscaped office concept originated in Germany.

The idea is to improve the open office by introducing carefully placed partitions and large plants to create some privacy and grouping effects. This is coupled with carpeting, general soundproofing of ceilings and walls, double glazing, modern furniture and decor, and often a screened rest area with a coffee machine. Added luxuries are air conditioning, improved scenic views, blinds to prevent glare and curtaining.

To summarise, the important factors to remember in office layout are:

(*a*) Use a scientific approach in redesigning layout.
(*b*) Consult staff to avoid personality clashes.
(*c*) Do not restrict staff movement to a point where they are expected to sit at a desk for long periods.
(*d*) Write for catalogues on modern office furniture.
(*e*) Use specialist companies if this is thought desirable.
(*f*) Plan carefully using work study techniques.

Layout checklist

1   Avoid overcrowding.
2   Ease of daily cleaning.
3   Staff not facing directly into light.
4   Proximity of cloakrooms and toilets.
5   Comfortable furniture.
6   Main gangways about 5 feet wide and minor gangways about 3 feet.
7   Non-slip floors and stairs.
8   Fencing any exposed moving parts of office machines.
9   Minimise staff movement.
10 Place filing cabinets near staff using them.
11 Group together staff with related activities.
12 Adequate space between desks.
13 Positioning supervisors at appropriate points.
14 Separate noisy machines from staff who are engaged in work requiring high concentration.

15 Remember cost of resiting telephones and other communication devices.
16 Put close work near to natural light.
17 Minimise paper movement by designing according to work flow.
18 Avoid placing desks near to draughty areas or by radiators.

Office furniture

The purchase of good-quality office furniture should be considered a sound investment in view of its effect on morale, the general well-being of staff and the reduction of fatigue. In some concerns there is a tendency to furnish some departments lavishly while others have to suffer the indignities of worn-out equipment suitable only for the bonfire. Excuses given for this fiasco are that it depends on where the public is admitted, the budget allowance for the department is too low and the departmental head lacks power. Such a situation is designed to cause trouble and ill-feeling between the staff of various departments and there is, of course, bound to be low respect for senior management.

The main points to remember when buying office furniture are:

1 Assess the range available by contacting a cross-section of appropriate suppliers.
2 Consider space availability, bearing in mind the various designs available such as modular constructions.
3 Decide upon the price range considering funds available, construction (steel, alloy or wood) and suitability.
4 Consider the ergonomic aspects, discussed later.
5 Is it easy to clean and maintain?
6 Is it functional and lightweight?

Desks

The working area is used mainly for the clerical activities associated with the job, to accommodate any equipment and machines, to store incoming, outgoing and pending paperwork, and to accommodate any reference manuals and stationery. The amount of drawer space required for a job tends to be over-estimated because many staff seem to be great hoarders of a bewildering range of bits and pieces.

The main considerations in the choice of a desk are the size of its working area, reducing movement to the minimum, reducing fatigue, ergonomic viability, any security requirements, reasonable space for personal requirements, prestige, standardisation and cost. The importance of providing suitable desks is stressed because they are the centre of productivity for each employee. Most of the work is carried out on the desk and as a clerical tool it must be up to standard.

Chairs

Many clerical staff spend most of the working day seated and this factor alone highlights the amount of care required in choosing suitable chairs if fatigue is to be minimised and comfort maximised.

The main points to look for when examining chairs are that they should be durable, should provide appropriate back support, be fully adjustable and encourage good posture. One feature often overlooked is that when the chairs are installed it should not necessarily be left to the employee to make the adjustments. Often specialist advice is both advisable and desirable.

Miscellaneous items

The very wide range of ancillary equipment often leads to haphazard buying based on information to hand or whether a particular representative happens to be calling at the time. These items should warrant just as much care as desks and chairs and often uniformity is an advantage and more pleasing in appearance.

Physical conditions

Finally, there remain the physical features such as floors, ceilings, walls, woodwork, cloakrooms, decor, and colour schemes. Also included under this heading is the general environment, consisting of lighting, heating, ventilation, noise and cleanliness. Similar criteria to those mentioned under office furniture apply here. To avoid upsetting staff and high-lighting favouritism there should be set standards throughout the concern and a planned, fair programme of redecoration and maintenance.

Apart from the ergonomic aspects discussed next and their effect on the staff, there is a strong psychological aspect which is probably still not thoroughly appreciated. Surroundings and environment are important to people, although sometimes they will not admit it. A modern approach is essential and the image of the concern is also governed partly by this factor.

Ergonomic aspects

The scientific study of human needs in working situations utilises various disciplines, such as anatomy, physiology and psychology, to formulate suitable employment conditions. In recent years considerable ergonomic research has resulted in the introduction of new concepts associated with reducing fatigue and improving working efficiency and the employment environment. Many practical recommendations are now available.

Some of the important factors affecting conditions in the office that have been investigated are:

1 Fatigue
Most people have experienced various forms of fatigue, such

as physical, mental, visual, nervous and chronic fatigue. Feeling tired (not necessarily through overworking) is most unpleasant when there is no opportunity to rest and recover, and this is often the case in an employment situation. Fatigue during employment may be caused through a poor working environment as well as by lack of job interest and insufficiently demanding tasks. The trend towards much brighter homes and gayer surroundings aggravates the situation where staff have to work in dingy offices.

In addition to the aforementioned factors, other causes are the amount of pressure felt by staff during working periods, the duration of these periods, the number of rest pauses, the degree of responsibility and their state of health. One example is research undertaken by S.E. Seashore and B. Georgopoulos in the USA which indicated that productivity was highest in departments where staff felt the least pressure. Apparently low performance can be directly attributable to a high degree of unreasonable pressure exerted by supervisors and managers. This is perhaps the opposite to what might be expected.

2 The work place

Another sector closely connected with reducing fatigue is the use of the most appropriate dimensions for office furniture. Although research findings in various countries vary a little, a reasonable guide is to use the findings from Switzerland: these are given in a book by E. Grandjean entitled *Fitting the task to the Man*. He recommends following dimensions:

(a) *Standing position*. The height of the working surface should be about 90–95 cm for men and 85–90 cm for women.

(b) *Sitting position*. The height of the working surface should be about 74–78 cm for men and 74 cm for women. For typewriting the surface should be a little lower: about 65–68 cm for men and 65 cm for women.

(*c*) *Chair height.* E. Grandjean's recommendations are 45–53 cm for desk work and 40–48 cm for typewriting. His investigations also indicated that there should be a gap between chair height and desk level of 13 cm; back rests should be adjustable from 14–24 cm vertically above the seat level and adjustable in depth from 34–44 cm from seat front edge; and seat depth should be at least 35 cm.

(*d*) *Working area.* The two dimensions that involve grasping distance on the desk top are 35–45 cm optiminimum from lowered elbow and 55–65 cm maximum from the shoulder.

(*e*) *Head position.* A critical overall feature that affects fatigue is the position of the head when the above-mentioned dimensions are introduced. Lehmon and Stier conducted some research on this feature and they found that when standing the work should be located along the line of sight 32–44° below the horizontal and when sitting the angle should be 23–37°.

3 The environment

The final sector includes the remaining physical features of the office and the general atmosphere conditions:

(*a*) *Decoration.* To avoid glare particular attention to brightness in various sectors of vision are essential. The main points are that large surfaces should have equal brightness; excessive contrasts in brightness should be avoided in the middle vision range; bright areas should be concentrated on the immediate working point; and the use of darker surfaces on the fringe areas is recommended.

The choice of colour is also important. Some colours such as green and blue tend to give a feeling of coolness and are soothing, while others such as red, orange and yellow feel warm and are stimulating. The use of appropriate colours can create more acceptable working surroundings.

(*b*) *Lighting*. Although natural lighting is ideal this is not always possible; artificial lighting has, however, improved considerably since the introduction of fluorescent lights. The main points are:

    (i) The degree of light intensity should depend upon the type of work. An indication is given below.

	Nits
Using desk type office machines	1600
General clerical duties	1100
Filing and duplicating	800
Corridors and gangways	200

  (ii) Quality of lighting is important. Lights should be non-glare and diffused evenly to avoid shadows.

 (iii) The light source should be above the visual field.

 (iv) A check should be made to see that polished surfaces on the desk are not reflecting into the eyes.

(*c*) *Temperature*. There is a tendency in offices towards higher temperature requirements. Lighter clothing is often worn and about 20–24° C is considered reasonable for this reason.

The comfort zone is not affected very much by the relative humidity of the atmosphere but if dry air is inhaled for long periods it affects the mucous membranes in the throat and nose. Feelings of stuffiness and soreness are unpleasant and cause poor concentration. Colds are said to spread more easily in these conditions. A relative humidity of 45–65% is acceptable.

(*d*) *Fresh air*. The dangers of air pollution are becoming increasingly recognised, but so far there are few signs of any positive action being undertaken in most offices. Some large concerns have introduced air conditioning but these are in the minority.

Air pollution occurs both internally and externally, therefore efficient air conditioning is not simply a question of opening windows. Within an office the air composition is constantly changing because of oxygen loss, body odours, humidity changes, temperature changes and the addition of carbon dioxide. Externally a vast range of fumes pollute the atmosphere, the intensity depending upon site location.

Although an assessment of work performance is difficult, it is generally thought that drowsiness, loss of concentration and feelings of discomfort are partly attributable to air pollution. Performance improvement probably outweighs the expenditure on air conditioning.

(*e*) *Noise*. The overall effect of too much noise in an office can be very distressing and may lead to poor mental and physical health. Performance is affected through concentration loss, difficulty in hearing clearly, increased mistakes, lower morale and increased fatigue. Noise is a source of annoyance, especially when steps could be taken to reduce it but no action is forthcoming from management. There are many sound-proofing materials available for ceilings, walls, doors and floor; and, of course, double glazing for windows.

A better approach is to stop the noise at source if possible, or at least to reduce it. Noise is generally located through proximity to road and rail traffic, the factory, other factories and airfields. Within the office other sources of noise are telephones, typewriters, office machines, conversations and the movement of people. Research has shown that noise can raise the heart rate, blood pressure and metabolic rate, increase muscular tension and decrease the rate of digestion. Intermittent noises are more distracting than constant noise and, of course, the higher the volume the more annoying it becomes.

In recent years music has been introduced in many offices throughout the USA and there has been some argument as to whether or not it is beneficial. Opinions from employees are very mixed: some are in favour while others claim that it is distracting. Surveys indicate a varying rise in performance when soft music is played at intervals during the day to a carefully planned programme.

Safety

Compared with the factory and the home, the number of accidents in offices is negligible, but office accidents are on the increase and are now considered to be a serious problem.

Any accident—even a minor one—is costly considering the local upheaval it causes. Other employees stop working to see if they can help or to discuss it; the injured member of staff needs assistance and immediate treatment; reporting to the supervisor has to be undertaken by someone, and to the office manager if the accident is serious; furthermore, if it incapacitates, the various problems that follow often involve a considerable amount of time.

The office manager is responsible for ensuring that accidents are reduced to a minimum and that, through his supervisors, staff are encouraged to be safety-conscious. Within this sphere he should see that first-aid kits are available and fully stocked; that at least one employee in the office has some training in first-aid; that any fire precautions are known to everyone; and that all fire-fighting equipment is available and operational. Finally, he should ensure that any accidents are reported according to company and legal requirements.

Causes of accidents

Although each accident is probably a combination of circumstances, the main causes are:

1   Loss of concentration through a distraction, emotional problem or some form of tension.
2   General apathy created by the situation within the office.

3 Carelessness caused by overconfidence or poor attitude.
4 General indifference.
5 Disobedience of instructions given to avoid accidents.
6 Negligence through, for example, removing a guard on a guillotine.
7 Lack of training.
8 An unforeseen situation.
9 Poor maintenance of equipment.
10 Unsuitable equipment.
11 General fatigue or drowsiness.

Typical office accidents

The main types of office accidents are easily foreseeable and clearly indicate to the office manager the areas of improvement:

1 Slipping on poor flooring.
2 Tripping over obstacles such as parcels, small items and leads from telephones and machines.
3 Tripping over poorly maintained stairs.
4 Catching clothing and the body on sharp protrusions such as corners of desks, extended drawers, protruding parts of machinery and equipment.
5 Using chairs to stand on for reaching high shelves.
6 Colliding with other people, with open filing drawers or with clear-glass doors.
7 Opening windows without using a pole or leaning out of them.
8 Electric shocks from poorly maintained points and machines, or overloading electric points for tea-making.
9 Incorrect use of machines and equipment.
10 Fires and small explosions through incorrect use of inflammable liquids or gas.
11 Leaning back on chairs or sitting on the corner of a desk that suddenly tips up.
12 Practical jokes or horse-play.

Accident prevention

The office manager should take every opportunity to impress on his supervisors and staff the need to be safety-conscious. He should also think carefully about the main causes of accidents and about typical ones, thus arriving at a suitable long-term plan to reduce the probability of similar accidents recurring. Many lines of action directly coincide with policies he will be adopting in connection with other managerial aspects and it becomes obvious that safety precautions have to be tackled on a broad front.

A safety officer may be engaged in a large firm and full co-operation with him is essential. In some concerns safety com-mittees are established and campaigns are launched which include films on safety, refresher courses, warning posters and pamphlets.

Safety check list

1 Keep all gangways clear.
2 Keep all corridors clear.
3 Maintain floors and stairs regularly.
4 Avoid leaving parcels or any items lying around in the office.
5 Erect warning notices of any temporary or permanent hazard.
6 Encourage tidiness.
7 Study work flow between employees and rearrange to avoid possible collisions.
8 Clear-glass doors should be fitted with prominent warn-ing signs.
9 Avoid placing articles in precarious high positions.
10 Use step-ladders rather than chairs to reach high positions.
11 Balance filing cabinets to avoid top heaviness.
12 Use scientific loading of store cupboards.
13 Discourage horse-play and practical jokes.

14 Stress through notices and reminders the dangers of lighted cigarettes, inflammable liquids and any other inflammable items used in the office.

15 Regularly maintain all electrical wiring and points and do not allow misuse.

16 Ensure that the first-aid kit is to hand and well stocked.

17 Regularly check that all aids that promote safety are available.

18 Check machines and equipment regularly.

19 Remind supervisors periodically of the importance of accident prevention.

9 Controlling office work

The meaning of control

Control is a confusing and often misunderstood term because of its many meanings. Whenever the office manager uses this term he should always qualify the exact meaning he has in mind, otherwise complications will surely follow.

Consider a few dictionary definitions:

(a) Power of directing and restraining.
(b) Right of supervision.
(c) Means of checking or verifying the results of book-keeping or experimentation, or of safeguarding the constitution.
(d) Personality actuating a medium (spiritualism).
(e) Devices giving stability to an aircraft in turning, etc.
(f) Commanding, dominating.
(g) Standard of comparison for checking inferences deduced from experiment.
(h) Hold in check.
(i) Check, verify.
(j) Regulate.

A controller, often spelt comptroller, is defined in the dictionary as an officer who checks expenditure of the royal household or certain public offices such as the Mint. In business and office work it is advisable to interpret control as the direction of activities to achieve an objective in accordance with a predetermined plan and established standards. Thus control is an active continuous technical process of adjusting to constantly changing situations. This generally accepted meaning in business implies that control is a composite term encompassing a number of features, each one being inter-related and entirely dependent on all the others for effective-ness.

Elements of control

The features mentioned above form a logical sequence:

(*a*) Establish standards at the planning stage of operations.
(*b*) Check results through inspection and compare with the plan.
(*c*) Correct deviations from the plan by locating the cause and making suitable adjustments.

A typical control procedure in diagrammatic form using this sequence is shown in Fig. 20.

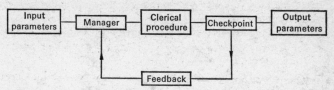

Fig. 20 A control procedure

In practice the absence of any feature signifies loss of control. If this dangerous situation applies an immediate appraisal should be undertaken.

The main elements to be investigated would be:

1 Examine the organisation to check on the division of responsibility and the identification of individuals (or job titles) bearing responsibility for each section of the work.
2 Check all job descriptions and, if historical, update to include any missing control features.

3 Ensure that standards exist for methods of working, performance, quality of work and cost of each clerical operation.

4 Examine the work flow within the procedure and check that the layout is consistent with the requirements.

5 Examine and revise the plan and schedules to ensure that the work is in correct sequence and assessable.

6 Consider the present situation to determine why control was lost.

This investigation will highlight the following aspects which may need attention:

Reorganisation, revision of job descriptions, method study, revised layout, work measurement, planning, scheduling, budgeting, motivation, quality control, procedure and system revision.

Some of these aspects have already been discussed elsewhere and the remainder will be examined shortly. Before continuing, however, a brief look at control theory should summarise the points made so far.

Theory of control

Treating control as a continuing process indicates a cycle effect which not only ensures eventual achievement of aims but also stresses problem areas warranting intensive investigation.

Fig. 21 indicates a typical cycle associated with typing a letter, where an error occurs and a retyping operation follows. The sequence is straightforward and illustrates the importance of adequate feedback of information. Failure to provide sufficient feedback could mean frustration and wasted time as the letter may have to be retyped more than once. In practice failure to recognise the importance of the control cycle stages incurs considerable expense.

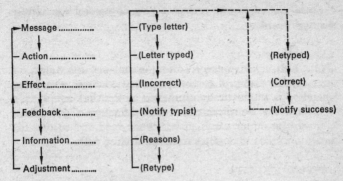

Fig. 21 The control cycle

The control sequence is:

(*a*) feedback notifying controller of failure,
(*b*) provide information on failure,
(*c*) adjustment to rectify the mistakes,

followed by:

(*d*) repeating the original message, suitably modified,
(*e*) feedback notifying controller of successful completion.

The critical feature is that the first three stages may cycle continuously until a passable piece of work is completed. Continuous cycling might indicate that considerable typing training is needed.

Forms of control

Although control theory has been explained, there may be some doubt about the level or form of control envisaged. From very simple forms such as steering a bicycle these range right through to complex forms such as successfully flying an aircraft halfway round the world.

In the office world certain forms of control are clearly distinguishable:

1 Operational control

At the clerical activities level a simple control exists where, for example, the degree of accuracy required is known, a verifying operation is automatically conducted by the clerk and when a mistake occurs he corrects it. A typical analogy of operational control in a motor car is to watch the road and correct the steering as the car deviates from the desired path.

2 Supervisory control

The next level is isolated from actually doing the work and involves a supervisory activity. At this point the work is often distributed in accordance with a plan to staff, who return it processed to the supervisor, who checks against established standards and then returns it if errors are located. By way of a reminder: when errors occur the supervisor's job is to be helpful and to advise on how to avoid them in future, not to be critical and punitive.

Continuing with the car analogy, a plan would be given to travel from A to B, the proposed route would be followed and deviations made to overcome obstacles during the journey. If the car develops a fault there is no point in kicking it (although this has been known to work), but generally remedial treatment is necessary.

3 Managerial control

At departmental office management level, the emphasis changes to concentrate on longer term aspects of control and include the expense feature in accordance with a budget.

Overall control of a procedure (or procedures) involves the establishment of procedural aims and standards; the assessment of feedback from various control points in the department; deciding whether deviations or problems are of sufficient

major importance to warrant the manager's attention; solving
the problems associated with major aspects; making decisions;
and revising certain features associated with the plan, procedure, personnel or budget items.

Thus overall control is a predominant part of the office
manager's job. Within the composite skill the main skills
involved are planning, which includes setting standards,
checking, problem-solving, revising departmental policy, and
decision-making.

This level in the motor car analogy would involve the
formulation of the plan to travel from A to B, along with an
estimated time of arrival and an assessment of the cost of the
trip. If the trip is unsuccessful because of a breakdown, for
example, consideration would be given to servicing and changes
in the maintenance programme.

4 Senior management control

Overall control of all systems involves similar activities to those
mentioned above, but long-term considerations at top level
involve the master budget, automation and mechanisation
policy, the whole question of management information and the
optimum use of information technology, and assessment on the
control cycle principle.

The car analogy at this level is characterised by objective
assessment of the car's performance, deciding whether to keep
it, determining on a policy of exchanging or selling, choosing
a new model and justifying the expenditure by determining
the advantages.

General aspects

Confusing terms

The breadth of control sometimes leads managers into thinking
that control is identical with the term management. The main
aspects of management are often referred to as forecasting,

planning, organising, co-ordinating, commanding, controlling and motivating. Thus control is only one aspect; nevertheless it is a very important one that is often neglected. A good organiser should not be confused with a good controller. The organiser may establish the control points in the organisation structure, but this activity is static until motivation is successful and control is applied.

Similarly, communication differs fundamentally from control. Communication ensures that there is an awareness of standards, that appropriate channels for feedback are established and that information is available on adjustments required. Control, however, is a scientific cycle of adjustment, a technical feature or principle demanding the development of various skills, while motivation is the technique that achieves activity. Without motivation the control cycle would simply oscillate or repeat the same feedback and the same suggested adjustment, continually reporting failure.

Control phrases

Phrases often used in connection with control are: losing control, gaining control, in control and no control. These phrases are often misused and to clarify them suggested definitions are:

1 Losing control. Loss of awareness of the situation, thus no corrective action is possible.

2 Gaining control. Establishing a standard and awaiting feedback on performance.

3 In control. Standards set, checks operating, standing by to receive feedback and make adjustments; or the process of adjusting.

4 No control. No standards available, no checking arrangements or no attempt to adjust to the changing situation.

Control parameters

A well-worn saying that is worth repeating is, 'If you cannot measure it you cannot control it'. Thus input and output variables in a control system are assumed to be measurable in terms of quantity or other forms of measurement. These variables are known as parameters.

In the office there is an attempt to control many factors such as people, forms, paper, materials, procedures and systems. Some of the parameters are cost of staff, paper and materials; cost of the procedure and system; input and output of paperwork through various sections, speed in producing results, quality of work, efficiency and effectiveness factors; absenteeism; lateness, wasting time and tea breaks; and the various costs of the office. This brief cross-section of parameters indicates the vast control areas, and unless every parameter is subjected to control the office manager cannot possibly be effective. Neglecting to measure certain parameters has led even reputable companies of long standing towards disaster.

The tools of control

The office manager should familiarise himself with the main tools of control which, in logical sequence, are:

1 Establishing standards.
2 Planning the control programme.
3 Scheduling the work.
4 Utilisation of office machines.
5 The use of statistical method.
6 Checking the results.
7 Feedback of information.
8 Adjusting to overcome deviations.

Each aspect is now discussed.

Standards

Establishing the standards means setting up, either crudely or through the use of scientific methods, a gauge or yardstick that can be used to compare with actual results. If an O & M department exists, much of the burden is usually, but not always, removed from the office manager. Much depends upon the size of the O & M department, how quickly the O & M people work and the size of the firm. Waiting a few years is not a good idea; it is better to start immediately with some intelligent estimates gleaned from supervisors and staff.

Many of the standards will be in terms of quantity, however many invoices are completed; and of quality, however many errors are acceptable. The time factor will also be established in association with quantity—for instance, x invoices to be completed in y minutes. In addition, the expenditure for various items will naturally be in terms of cash over set periods. More intangible forms of standards are appearance and impression, which apply when attempting the very difficult task of assessing effectiveness. Standards for all the measurable activities are invaluable and essential when carrying out planning, which will be discussed next.

Planning

Recalling the meaning of control for a moment immediately highlights the need for a detailed written plan indicating the objectives and how they are to be reached. For control to operate efficiently the plan must be based on realistic performance and standards conforming to the resources available. It must also be economically viable, which implies the optimum use of all resources to a set time-scale and readily adjustable as the situation changes.

Put another way, the main features are:

(*a*) The aims.
(*b*) All physical resources.

(*c*) The schedule.
(*d*) The staff involved.
(*e*) The methods to be employed.
(*f*) The location of all activities.
(*g*) The work involved.
(*h*) Built-in flexibility for revision of above features.

These main features are governed at similar levels to those outlined under the heading of forms of control:

(i) *Operational level.* Each member of staff plans his work—often described as task planning—with the aim of completing the jobs allocated to him in a logical sequence and to a set timetable.

(ii) *Supervisory level.* Office supervisors plan in the short term by scheduling for the week, progressing daily, controlling continually and motivating. Thus they are attempting to reach the aims for the section in accordance with the broad plan.

(iii) *Managerial level.* The office manager is responsible for tactical planning in the medium term to achieve the overall plans within the budget and time-scale.

(iv) *Senior managerial level.* Strategic planning is undertaken based on company policies involving objectives, finance, the market, production compatibility and administrative effectiveness.

Tactical planning. The office manager's role as a tactical planner should be absorbing and part of his weekly programme to allow for revision and thought, and formulation of new plans. All aspects of his responsibility should be planned, otherwise he will possess no guide to his own performance and rate of development. He must constantly refer to the plans and assess the aspects he managed to account for and those he overlooked, which become obvious as feedback occurs. Control is simply not possible without planning.

General rules for planning

(*a*) The time-scale must be employed in the plan.

(*b*) Up-date information on resources, such as machines, equipment, space, materials, etc.

(*c*) Gather as much information as possible on staff.

(*d*) Utilise the O & M department.

(*e*) Build in co-ordination and co-operation features.

(*f*) Plans must be in detail.

(*g*) Work within the budget.

(*h*) Do not economise to a point where performance and effectiveness might suffer.

(*i*) Check with supervisors and staff that projected plans are workable.

(*j*) Seek opinions and constructive criticisms and admit oversights.

(*k*) Allow for flexibility.

(*l*) Issue the plans on time.

(*m*) State the objectives clearly.

(*n*) Do not delay planning. If delay is inevitable, look closely at the organisation structure and the problem areas to find out why.

(*o*) Sell the plan to everyone who is involved.

(*p*) Try to be imaginative when planning.

(*q*) Resist the temptation to back out if the plan fails.

(*r*) Constantly check and revise as required.

Revising the plan. Eventually a stage is reached where, subsequent to the sequence of checking, problem-solving and decision-making, the plan should be revised.

This is a logical sequence which avoids unnecessary crisis alterations:

(*a*) List the factors that can be changed, for example whether there is sufficient space available to engage more staff.

(*b*) Consider the budget.

(*c*) List the choices of action based upon the changeable and unchangeable factors.

(*d*) Gather any further information vital to the choice.

(*e*) Determine feasibility of choice, for example the market situation for the engagement of more staff.

(*f*) Decide on the most suitable line of approach.

(*g*) Draw up a plan within the proposed changes.

(*h*) Schedule the installation of the new plan.

(*i*) Progress the schedule to the point of installation.

(*j*) Follow-up to assess the effectiveness of the new plan.

Scheduling

An advanced stage of planning incorporates the schedule, which is basically a timetable of each activity giving, for example, the standard, number of items, starting and finishing

Sales invoicing schedule						
Week commencing_____ Dept._____						
Name	Operation	Mon.	Tues.	Wed.	Thurs.	Fri.
A.Round	Typing invoices					
C.Tiree	Credit checks					

╱──╲ = work planned
▨▨▨ work completed

Fig. 22 Example of a Gantt chart for scheduling

times, and the name of the employee performing the work. Incorporating the actual times in an operational chart provides visual indications for control purposes; many charts are available for this use and these are mentioned in the statistics section shortly. An example of a typical Gantt chart is given in Fig. 22.

Charts of this nature are recommended because the correct situation is immediately apparent so long as they are constantly up-dated; they show clearly the forecast; each employee's responsibilities for workload are clearly portrayed; peaks and deadlines may be plotted; and control is simplified through temporary staff transfers from one job to another as indicated by peaks and troughs in each job loading.

A master schedule to show workloads over longer periods, of say a quarter, facilitates finer control of the peaks and troughs. Each item recorded should show the load portion, which will be either to schedule, above or below for each period of, for instance, one week. Thus forecasting, control and plans for reorganisation may be partly based on this schedule.

Machine utilisation

The increasing use of the computer and peripheral equipment has highlighted the need to schedule the loading of office machines whenever this is economically viable. The high cost of some machines warrants careful planning and scheduling to provide optimum usage. Two typical efficiency ratios for this purpose are:

$$\text{Machine utilisation:} \quad \frac{\text{running time} + \text{set-up time}}{\text{total working hours of section}} \times 100$$

$$\text{Machine effectiveness:} \quad \frac{\text{running time}}{\text{running time} + \text{stoppages}} \times 100$$

Statistical method

Underlying the plan is the use of statistics for abstracting, classifying and comparing information during the control process. The systematic collection of numerical facts is an important technique which the office manager should use, along with the ability to interpret data in graphical presentation and to use statistics in control processes. The bibliography should be consulted on this point and further reading is essential before embarking on the use of sophisticated techniques associated with statistical method. The opportunity should also be taken whenever possible to discuss the problems with a specialist.

A typical statistical investigation would conform to the following sequence:

(a) State the aims of the investigation.
(b) Gather all appropriate information.
(c) Collate the data.
(d) Analyse by one or more of the following methods:

   (i) tabulation,
   (ii) graphical representation,
   (iii) numerical techniques.

(e) Interpret the findings.
(f) Utilise information.
(g) Check accuracy through feedback.

Analysis of information.
The main aspects are associated with:

(a) Tabulation, graphs, charts and numerical techniques.
(b) Statistical quality control which employs the theory of probability.
(c) Operational research.
(d) Time series for predicting trends.

Each aspect is now briefly described to indicate the range of methods and their uses.

Tabulation. A reasonable guide to interpreting information is to classify and tabulate. The information is arranged in logical sequence to include the subject, division into suitable groups, the characteristic of each group and the values of each characteristic. Various tables are in use such as simple tables, complex tables and frequency tables.

Graphical representation. Pictorial representation has the advantages of being simple and easily understood. The main types are:

  (i) Bar charts consisting of simple, multiple and component forms.
 (ii) Pie charts.
(iii) Pictograms.
(iv) Graphs.
  (v) Trend charts.
(vi) Z charts.
(vii) Frequency distributions.
(viii) Histograms.
(ix) Frequency polygons.

Numerical techniques. These include:
  (a) *Averages.* Measures of central tendency assist analysis by indicating more clearly the true significance of a number of figures. The information is condensed by using appropriate formulae, thus showing the critical relationships which would not be apparent in their original form. The main types of average or location are:

   (i) the arithmetic mean,
  (ii) the median,
 (iii) the mode.

  (b) *Dispersion.* The wide dispersion of groups around a central point tends to lose its significance when averages are used. To overcome this problem measures of dispersion are employed that show clearly the extent of this spread around the central point:

   (i) the range,

     (ii) the mean deviation,
    (iii) the quartile deviation,
    (iv) the standard deviation.

(c) *Skewness.* A further refinement indicates the degree of symmetry within a distribution of figures. Asymmetrical curves are called skewed and most frequency curves are in this group. A measure of skewness can also be supported by other measures known as quartile measure of skewness and the third moment of skewness.

Statistical quality control. Control of actual processes is simplified and more accurate if a set of control limits is established by determining the range within which the chance variables most probably will occur. Violation of the set limits is immediately highlighted but, of course, sampling at regular intervals is essential to show promptly the current trend. This method relies on the theory of probability and is often used in production control.

Operational research. This highly sophisticated technique already mentioned in Chapter 1 applies scientific analysis and refined reasoning to establish a quantitative basis for measuring likely courses of action. The techniques in current use are critical path scheduling, linear programming, queueing theory, replacement theory and stock control theory. The application of OR is steadily growing and its use in decision-making is becoming more general.

Time series. Studying trends involves the collection of data over fairly long periods, say ten years, plotting the information and attempting to forecast the future pattern based upon the trend line. The forecast will not necessarily follow in sympathy with the trend. For example, in the marketing field, sales may vary depending upon international pressures, changing tastes, seasonal fluctuations and the appearance of new products.

Various methods are employed to separate the trend from the plotted data, such as sketching in the line of best fit through the plotted points, calculating the moving average and computing a regression line.

Checking results

The physical checking of results, although important, is an arduous and expensive sector of office work. Checking provides information for the essential element of feedback through carefully selected check points. Economic inspection techniques should be adopted to minimise the cost. Initially the cost of errors in the particular activity must be assessed and, based on this factor, an inspection point is established. The check may be conducted by the employee himself, by a colleague or by the supervisor. Staff feel less responsibility if checkers are employed, furthermore there is a tendency for checkers to make similar errors.

The whole question of accuracy is debatable and poses many fundamental problems. The degree of accuracy to be expected, the human factor, the overall cost of checking, the possible loss to the concern and preventive measures are some of the features that are very difficult to assess.

Many concerns accept the situation as an inevitable human imperfection and there is little attempt to be scientific. Others, however, concentrate on elaborate error reduction programmes which are in line with employee development schemes. To assess the logic of this approach the following factors are mentioned:

(*a*) *Reasons for checking.* To increase accuracy, avoid serious delays, give management more confidence in reports, avoid costly blunders and increase goodwill and prestige.

(*b*) *Responsibility for errors.* Four main areas are apparent:

(i) Fault of the employee doing the work.

(ii) Partly the fault of the employee.

(iii) Fault of supervision.

(iv) Fault of management.

(*c*) *Causes of errors.* There is a multitude of causes and determining the real causes as against the apparent ones is the true problem. A cross-section is given, bearing in mind the true problem:

(i) Employees: carelessness, poor concentration, poor training, no confidence, poor memory, mental difficulty, overworked, underworked, poor judgement and poor physical health.

(ii) Supervisors: ambiguous instructions, confusing messages, poor co-ordination, forgetfulness and insensitivity to the situation.

(iii) Managers: procedure design, organisation faults, lack of enthusiasm, neglect of personnel policy and incorrect priorities.

(*d*) *Acceptable standards.* There is no definite guide to standards of accuracy; every situation is unique and really depends upon an analysis of the chances of errors occurring. Probably the best approach is to assess employees who possess average capability, bearing in mind personnel policy and the effectiveness of management and supervision. Coupled with common sense and a sensitive approach, a reasonable guide should emerge. Naturally the standard must be raised in sympathy with the importance of the work and its effect on other departments who take on additional associated tasks.

(*e*) *Type of checking.* Checking may be undertaken in various ways such as calling-back, comparing with correct work, repeating calculations and reading through for errors. Calling-back (one person calls out the information while the other checks) is often not recommended because concentration is easily lost by both parties, the slightest noise tends to distract, calling interferes with other employees and there is a tendency for both to develop tension with this form of checking.

Complete or 100% checking is obviously very expensive but is warranted where an error may prove to be very costly. However, 100% inspection is not infallible and in some cases work is double and even treble-checked. Spot checks, often known as random checking or acceptance sampling, is a systematic method using the theory of probability. The sample size is determined from pre-calculated tables and the degree of certainty required.

Feedback

The results of checks have to be communicated to appropriate higher control points. At the office manager's level the contact points will be through routine and special written reports, verbal reports, meetings and personal checks (conducted as subtly as possible) with supervisors and staff.

There is no excuse for poor feedback: ample opportunities occur during daily contact and the other means mentioned should be more than sufficient provided the right working atmosphere is created. Poor feedback is an excellent indicator that something is seriously wrong with the control system or with the managerial approach.

Adjusting

The control cycle ends at this stage which also precedes another closely associated skill in the management skill cycle: anticipation (or forecasting). The aims of adjusting are to raise the quality of work and to reduce the number of checks. The approaches have been mentioned and it should be remembered that real causes of errors often lie within the provinces of training, selection, job interest and conditions. The process of adjustment must be systematic and not haphazard. Avoiding the 'fire-fighting' label is paramount: the aim should be to gradually reduce the crises and build up enthusiasm and a quality-conscious spirit.

Budgets

A departmental budget is simply a pre-planned estimate of all the items of expenditure. All departmental budgets are collated and form the master budget through which co-ordination and control are achieved at top management level.

The office manager is responsible for budgetary control within his department, which means that he should receive at regular intervals (generally monthly) operating statements that show the standard cost, actual cost and the variance (the difference) for each expense item. He should then take appropriate action to bring the expenditure back into line with the budget if there is an adverse variance, or recommend certain action to his superior based upon the reasons for the deviation. Some items will vary for reasons outside the office manager's control, such as salary increases, price rises in stationery and increased electricity charges per unit. Also, an increased work load may force up the number of staff employed.

For these reasons, and many others, budgets must be flexible and are often revised during the year. Nevertheless there are many items that are directly attributable to the office manager's ability to control the budget effectively and these are the ones on which he will be judged. In addition, he is usually consulted and asked to recommend any changes.

10   Work study in the office

Background

The need to establish standards against which individual
performance may be compared for planning and control purposes has already been stressed in the previous chapter. Work
study—often loosely described as the scientific study of any
form of work—provides these standards along with other
advantages:

1 A more accurate assessment of job values for salary
   adjustments.
2 The reduction of frustration and tension by eliminating
   unnecessary tasks in procedures.
3 The more economic use of all resources associated with
   clerical work.
4 A fairer allocation of workload among employees, thus
   tending to increase morale and productivity.

The above points alone should indicate to the office manager
the importance of work study and the likely effect on staff if
it is neglected. Remember that employees generally feel that
they work for the manager, and if the recommended method
of working and control are poor they tend to blame him for
technical incompetence, insufficient interest in them and
general indifference towards their frustrations.

Unless a scientific approach is adopted, misleading judgements will occur in assessing workloads and performance.
Staff effectiveness cannot be assessed accurately solely by such
methods as spot checks, looking in to see if a person appears
busy, checking on the backlog of work and judging by past

records. The whole process must be considered, which includes examining the organisation, the procedure, the method of working, the time it should take to complete the various tasks, the forms, machines and equipment, working conditions and so on.

No doubt such an approach appears to be common sense, but on the whole companies have not yet adopted the technique. The reasons often submitted for this tendency to lag behind the shop floor, where work study has been practised for over fifty years, are that some managers are out of date, they have strong misconceptions about office work and they do not seem to appreciate the savings and increased effectiveness that follow. The office manager, therefore, must expect prejudice and scepticism from some senior managers, especially the experienced manager who perhaps has professional status but lacks administrative know-how.

Gradually attitudes towards clerical work study are changing however, as new professional managers take over, and in recent years the trend has accelerated due to the efforts of specialist consultants and the advent of more sophisticated techniques that have proved popular among large concerns.

Organisation and Methods (O & M) is the name generally used for clerical work study; other titles associated with this specialist activity are systems analysis and clerical methods planning. Recently the tendency is to include O & M under a management services department which may also involve OR, value analysis, corporate planning, market research and DP management, but such an arrangement is limited to the medium- and large-scale concerns.

Probably the most striking example of the strong need for O & M is that given by Professor Parkinson, who propounded 'Parkinson's Law' which, in brief, states that an individual will expand the work allocated to him to fill the time available for its completion and in view of this subordinates will multiply in number at a fixed rate, regardless of their output. Thus the number of staff and the amount of work to be produced are not at all related to each other. Some of the causes attributed to this law are:

1　Poor control: if staff are not allocated sufficient work on a scientific basis they will spread the lighter load over the whole day.

2　'Empire-building' or 'Pyramid building' is a natural way for a manager to improve his status and the appointment of additional staff automatically creates more work.

3　Increases in staff often mean the appointment of more supervisors to control them and they in turn create more communication problems.

4　Unless carefully monitored, there is a tendency for work to create more work.

This chapter indicates various approaches that can be adopted by the office manager to solve these problems, even in circumstances where an O & M department is established. Work study is a continuing process that should involve everyone in the concern, thus reducing resistance to change, which will be discussed later.

The broad pattern

A broad approach is essential because if artificial barriers are raised during the study of clerical work an important aspect may be overlooked. Indeed, everyone should be involved if possible, otherwise the exercise could easily be wasted. For example, it is pointless studying and improving part of a procedure only to discover by chance later on that the information provided to a manager is simply filed and has no use whatsoever. This happens all too often!

A logical point at which to start, therefore, is by checking on the need for the information, the objective. Before proceeding with the sequence of events it should be understood that the achievement of the work study objectives which were outlined as advantages at the beginning of this chapter is an all-embracing aim and should incorporate all the specialised inter-related approaches outlined in previous chapters. Thus the office manager, if he adopts both this broad questioning approach and a constant 'seeking for improvement philosophy' explained throughout the text, will prove to his staff and himself his capability as an administrative specialist.

The importance of this pattern should also be emphasised because of the chain reaction which often occurs when a change is introduced: for example, an increase in the number of staff to cope with an additional workload often involves space and layout changes, and reorganisation, in addition to possible rearranging of jobs and so on.

A proposed sequence is now listed, followed by a short discussion on the main aspects of each approach:

1 State the objectives
2 List the known problems
3 Examine the problems
4 The system and procedure
5 Forms
6 Clerical staff
7 Supervisors
8 Organisation
9 Machines and equipment
10 Furniture and layout
11 Office services

1 State the objectives
The clarification of objectives at this initial stage is concerned with the operational and informative value of the procedure rather than with the general aim of improvements in, for example, the method or the quality of work. An example should illustrate the point: in a share registration office some of the

operational objectives are to pay the correct dividends on time, deal with share transfers and probates; on the informative side, to notify management daily of the number of deals, the current share price and any large transactions.

The validity of each objective is a primary consideration and is probably the most difficult to assess in terms of information to management. Every attempt must be made to seek justification, however, by employing diplomatic measures if antagonism from managers is to be avoided. One drastic and hardly diplomatic approach is to stop the flow of information to a manager where the value is suspect. The absence of such information may not be noticed for several months, in which case it becomes more difficult for him to justify recommencing due to the time-lag and obvious low usage rate. Moreover, the thirst for information can become an expensive obsession which defeats the object when the manager's optimum rate of absorption—in terms of time available and usefulness—is overstretched to a point where his effectiveness suffers and the cost-benefit ratio drops below an acceptable level.

2 List the known problems

Before proceeding further, drawing up a summary of the problems helps to clarify the present situation. These symptoms can be misleading as the true cause is generally obscure and very difficult to locate. A typical case of high staff turnover which is generally particularly troublesome may not necessarily be due to one cause or to the most obvious cause in the particular situation under review. Many possible causes and combinations may apply, such as a personality clash, poor selection, poor training, a narrow job, dissatisfaction over salary or welfare arrangements, unfair work load, low morale, poor supervision or lack of promotion possibilities.

The type of problem that initially emerges is generally associated with features such as output, quality of work, delays, errors, lack of co-operation, excessive overtime, high over-heads, rising costs, staff discontent and machine faults.

3 Examine the problems

Effective problem-solving at this stage highlights the areas that must be investigated in depth. Although the true causes may be elusive, in all probability the immediate causes when studied deeply will eventually reveal the situation. This information is invaluable, not only from the work study aspect but also in governing the office manager's approach to his job.

4 The system and procedure

With the causes of the problems firmly in mind, the system and the particular procedure should be examined, remembering all the relevant points detailed throughout Chapter 5. This feature inevitably develops into a major operation as it becomes apparent that successful decisions will hinge upon detailed investigations utilising method study and work measurement techniques that are discussed later.

5 Forms

An inherent part of the investigation is concerned with forms and their design, in addition to the documentation aspect covered in Chapter 5. Poorly designed forms may cause considerable unnecessary expense and frustration to staff and this aspect is also covered later in the chapter.

6 Clerical staff

The office manager should never lose sight of the fact that the most important resource available to the concern is its staff. Unless he is prepared to put them first, all attempts to improve the situation will be wasted. They decide whether the proposals will be successful and if this point is ignored the scheme will inevitably not work well.

Even in circumstances where changes appear to be successful, if staff support is lacking they will find ways of ensuring that their effectiveness suffers. Proposed changes and economy, therefore, must always be measured against the benefit obtainable. Unfortunately some managers think only in terms of costs and do not relate them to other benefits which tend to fluctuate in sympathy. Thus a 'penny-pinching' philosophy may reduce the total bill for clerical activities, but productivity, including all the obscure information aspects associated with effectiveness, suffers drastically.

A number of points should be remembered if the office manager is to achieve staff support. Firstly, never underestimate staff capability. Generally the individual who is doing a particular job knows most about it, is up to date and possesses many ideas on how to improve it. Next, whether those ideas are ever put into practice depends mainly upon the ability of the manager to create the right frame of mind in the individual so that he will be prepared to contribute. This unique knowledge can also be used effectively in discussions on ways of improving the procedure in general terms.

Staff receptivity to work improvement programmes is strongly associated with the psychological and social aspects, and personnel aspects discussed respectively in Chapters 3 and 7. Thus, to achieve support staff must feel productive and not disruptive, which involves such factors as eliminating obvious changes that are guaranteed to upset people, considering their feelings, using their ingenuity, insisting on fairness and justice and arranging work improvement programmes so that maximum participation from staff is an essential requirement.

One school of thought insists that work study and motivation theory conflict. However, provided that both concepts are fully understood, it is possible to combine the two successfully. The mistake often made is to attempt a more regimented approach to the job by stating categorically how the tasks should be done. This naturally removes some freedom, which is against the motivation concept of enriching the job. Although streamlining is often necessary, this must be accompanied by adding enriching tasks designed to compensate for any tendency to narrow the job down to frustration level.

Similarly, there could be a reaction against increasing the workload unless the aims are carefully explained. People generally jump to the wrong conclusions and they are highly suspicious of management's intentions, which is only to be expected considering the off-hand treatment they often receive.

A work-simplification programme and an approach to work measurement, both of which are designed to overcome these problems outlined, are discussed later.

7 Supervisors

In practice the office manager who is responsible for a large department, for example, will immediately recognise the impossibility of attempting clerical work study without the support and help of his supervisors. In this case his preliminary operations will include consulting and carefully explaining the techniques to them, followed by a training scheme designed to make them proficient in the use of desirable approaches in O & M.

The sincere enthusiasm of supervisors is critical. Unless they wholeheartedly agree with the ideas they will feign acceptance to the office manager and promptly spread alarm about the scheme among the staff. Winning supervisory support is not always easy, especially if the changes mean more work for them and they see the risks of upsets and resistance. The advantages must be logically emphasised with practical examples couched in similar meaningful terms.

8 Organisation

An examination of the organisation structure within the department is essential if, for example, the proposed changes involve a redistribution of staff. The techniques and approaches outlined in Chapter 2 are utilised at this stage. The question of reorganisation, perhaps through contraction or expansion of staff, cannot be ignored or omitted from the broad pattern. The principles of organisation, although flexible, demand consideration and adjustment to achieve effective supervision and control which were discussed in the previous chapter.

9 Machines and equipment
The whole question of mechanisation and automation permeates O & M and often hinges on foresight at higher levels in the organisation through consideration of expenditure problems, information requirements and administrative capability. In many instances the office manager also has the opportunity of purchasing machines for his own department. The decision to buy is naturally made in conjunction with method study and reorganisation possibilities. An approach to this aspect was outlined in Chapter 5 on data processing.

10 Furniture and layout
Contemplated changes may also affect the suitability of furniture, working conditions and layout. Further expenditure may be incurred and the possible disruption of working groups should be considered if layout changes are inevitable. Hidden costs of this nature are not necessarily taken into account at the time; these problems are covered in Chapter 8 on the office environment.

11 Office services
Finally, the broad pattern should include an examination of all the office services that may be affected by the proposed changes. These services, which include filing, typing, mailing and duplicating, were dealt with in Chapter 6 on business communication.

Further considerations

The broad pattern just described has indicated the main areas that have been discussed throughout the text. Certain specialist techniques directly connected with work study have also been mentioned; these comprise a programme for the improvement of clerical work, method study, work measurement and form design. To conclude the chapter, each one is now outlined.

A work improvement programme

One of the main snags with a work study assignment undertaken by specialists is the resistance members of staff may offer to the proposed changes. The main reasons for this are: a feeling of being criticised, a certain amount of humiliation, fear of redundancy, personal doubts about the revised arrangements, difficulty in breaking habits and fear of a loss in status.

The causes of these disturbing feelings may be attributed to lack of information and little participation in the programme. To achieve enthusiasm and sincere acceptance, therefore, employees must actively participate. Constructive participation, however, is not simply a matter of arranging for talks and asking for suggestions which may be catered for in suggestion schemes. There must be some very basic training in the techniques of work simplification, method study and work measurement.

The thought of training all staff in these techniques may sound too ambitious and costly but, considering people's ingenuity, capacity and the vital requirement of fostering the correct attitude, there seems to be no choice. Fortunately basic training in work study is straightforward and does not demand extensive courses to cover the essentials that are suitable for this purpose. Such schemes have been undertaken by some famous companies in the USA and it is claimed that the benefit in terms of morale and productivity has been worth while.

The training programme generally includes a basic procedure for method study, principles of motion economy, the basics of work measurement, activity-sampling and developing a questioning attitude. More sophisticated programmes cover systems analysis, records management, communications, problem-solving, form design and more complex techniques.

If a suggestion scheme is operating, the usefulness of its continuance after work simplification training inevitably becomes questionable. The philosophy behind the training programme is to encourage staff to adopt an improvement approach constantly incorporating new ideas, which tends to move against the suggestion scheme concept. Theoretically sound perhaps, but the reward system must be strengthened and consolidated if the new concept is to replace suggestions. Some concerns even operate both schemes on the grounds that the suggestions are now more constructive, but the clash between the two would seem inevitable.

Method study

The recognised definition of method study is the systematic recording and critical examination of existing and proposed ways of doing work as a means of developing and applying easier and more effective methods and reducing costs. A logical five-step sequence of study is:

1 Select the part of the procedure to be examined.
2 Record all the relevant facts.
3 Examine the recorded information.
4 Develop a more effective method.
5 Install and maintain the new method.

Although a procedure manual may exist in the concern, there is a constant danger of obsolescence due to gradual and sometimes drastic changes in the company's information and operational requirements. To overcome this problem method study should be a continuous process, but this is not often possible. The five steps are now outlined.

1 Selection

The part of the procedure to be examined should be decided by, firstly, considering the predominant problems such as bottlenecks, complaints, trouble-spots and high cost areas; secondly, assessing the time available and the scope of the study that may be undertaken; and, thirdly, the degree of urgency in terms of priority requirements.

2 Recording

Recording the investigation may be done in various ways, the main ones being through a narrative, charting, compiling a diagram, building models or, occasionally, filming. The investigation is generally planned to cover the procedure flow, work content, methods, location, duration and staff involved. The study may include interviews, observation and work sampling according to circumstances. The recording techniques are now examined:

Procedure narrative. This technique was mentioned in Chapter 5 and is generally used in procedure manuals. The tendency to present a mass of information which is difficult to examine is often noticeable, but the narrative is generally supplemented by diagrams to clarify the sequences. A typical narrative involves at least three subjects: the activity, the document and the employee. The layout for payroll preparation may be arranged as follows:

Activity	Document	Employee
Receive	time card	time office clerk
Record total hours	time card	time office clerk

Activity	Document	Employee
Calculate basic pay	time card	time office clerk
Calculate overtime	time card	time office clerk
Calculate total pay	time card	time office clerk
Transport	time card	time office clerk
Receive	time card	wages clerk
Check calculations	time card	wages clerk
Record	payroll	wages clerk
File	time card	wages clerk
Transport	payroll	wages clerk
Receive	payroll	wages supervisor
		and so on

Documentation chart. To supplement the narrative all the documents associated with the procedure are pasted on a board or piece of cardboard in activity sequence. They may be coupled with routing lines and other relevant information to represent a composite pictorial display of the procedure. This approach highlights the paperwork involved, and if a revised chart is drawn up it should indicate vividly the possible savings.

Process charts. Another method of recording is to portray the sequence of activities in a procedure or a job by means of symbols on a chart. Various types of chart may be used: an outline process chart demonstrates the main aspects of one job by indicating the main operations and checks; the flow process chart, which illustrates the main activities in a procedure or part of a procedure; and a two-handed operation analysis chart, which records the activities of both hands in relation to each other during a task or number of tasks.

An example of a flow process chart is shown in Fig. 23 and a two-handed operation analysis chart in Fig. 24.

Diagrams. A useful way of assessing the movement of documents and staff to see whether any excessive backtracking,

Flow process chart

Procedure: Re-ordering procedure – Stores no 1
Chart starts: Checking stock cards
Chart ends: Copies of official order filed

O = Operation D = Delay	Prepared by: R.A. Nance
□ = Check ▽ = Storage	Department: Purchasing
⇦ = Transport	Date: 20.9.73

Present method		Proposed method
O■ ⇦D▽ Check stock card	O□ ⇦ D▽	
●□ ⇦D▽ Write stores requisition	O□ ⇦ D▽	
O□ ⇥D▽ To chief storekeeper	O□ ⇦ D▽	
●□ ⇦D▽ Sign	O□ ⇦ D▽	
O□ ⇥D▽ To purchasing department	O□ ⇦ D▽	
●□ ⇦D▽ Sort into suppliers' names	O□ ⇦ D▽	
O□ ⇦● ▽ Hold until batch complete	O□ ⇦ D▽	
●□ ⇦D▽ Enter missing details	O□ ⇦ D▽	
O□ ⇥D▽ To typist	O□ ⇦ D▽	
●□ ⇦D▽ Type official order	O□ ⇦ D▽	
O□ ⇥D▽ To order clerk	O□ ⇦ D▽	
O■ ⇦D▽ Check with requisition	O□ ⇦ D▽	
O□ ⇥D▽ To purchasing officer	O□ ⇦ D▽	
●□ ⇦D▽ Sign official order	O□ ⇦ D▽	
O□ ⇥D▽ To general manager	O□ ⇦ D▽	
●□ ⇦D▽ Sign official order	O□ ⇦ D▽	
O□ ⇥D▽ To order clerk	O□ ⇦ D▽	
●□ ⇦D▽ File no 4 copy	O□ ⇦ D▽	
O□ ⇦D▼ Permanent storage	O□ ⇦ D▽	
O□ ⇥●D▽ Copies 1/2/3 to mailing clerk	O□ ⇦ D▽	
●□ ⇦D▽ Write envelope , insert copies 1/2	O□ ⇦ D▽	
●□ ⇦D▽ Stamp, enter in mailing book	O□ ⇦ D▽	
O□ ⇥D▽ Copy no 3 to stores	O□ ⇦ D▽	
●□ ⇦D▽ File no 3 copy	O□ ⇦ D▽	
O□ ⇦D▼ Permanent storage	O□ ⇦ D▽	
O□ ⇦D▽	O□ ⇦ D▽	
O□ ⇦D▽	O□ ⇦ D▽	

Fig. 23 A flow process chart

	Two–handed operation analysis chart		
Procedure: Sales invoicing			
Job description: Preparation and mailing payment demand letter			
Chart starts: Pick up letter for insertion in envelope			
Chart ends: Place sealed envelope in OUT tray for franking			

o =Operation	d =Delay	Prepared by: R.A. Nance
□ =Check	∇ =Storage	Department : Sales
⋄ =Transport		Date: 20.4.73

Left hand	Left symbols	Right symbols	Right hand
Pick up letter, move to work area	●□◆D∇	O□⋄D∇	
Fold letter and crease	●□⋄D∇	●□⋄D∇	Assists left hand
	O□⋄D∇	●□⋄D∇	Pick up and transport envelope
Open envelope flap	●□⋄D∇	●□⋄D∇	Hold envelope
Pick up letter, move to envelope	●□⋄D∇	●□⋄D∇	Hold envelope
Insert letter in envelope	●□⋄D∇	●□⋄D∇	Hold envelope
Move envelope to mouth	O□◆D∇	O□◆D∇	Move envelope to mouth
Lick envelope flap	●□⋄D∇	●□⋄D∇	Lick envelope flap
Fold over flap and secure	●□⋄D∇	●□⋄D∇	Fold over flap and secure
Put in OUT tray for franking	O□◆D∇	O□⋄D∇	
	O□⋄D∇	O□⋄D∇	
	O□⋄D∇	O□⋄D∇	
	O□⋄D∇	O□⋄D∇	
	O□⋄D∇	O□⋄D∇	
	O□⋄D∇	O□⋄D∇	
	O□⋄D∇	O□⋄D∇	
	O□⋄D∇	O□⋄D∇	
	O□⋄D∇	O□⋄D∇	
	O□⋄D∇	O□⋄D∇	
	O□⋄D∇	O□⋄D∇	
	O□⋄D∇	O□⋄D∇	

Fig. 24   A two-handed operation analysis chart

bottlenecks, or long runs are occurring is to draw a flow diagram. A layout of the area is drawn up allowing for sufficient space to couple each working point with lines indicating the sequential flow of documents. The completed exercise highlights the faults. Fig. 25 illustrates a reordering procedure similar to the outline given in the flow process chart (Fig. 23). A similar process may be undertaken using a string diagram.

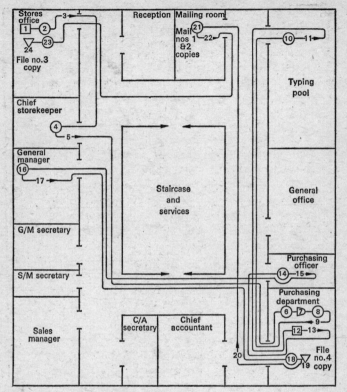

Fig. 25 A flow diagram

Pins are inserted at the operational points which allow for
string to be wound between them, representing the flow lines.
The lengths are measured after the string is unravelled and
scaled up to find the distances travelled.

Models. Three-dimensional and two-dimensional models also
help to illustrate vividly the methods used and possible im-

provements. Various choices of layout and flow may be experimented easily with before deciding upon the most suitable arrangement.

3 Examination

A critical examination of the facts is an important stage that should be undertaken in an objective way. Complete elimination of personal bias is not possible, but every attempt must be made to keep an open mind and a broad outlook.

The first step is to use the questioning technique to find out as much as possible about the present method and its justification. Standard questions apply to the main aspects of any job or sequence of activities:

(a) The purpose: why is the work necessary? What is the aim? Is the end product actually used?

(b) Location: where is the work done? Why is the work located in this position?

(c) The employee: who performs the work? Is there a special reason why he does it?

(d) The sequence: when is the work performed? Why is it performed at this point? Why is it done at this time?

(e) Means: how is the work performed? Why is it done this way?

The second step is to utilise the answers from the above questions by subjecting them to a more detailed analysis. This may be achieved in various ways, but the straightforward method is to ask further questions. Some typical ones are:

(a) The purpose: are alterations or eliminations possible without abandoning the purpose? Could parts of the work be omitted?

(b) Location: are there more suitable places? Are there other locations available?

(c) The employee: are there others available? Who else could do the work? Is the employee suited for the work?

(*d*) The sequence: could the sequence be changed easily? Are there advantages in altering the sequence?

(*e*) Means: what are the alternative ways of doing the work? Is motion economy fully utilised? Are the most suitable machines and equipment employed? Are the working conditions suitable?

4 Development

Developing the new method may be approached in various ways. One way is to consider each aspect mentioned above, attempt to answer all the questions and assess the benefits of the findings. The main factors in this process are the purpose, location, staff, sequence, documentation, forms, machines, equipment and working conditions. These will be considered in conjunction with the many features associated with the procedure such as the time factor, accuracy requirements, the budget, prestige, peaks and troughs of workload, staff turnover and training.

Alternatively, the work may be examined from four main angles: elimination, change of sequence, combination and simplification.

(*a*) *Elimination.* This aspect has been stressed several times and it should be the primary consideration. Maximum saving is naturally possible and staff are released for more important tasks.

(*b*) *Change of sequence.* A change in the sequence of operations may improve flow of work or possibly avoid unnecessary work. For example, the transportation of documents to various points is often out of phase, which means that excessive distances are involved. These can be avoided by careful routing and rearranging the sequence of operations.

(*c*) *Combination.* Each operation should be examined with a view to combining it with a preceding or subsequent one. The possibility of saving time by avoiding a movement from one point to another and combining the two operations together should also be considered.

(*d*) *Simplification.* There are always easier methods of performing tasks. A careful examination invariably reveals certain areas where simplification is possible, such as:

(i) Motion economy is always worth investigating as both time and fatigue are reduced if more economical ways can be devised. The principles of motion economy are discussed shortly.

(ii) The suitability of staff for particular jobs should be considered. Selection has been discussed under personnel aspects, Chapter 7. Surprising savings and improved performance are possible if more attention is given to this aspect.

(iii) Another neglected area is the control and design of forms and documents. Possible savings and avoidance of frustration are included in the discussion on form design later in this chapter.

(iv) Unfortunately the introduction of machines and certain equipment does not necessarily simplify operations; in fact, to simplify may mean abandoning these tools. Naturally careful thought is essential, but it is not unheard of for this step to be taken, especially if insufficient justification existed for the original mechanisation. Reverting to a manual method should not be looked upon as a retrograde step. It can be a sensible move if there is sufficient evidence to prove the case for it.

5 *Installation and maintenance*

The final step of installation and maintenance is really the testing time for new ideas. Success depends not only on the validity of the new method but also on the degree of care and attention during installation, and on the amount of detail in the plan. Unless these features are effective the amount of co-operation from staff will be negligible.

Motion economy

Frank Gilbreth formulated certain principles of motion economy with the aims of minimising fatigue and wasted time. The principles that are most useful in clerical activities are:

1 Minimise movements
Place all documents, reference books, writing equipment and machine aids within the normal working area and in standard positions for easy reference. The normal working area is the space covered between the arcs drawn by the tips of hands to the elbows when the upper arms are vertical to the body.

2 Simultaneous movements
Both hands should be used simultaneously so that balance is maintained whenever possible.

3 Simplify movements
Use the simplest movements, hand movement rather than arm movement and so on.

4 Natural movements
Make the best use of the shape and design of the body by adopting natural movements rather than using awkward, straining movements.

5 Rhythmical movements
Try to develop a natural rhythm whenever a cycle of operations is involved.

6 Continuous movements
Smooth and curved movements are less fatiguing.

7 Habitual movements
If precise repetition is possible the mental effort exerted is reduced, as the cycle encourages a reflex action.

Clerical work measurement

The importance in planning and control theory of knowing how long a task should take has already been stressed. These time standards are invaluable and may be utilised in many ways, such as determining staffing levels, justifying mechanisation, assisting in costing and budgetary control, scheduling workloads and providing data for a salary structure and job evaluation.

Although time standards have been accepted as feasible in the factory, a certain amount of controversy has surrounded work measurement in the office. Contestants put forward many arguments: clerical staff are involved in considerable brainwork, many queries arise, the work varies considerably, some activities are discretionary, the standards are already known, many minor operations do not justify measurement, the work is spasmodic and supervisors already ensure that a fair day's work is achieved. Unfortunately these arguments do not hold good when they are further investigated. An even stronger case for establishing time standards often emerges when, for example, simple tests are conducted to see how much time is spent by staff working and not working: the results indicate from 40% to 60% utilisation (actual working time).

There is a need to stress, however, that the initial object is not to measure the performance of an individual employee but, as the name implies, to measure the work content of his job. Moreover, the fact that most clerical staff decide to enter administration in the hope that repetitive, boring work (as seen on the shop floor) will be avoided is a point to remember. Thus work measurement should not stress the repetitive aspect or over-emphasise rigid control features, otherwise staff will react strongly against it.

The approach should be to indicate the advantages to staff: each individual will have a clearer idea of what is required from him; crises are easier to avoid; peaks and troughs of work-load are more controllable; unfair loading of work on certain employees can be avoided; a fairer salary structure can be introduced; individual performance is more apparent; and realistic targets can be set.

The upsurge of interest in clerical work measurement in recent years is due not only to the alarming increase in office workers but also to the rising interest in the study of communication and control mechanisms in machines and living creatures, which is known as cybernetics. The science of cybernetics is very involved, but even a scanty knowledge clearly indicates its enormous potential in business and the vital part played by measurement and control.

Considering the organisation side of O & M for a moment, the cybernetic approach is to view organisation in terms of planning, standards, control, feedback, information, channel capacity, 'noise' in the system and so on. This approach should be compared with the traditional view known as the sociological approach which involves authority, responsibility, power, roles, duties, accountability and so on. Also, the economics approach should be considered, which includes such terms as organisation thinking, price, costs, capital, revenue, income and expenditure.

From this introduction the next step in any proposal to introduce work measurement and control, which naturally follows, is to decide upon a suitable method of measuring and to adopt a reporting procedure for control procedures. Various techniques are now considered.

Work measurement techniques

The criteria for deciding which work measurement technique to employ depend upon the degree of accuracy required, which rises in sympathy with the expenditure that can be afforded, and the objectives, which may be short or long term. The uses of work measurement have been mentioned and the choice, depending on the extent of the programme, will also affect the decision. Ideally, a specialist should be employed as there are certain dangers if the office manager undertakes the task without expert guidance. The techniques available are many and varied. Within the space allocated it is only possible to give a brief survey, further reading being essential.

Self-recording. A simple, inexpensive and consequently not very accurate method is to invite members of staff to record the times required to perform the various tasks involved in their jobs. Although the times will be subjective and specialists may frown at using such a simple technique, it is useful if funds are low, if there is little top management support, or as a quick means of establishing standards to start a control system.

The recording technique is to design a form with columns to accommodate headings such as: task, day, starting and finishing times, number of operations or documents completed, total time and average time per document, and any other appropriate information required. The clerk fills in the details and spot checks conducted by the supervisor help to maintain some form of accuracy. The personal involvement of the clerk helps and surprisingly good standards of recording are often produced. There is only a negligible tendency to cheat and in any case consistent misrecording is very difficult over a period of a few days.

Estimating. There is no doubt that intelligent guesses about work timings are possible if sufficient experience and knowledge of the job exists. A discussion with the clerk to see if he agrees with the proposed standards also helps to gain his support and clarify the times. Although crude, such an arrangement does bring realistic control into being, which is probably more important than determining exact standard times. After all, if the standards set are incorrect, the obvious thing to do is to revise them in the light of experience.

Activity sampling. A popular technique to determine the times *being taken* rather than the times that *should* be taken is to conduct periodic observations of the activities under investigation. The observation times are calculated by using the laws of probability. Although this technique takes more time, its uses are wider. For instance, it can determine the total time a clerk is working in a day, assess the job content, assess machine running time and check backlogs of work.

Observing a secretary for a day might indicate, for example, that she is working only 65% of the time and that during actual working time she spent 25% of her time on shorthand, 40% on typing, 10% on filing, 5% on answering the telephone and 20% on other tasks. From this information utilisation ratios can be calculated and planning may be undertaken to avoid boredom and frustration.

Time study. Most specialists deplore the use of a stop-watch in the office. They argue that sufficient accuracy is achieved through the use of an ordinary watch. Four steps should be taken to arrive at a standard time: timing, rating, applying a relaxation allowance and calculating the standard time. The essentials of timing are that the task must have a regular sequence and that the job is capable of being divided into suitable elements. An element is part of the work that is easily recognisable in terms of starting and finishing points. Rating briefly means being able to assess the rate of working so that an allowance may be added or subtracted to compensate for this factor. A relaxation allowance is added to provide for those periods when clerks are not expected to work. From this information a standard time may be calculated.

Predetermined motion time systems. PMTS are times calculated on the assumption that experienced staff will perform various motions in about the same time. Thus a complex series of body movements required to carry out office work may be measured and used to build up standard times for clerical operations.

The well-known systems are Mulligan standards, master clerical data and other systems derived from Methods Time Measurement (MTM).

Forms

A form may be described as a sheet of paper or card with printed information (or questions) indicating the data required in the blank spaces provided.

From this definition its main aims are apparent:

1 To provide concise and sufficient information according to procedural requirements.
2 To minimise repetitive information writing by printing the essential data on the form.
3 To provide a number of copies of similar information for injection at various points in the procedure.
4 To indicate clearly their filing location, reference and identification.
5 To record systematically so that the data appear in the same place each time for operational effectiveness.

Forms control
To achieve the above-mentioned aims and combine effectiveness with economy, a strict forms control system is essential.

Without control there is a clear tendency for managers and supervisors to introduce forms in a haphazard, wasteful way. Furthermore, the creation of forms bears little relative cost compared with the costs of subsequent form-filling operations, filing and storage. There are also many side-effects, such as haphazard ordering, which results in storage problems for blank forms and wastage if the form is obsolescent, careless use of forms and little incentive to revise or consolidate them. To overcome these problems the elements of control described in the previous chapter must be applied.

(*a*) *Establish standards*. The first step is to establish as many standards as possible, such as the design of forms, which is dealt with shortly; seeking out the best suppliers or method of reproduction; establishing an average usage rate; setting minimum, maximum and reordering levels; and a set procedure for requisitioning forms, including authorisation. Certain records will be needed, such as a forms file containing a copy of each form suitably coded, a list for easy form reference and for indicating the function of each form, and a stock record card. A plan is thus established which should include a procedure for forms requisitioning and up-dating the records.

(*b*) *Check results*. The second step incorporates regular checks on usage, obsolescence, and obsolete forms through inspection of the records and regular contact with the form users. Constant justification is essential, as well as checks to ensure that no form is raised without official authorisation.

(*c*) *Correct deviations*. As changes occur, the main features of adjustment are combining forms, abandoning forms, redesigning, seeking out more economical ways of reproducing, notifying sections of excessive usage and reordering to requirements. In the large concern a forms controller is appointed to undertake these responsibilities, or a member of the O & M department may be given the job as part of his workload. If control is not centralised or is non-existent, the departmental office manager should take the initiative and set up his own control system.

Form design

The essential requirements of the form should be examined first. These should be listed and alongside each item the degree of latitude and choices noted. Typical requirements that affect design are size, shape, type of paper, location of usage, the amount of data to be recorded, the sequence of data related to other documents in use at the same time, appearance, identification, method of writing entries, filing facilities, any mailing restrictions and security.

The most glaring faults are lack of regard for location, (for instance if a van driver's forms have to be completed in rough weather); insufficient space for entries; items omitted; data out of sequence, which means that the user has to dodge around from one part to another when extracting data; and ambiguity.

The technicalities involved in good form design make it a weighty subject and if the reader has to undertake this task, he should refer to the bibliography and select a suitable textbook before attempting it. Important points are easily overlooked and the evidence indicating the designer's failings is on display to many employees, often for a long time after.

When the essential requirements have been determined, and the technicalities learned, it is useful to draw up a check list so that any important feature is not overlooked. Such a list will probably cover more than fifty points if it is conscientiously compiled, but of course it can be used every time a new or revised form is contemplated.

Conclusion

The main aspects of clerical work study have now been briefly outlined. Provided that this discipline is operated in balance with the other considerations and disciplines illustrated in previous chapters, there should be a distinct improvement in control and productivity.

Successful application rests heavily on the office manager, his supervisors and the staff association, and above all on the ability of senior management to demonstrate their belief in the importance of their staff. There should be nothing to hide from employees. Ample consultation and participation are fundamental and should not need stressing. Redundancies are not necessary because normal staff turnover takes care of them and no one will be working harder just because of a clerical work study, for in fact the frustration of being idle is often more tiring than working.

Certainly the office manager will feel he is managing effectively, which encourages more enthusiasm and confidence in himself and in his staff. Provided that he also develops a sensitivity towards employees, treats them as equals and practices the managerial skills conscientiously, his performance should improve and his success in administration will be assured.

Appendix 1

Statutes affecting office management

Offices, Shops and Railway Premises Act, 1963
Factories Act, 1961
Contracts of Employment Act, 1963
Occupiers Liability Act, 1957
Sale of Goods Act, 1893
Copyright Act, 1956
Patents Act, 1949
Registered Designs Act, 1949
Merchandise Marks Act, 1887 to 1953
Companies Acts, 1948 and 1967
Restrictive Trade Practices Act, 1956
Industrial Relations Act, 1971
Terms and Conditions of Employment Act, 1959
Wages Councils Act, 1959
Truck Acts, 1831, 1837, 1896 and 1940
Payment of Wages Act, 1960
National Insurance Act, 1965
National Insurance (Industrial Injuries) Act, 1965
Law Reform (Personal Injuries) Act, 1948
Redundancy Payments Act, 1965
Industrial Courts Act, 1919
Conciliation Act, 1896
Industrial Training Act, 1964
Equal Pay Act, 1970
Race Relations Act, 1968
Supply of Goods (Implied Terms) Act, 1973

Appendix 2

British Standards Institution

The BSI is a recognised body in the UK for the preparation and promulgation of national standards. Booklet PD 4845 gives details of its work and organisation.

Booklets relating to clerical activities are given below.

Chapter 4
Adding Machines 1909
Amendment PD 5648
Duplicating Machines, Registration Testing 4588
Codes for Punched Cards 3174
Codes for Punched Tape 3480
DP Glossary 3527
DP—Problem Analysis 4058
Tape Spools 3732
UK 4—bit code 4731
UK 7—bit code 4730
Data Transmission, digital 4505
Dictation Machines 3738
Magnetic Tape for ADP 3658
Magnetic Tape for Data Interchange, 7 track 3968
Magnetic Tape for Data Interchange, 9 track 4503
Office Machines, Safety 3861, 4644
Paper Tape for DP 3880
DP Problem definition and Analysis Part I
   Flow Chart Symbols 4058
Typewriters 2481
Amendments PD 4582 and PD 5646

Chapter 10

Bibliography

Chapter 1
Office and Administrative Management, Littlefield and Rachel, Prentice-Hall.
Office Administration, Mills and Standingford, Pitman.

Chapter 2
Organisation and Innovation, C. Argyris, Wiley.
Organisations, Volumes I and II, J. A. Litterer, Wiley.

Chapter 3
New Patterns of Management, R. Likert, McGraw-Hill, 1961
Human Relations in Management, Huneryager and Heckman, E. Arnold, 1967.
The Human Side of Enterprise, D. McGregor, McGraw-Hill, 1960.
Management by Motivation, S. D. Gellerman, A.M.A.
The Motivation to Work, F. Herzberg, Wiley.
The Achieving Society, D. C. McClelland, Free Press.
Introducing Sociology, P. Worsley, Penguin.

Chapter 4
Business Equipment Guide, BED Business Journals (twice a year).
Electronic Business Data Processing, Schmidt and Meyers, Holt, Rinehart & Winston.
The Effective Use of Computers, P. A. Losty, Cassell.
Data Processing, McLachlan and Molsom, McGraw-Hill.

Chapter 5
System Design for Computer Applications, Laden and Gildersleeve, Wiley.
Office Organisation and Method, Mills and Standingford, Pitman.
The Student's Systems Analysis, P. Kilgannon, Arnold.
Management Systems, P. P. Schoderbek, Wiley.
How to Design Procedure, IAM.
Management of Change, J. R. M. Simmons, Gee & Co.

Chapter 6
Communication in Business, P. Little, Longmans.
Clear Thinking, Hy Ruchlis, Harper & Row.
The Rational Manager, Kepner and Tregoe, McGraw-Hill.
Decision Making, W. Edwards and A. Tversky, Penguin.
Report Writing, B. Trott, Heinemann.

Chapter 7
The Growth of White-Collar Unionism, B. G. Sayers, OUP 1970.
How to Interview, Bingham and Moore, Hamilton.
Personnel Administration, Pigors and Myers, McGraw-Hill.
Training for Development, Lynten and Pareek, Dorsey.
Salary Administration, McBeath and Rands, Business Books.
Job Evaluation, BIM.
Personnel Selection and Placement, M. D. Dunette, Tavistock.
Job Grading Schedule, IAM.

Chapter 8
Fitting the Task to the Man, An Ergonomics Approach, E. Grandjean, Taylor & Francis Ltd, 1971.
Office Accommodation, IAM.
Office Landscaping, F. Duffy, Anbar.

Chapter 9

Control Techniques for Office Efficiency, E. V. Grillo, McGraw-Hill.

Use and Abuse of Statistics, W. J. Reichman, Penguin.

Business Statistics, Freund and Williams, Pitman.

Management Accountancy, J. Batty, Macdonald & Evans.

Network Analysis for Planning and Scheduling, A. Bettersby, Macmillan.

Control of Quality in the Office, IAM.

Chapter 10

Cybernetics and Management, Stafford Beer, EUP.

Work Measurement in the Office, Hamill and Steele, Gower Press.

Work Study in the Office, Cemach HP, Maclaren & Sons.

Measurement and Control of Indirect Work, D. A. Whitmore, Heinemann.

Organisation and Methods, Milward, Macmillan & Co.

Design of Forms, HMSO.

Multiple Part Business Forms, E. Lennox, Cassell.

Index